HUMOR
of the Old Deep South

HUMOR
of the Old Deep South

Edited by

ARTHUR PALMER HUDSON

Volume II

KENNIKAT PRESS
Port Washington, N. Y./London

HUMOR OF THE OLD DEEP SOUTH

First published 1936
Reissued in 1970 by Kennikat Press
Library of Congress Catalog Card No: 75-86026
SBN 8046-0616-1

Manufactured by Taylor Publishing Company   Dallas, Texas

CHAPTER IX

BARKEEPERS AND BONIFACES

IN MISSISSIPPI, Alabama, and Louisiana, with occasional exceptions in the larger cities, inns, hotels, and taverns throve on an evil reputation. This they shared with their sister places of public accommodation over the South generally. Even as late as the forties, fifties, and sixties, travelers like Sir Charles Lyell, William Howard Russell, and Frederick Law Olmsted [1] complain bitterly of vermin-infested bedrooms, brawling tap-rooms, meager or repulsive bills of fare, greasy, slatternly servants, and rascally landlords. Only occasionally, and that usually from a local resident or traveler, like J. F. H. Claiborne, or the editor of the Natchez *Free Trader*, does a more genial note enter into the descriptions of these places and their inmates. In possibly the most comprehensive treatment of the American institution, Elise Lathrop's *Early American Inns and Taverns*,[2] Alabama rates records of only twenty-eight; Louisiana, eight; and Mississippi, undiscoverable, as so often, in the tabular hiatus *Minnesota. . . . Missouri*, not one. Concerning Mississippi, the only matter of record is that "A traveler in 1860 mentions that Fort [*sic*] Gibson had a tavern, and speaks of a few log cabin taverns, but for the most part he stopped at houses along the way for food or lodging, either being entertained free, if the house belonged to people of means, or paying the usual charge of one dollar for supper, lodging, breakfast and horse food." [3]

The implications of such a statement are, on the face of it, somewhat absurd. Even the few following selections should serve to cor-

---

[1] In books quoted elsewhere in the present book. Charles Joseph Latrobe (*A Rambler in North America*, London, 1835, Vol. II, p. 13), an English traveler and writer, complains in 1835 that in Georgia "Both the mode and style of entertainment for the traveller was vastly inferior to that of the more northern states," and gives many detailed deficiencies.

[2] New York (Robert M. McBride & Company), 1926.

[3] *Ibid.*, pp. 233-234.

rect them. Bad though most of them must have been, there were plenty of inns and taverns in Mississippi in 1860; there had been a good many for forty or fifty years, besides the apparently lone one at "Fort" Gibson and its vaguely traditional contemporaries. It is not the taverns that were, but the records of them, that are hard to find.

The generally unsettled, undeveloped, and backward state of civilization in these states, as in the other states of the lower South, of course in part explains the admitted comparative scarcity and poor quality of inns and taverns. But sectional customs and prejudices had a good deal to do with it. Soon after Columbus, Mississippi, successfully thwarted an effort to bring what is now the Mobile and Ohio Railroad to its haughty back doors,[4] an enterprising newcomer applied for a license to erect and operate a hotel. He was vigorously denied by the planter aristocrats. "No," one of them is reported to have said; "we don't need or want any hotel in Columbus. If a stranger is good enough to stop in our town, I'll entertain him in my own home. If he's not, he can stay with the niggers or keep moving, as he chooses."

The following selections, however, are not documents on the question of inns or no inns. They are meant to give a few glimpses of people and their ways. "Billy Button" belongs with the duelists as much as with the barkeepers, but he was a barkeeper, after all, and he received his mortal insult in the discharge of duty. The recipe for mint juleps as the drink was served at the Mansion House is the best piece of lagniappe offered by the purveyors of this book. Almost equally tempting is the orally proclaimed bill of fare of the Washington at Vicksburg. Those who are dissatisfied with this or with old Claiborne's list of goodies at the "spacious Inn at the junction of the Gallatin and Monticello roads," may turn to Olmsted's reprint of D. Cockrell's at the Commercial Hotel, Memphis,[5] and see how they would come out. And readers who are indifferent to taverns *per se,* but prick up their ears at one as a *mise en scène* for bedroom farce of the Gallic variety, may smile at Henry S. Foote's yarn about a Simpson County Harry Bailey.

[4] To this day that charming city must be reached from the M. & O. by a little branch line.
[5] See *A Journey in the Back Country,* New York (Mason Brothers), 1860, p. 127.

DICK THE BULLY AND BILLY BUTTON

(Rodney, 1830's)

By H. S. Fulkerson [6]

A TRAVELING circus had dropped from the roll of its "dramatis personæ," at the town, a queer little nondescript of a man who played clown when the real clown was drunk or sick and who was known as Billy Button, so-called, I believe, on account of some part he played in the circus. He was one of those curious creatures who could amuse you with his nothings, but who could never excite in your mind any interest in him. Billy had undertaken the new role of bar-tender at the hotel. He was quick and sprightly and amused the patrons of the bar.

At this time the town was afflicted, as it had been for many months, with a boisterous, drunken fellow named Dick B——, who, though an arrant coward, boasted loud and long of his manhood, and his readiness to give "satisfaction" on the field of honor, or elsewhere, to any aggrieved party. He was a nuisance that everybody wanted to see abated.

One day Dick was very annoying, and the boys determined to try his courage. They took Billy Button into their confidence and made him a party to the scheme. A sham duel was arranged for with Billy and Dick as the principals. Dick was invited in to drink. He said something whilst drinking which Billy took exceptions to, as had been arranged. High words followed and ended by Dick's inviting Billy to settle the matter after the manner of gentlemen. Billy promptly accepted, the fight to come off immediately, in front of the hotel, with pistols, at ten paces.

The seconds were chosen, and the pistols procured and loaded with powder, and the party proceeded to the front. The distance was measured and the principals were ordered to take position. Billy stepped forward promptly and stood upon the line, pistol in hand. Dick was nervously looking about, and at length, in reply to his second, who had told him to take his position, said, "Hold on, can't this thing be settled in a friendly way?" "No, no," shouted Billy, the seconds, and the by-standers. Dick's second got behind him, pushed him up to the mark and leaned against him as a brace.

The word was given and both fired—Dick with his head tucked down. Billy fell to the ground with a thud as Dick's pistol went off. Dick

[6] *Random Recollections of Early Days in Mississippi,* Vicksburg, Miss. (Vicksburg Printing and Publishing Company), 1885, pp. 9-11. For biographical notes, see p. 307.

dropped his pistol and started at a killing pace for the swamp, followed by the mob shouting "murder" at every jump.

They caught him, brought him back, and let him into Billy's room. That warrior was writhing in the agonies of a mortal wound, his shirt all bloody with the reddest of red ink. Dick implored them to send for *all* the doctors. An opportunity was given him to escape. He embraced it; jumped the town and was cured for life of his boasting propensity.

MINT JULEPS AT THE MANSION HOUSE

(Natchez, 1840)

WE HAVE been told by some amphibious amateurs who smacked their lips when they said it, that our friend George Vennigerholtz, the bar-keeper at the Mansion House, does create most luxurious juleps at about 11 o'clock each day. He opened the season with them on the 29th of February. We know that his juleps must be superb by the twinkle in the eyes of those that drink them; we have seen their eyes and smelt juleps in their breath.

The editor of the New Orleans *Picayune* boasts that some landlord in that city sent him the other day one of the tallest juleps, the coolest, the biggest round, and the deepest that ever was seen since Noah's flood. Now we recommend small and delicate juleps, made gratefully cool and fragrant, with but little of the *live critter* in them. The way Reddings of the Louisville Pearl Street House makes his crack juleps is something like this:—

Take a large and deep cut glass tumbler, fill it with sufficient sugar and ice to the brim—half of the ice shaved into snow and the rest in lumps of moderate size. Lay on the top of it three fresh leaves of mint without any part of the stem attached. Pour on just half a glass of fine unimpeachable cognac brandy, then just half a glass of fine old Jamaica rum; then add half a glass of old ripe port wine. Then pour the mass rapidly for some time, back and forth in two tumblers; the longer this action continues, the better. Then plant a small bunch of mint on one side of the tumbler by putting the stems down into the ice, and having the leaves up about as high as the nose of the drinker should come. On the other side of the tumbler, where the mouth should come, rub the edge with half a fresh lemon.

Thus brewed, it is fit to drink—smells like a bouquet, and is worth a silver bit. Reddings always intended to send one down preserved in ice to Natchez, but the passage of the gallon law prevented.[7]

[7] *Mississippi Free Trader and Natchez Gazette*, vol. V (Thursday, March 12, 1840), p. 1.

On Saturday we were presented with a magnificent Julep from the Mansion House that probably excelled anything of the kind made on the continent of Columbus; in fact, it put our late recipe entirely in the shade. It was in a massive cut goblet, with the green forest of mint which crowned it frosted over with sugar snow, and the whole mass underlaid with delicate slices of lemon piled in the pyramid of ice. As for the liquor, it was so skilfully compounded that no one could detect its several parts. Ladies drank of it and supposed that some huge grape from the south side of the Island of Madeira had burst open on a sunny day and been crushed in the goblet.

This magnificent Julep was made by our friend Mr. John George Vennigerholtz.[8]

At the Shakespeare, opposite the Market House in Natchez, kept by Messrs. James McGuckn and B. Gay, there are many exquisite juleps made, which are a little "touch above the vulgar." They are made in the usual manner of John George Vennigerholtz at the Mansion House, so celebrated in the annals of the old Natchez tribe—but, as a dash of fragrance, each julep has a delicate moss rose placed in it. This is something beyond the usual "fixins" and tastes like cream and strawberries. We have tasted them and know it![9]

LIFE IN NATCHEZ[10]

THE epicureans of other cities seem "to keep their eyes skinned" in regard to the style with which we do up small matters in Natchez. One of the last numbers of the Philadelphia North American has the following:

"*Refinement.*—In Natchez they ornament the glasses containing mint juleps with moss roses."

This was a fact at the time we made the record; but, now at the present writing, we have newer and more exquisite delicacies. That same "moss rose" house, "the Shakespeare," now puts strawberries in their milk toddies.

Mr. Alexander, at the Steam-Boat Hotel, puts strawberries in his mint juleps, and it affords one of the strongest arguments in favor of temperance to see with what avidity the drinkers will dig among the lumps of ice for the strawberries, after the julep has evaporated.

We also see that the last number of the New York Enquirer has still further immortalized our excellent friend at the Mansion House,

[8] *Ibid.*, p. 2.
[9] *Ibid.*, March 19, p. 2.
[10] *Mississippi Free Trader and Natchez Gazette*, Natchez, April 16, 1840, p. [3].

John George Vennigerholtz, by copying one of our descriptions of his juleps, and comparing that same description to Governor M'Nutt's anti-Union Bank bond Proclamation—that *ne plus ultra* and bank humbug finisher.

We have a word of reproof to some of our estimable friends in the country, who have, more than once, taken pains to present us with mint juleps when we have made calls of friendship and affection. Our reproof shall be as soft as the gentle south winds; yet we beg them to make some little distinction between professional and private character. If "in the way of business" we praise the brewing of a most superb and princely julep, we beg them not to think that we desire no taller monument over our graves than *spires of mint!*

"The Ladies of Natchez drink mint juleps. So says the *Free Trader.* Do they ever get snapped?"—New Orleans *Sun.*

The Ladies of Natchez will never get "snapped" up by a New Orleans bachelor editor.[11]

Excitement was felt throughout the city yesterday in consequence of the price of Ice—held by the only house that has a large quantity, at eight cents per pound, Natchez currency. . . . The Mansion House and the City Hotel have full supplies at $8 per ton.[12]

MRS. RAY'S SPACIOUS INN

By J. F. H. Claiborne [13]

OUR first night was spent at Mrs. Ray's, a spacious Inn at the junction of the Gallatin and Monticello roads, and immediately on the Natchez Railroad. We know of no place where the traveller is made more comfortable. Roomy apartments, luxurious beds, a table bountifully and delicately spread, a hostess of the kindest disposition and most engaging manner, a fine gushing spring, with no scarcity of madeira, claret and Monongohala to render your libations more generous—these form a *tout ensemble* rarely to be found at a country ordinary. What

11 *Ibid.,* March 26, p. 3.
12 *Ibid.,* April 9.
13 "A Trip through the Piney Woods," first published in the Natchez *Free Trader and Mississippi Gazette,* of which Claiborne was junior editor, in 1841–1842; here reprinted from *Publications of the Mississippi Historical Society,* vol. IX (Oxford, Mississippi), 1906, pp. 514–515. With reference to the question as to the number of inns in Mississippi (discussed in the introduction to this chapter), Claiborne, who was traveling through one of the most primitive sections of Mississippi in the forties, mentions (p. 514) "Col. Buckhalter's Hotel," at Williamsburg, Covington County, and (p. 512) a resort at Stovall, near Columbia.

a delightful excursion for our citizens in the balmy periods of the season, a strawberry hunt near Mrs. Ray's, and a picnic in the magnificent pine forest about there! Who could not be eloquent? What lover could not woo and win, with a fine girl stooping to gather the ruby fruit, not half so rich as the blush upon her cheek? And then, there are huckleberries near Mrs. Ray's. Why, the heart of a mountaineer would leap at the very idea! There is to him poetry in the thought. The days of young romance come back dancing upon the memory, gilded with sunlit recollections of his early home—his first idolatry of woman, whose sainted image nor time, nor distance, nor other attachments, nor the "sere and yellow leaf" of misfortune, have been able to tear from its resting place. How many destinies are fixed for life, hearts cemented into one, in the colder North, in these autumn rambles over the sunny side of the mountain—these annual fruit-gatherings! But here is another attraction to Mrs. Ray's. Winter is coming; we have no sleigh rides; no music of the merry bells, as they sweep, like Laplanders, over the glassy valleys, reflecting back the joyous moonbeams and the smiling stars. This is not vouchsafed to us; but how delightful to wrap up in warm furs, and glide along in the cars, with the melody of clarionet and horn, flinging back their cheering echoes from the hills, to a ball at that pleasant inn, with a glorious supper of oysters and chicken salad, turkeys, terrapin and champagne! Why, it would be almost as pleasant as a New England sleigh ride! Now that there is suspension of arms, and politics for the moment is not *the* thing, we should look around us, and see how many sources of enjoyment and of improvement are within our reach.

HERE IS A SPLENDID GOOSE!

By William Howard Russell [14]

[Vicksburg], Friday, June 14th, [1861].— ....

Mr. MacMeekan, the proprietor of the "Washington," declares himself to have been the pioneer of hotels in the far west; but he has now built himself this huge caravansary, and rests from his wanderings. We entered the dining saloon, and found the tables closely packed with a numerous company of every condition of life, from generals and planters down to soldiers in the uniforms of privates. At the end

[14] William Howard Russell, *My Diary North and South,* Boston (T.O.H.P. Burnham), 1863, pp. 295-96. Of Jackson, Russell says, "There are of course a monster hotel and blazing bar-rooms—the former celebrated as the scene of many a serious difficulty, out of some of which the participators never escaped alive" (p. 298).

of the room there was a long table on which the joints and dishes were brought hot from the kitchen to be carved by the negro waiters, male and female, and as each was brought in the proprietor, standing in the centre of the room, shouted out with a loud voice, "Now, then, here is a splendid goose! ladies and gentlemen, don't neglect the goose and applesauce! Here's a piece of beef that *I* can recommend! upon my honor you will never regret taking a slice of the beef. Oyster-pie! oyster-pie! never was better oyster-pie seen in Vicksburg. Run about, boys, and take orders. Ladies and gentlemen, just look at that turkey! who's for turkey?"—and so on, wiping the perspiration from his forehead and combating with the flies.

Altogether it was a semi-barbarous scene, but the host was active and attentive; and after all, his recommendations were very much like those which it was the habit of the taverners in old London to call out in the streets to the passers-by when the joints were ready. The little negroes who ran about to take orders were smart, but now and then came into violent collision, and were cuffed incontinently. One mild-looking little fellow stood by my chair and appeared so sad that I asked him "Are you happy, my boy?" "I'se afeered, sir; I can't tell that to Massa." "Is not your master kind to you?" "Massa very kind man, sir; very good man when he is not angry with me," and his eyes filled with tears to the brim.

POLITICS AND BEDFELLOWS

By Henry S. Foote [15]

I RECOLLECT an anecdote I once heard from him [Judge Buckner C. Harris, of Copiah County]. . . . Judge Harris' judicial district embraced the county of Simpson, of which Westville was the seat of justice. Here there were several little taverns where plain accommodations were afforded. . . . A man had recently gotten possession of one of them, and very naturally desired to obtain as large a share of the public patronage as he could. A term of circuit court was to commence in a few days. So mine host . . . addressed a letter to the judge, urging him, when he should come to Westville, to give his hotel a trial, and to bring in his company all the attorneys he could, promising . . . to do all in his power to accommodate them.

The judge, painfully remembering that he had never had any but the most uncomfortable quarters in Westville on former occasions, readily closed with the proposal, and reached the hotel . . . on a bright Sunday

[15] *Bench and Bar*, pp. 107-108.

evening. He asked to be shown to the room . . . and proceeded to it. He found a gentleman and a lady in it, and . . . asked to be shown another. . . .

Some little delay occurred before this was done, and when he reached the second room, he found that also occupied.

He then came back to the bar and indignantly addressed the host . . . : "Pray, sir, are you keeping a bawdy-house? I found the first room . . . already in possession of a man and woman—the latter of whom I understand to be your wife—lying together upon the bed. On opening the door of the second room, I found the same woman lying on the bed there, but attended by another man. I wish to know what all this means."

"My dear judge," exclaimed the good-natured tavern-keeper, "I beg you will be composed. It is not possible that I can for the present say a single word concerning the matter. You see . . . I am a candidate for constable in this beat, and very hard run for votes . . .The election will come off tomorrow, after which I promise you there shall be no similar cause for complaint."

FOR SNAKE BITES AND THY STOMACH'S SAKE

By T. W. Caskey [16]

A TOTAL abstinence preacher and a strong advocate of the cause of temperance conducted a revival in a neighborhood near a saloon. Many souls were converted, and, among the number, the saloon-keeper himself. The converts not only professed religion, but, under the good man's preaching, they were also converted on the temperance question. The saloon-keeper was in trouble. He did not want to sell any more whisky, but everything he had in the world was invested in the stuff. To pour it out was in accordance with his feelings, but that meant financial ruin. The welfare of his family was not the only thing to be considered. He had bought much of his liquor on a credit, and the rights of his creditors were clearly involved. To pour it out would leave his family without a penny and himself without ability to pay his honest debts. He was greatly troubled, but finally decided to state the case to the preacher and ask for advice. The preacher was in doubt what to advise him to do, and decided to lay the case before the brethren. They all thought and prayed over it in great seriousness. The revival grew in interest. A deep religious feeling pervaded the entire community. Sinners repented, saints rejoiced, scoffers won-

[16] F. D. Srygley, *Seventy Years in Dixie. Recollections and Sayings of T. W. Caskey and Others*, Nashville, 1893, pp. 177-185.

dered, and wags grew serious. The preacher inveighed against sin in general, explained to all the way of life, and denounced drunkenness and the liquor traffic as a sin against God and a crime against mankind. The saloon-keeper groaned in spirit, but no one could solve his difficulty or suggest any way to lighten his burden.

Finally, under the excitement of the revival, the zealous new converts and the happy old brethren decided to buy the whole stock of liquor and pour it out. The preacher seized the idea with delight and urged them to carry out the good resolution.

Accordingly they started a subscription, to make up the money, and appointed a day considerably in the future to meet at the saloon and consummate the business. Unfortunately, the revival closed and the religious excitement collapsed before the day arrived when the faithful were to meet at the saloon, to purchase and pour out the condemned beverage.

The pilgrims gathered promptly, but each one had a sort of I-didn't-know-it-was-loaded and wish-I-hadn't-done-it expression on his countenance. But no one had the nerve to back down. The money was promptly handed over and counted down to the ex-saloon-keeper and late convert. The whisky now belonged to the church, but no one offered to pour it out. Evidently they all felt the sacrifice they were about to make. Truly, the spirit was willing, but the flesh was weak.

The saints . . . were all right in theory. It was in *practice* they so signally failed. For several moments after the whisky was bought and paid for, they sat in solemn silence and deep meditation. Finally one old brother said:

"My old 'oman's out'n camphor."

Of course that was a "feeler" only. For several seconds no one responded to it. The silence seemed almost dense. The devil was clearly at work on the new converts. By and by another old brother said:

"My old 'oman was a telling of me t'other day as how she needed some sperits to make bitters."

Another period of painful silence. Every man was fighting a mighty battle in himself against the world, the flesh and the devil. Two souls in that faithful little band had already showed signs of alarming weakness. Evidently they were hard pressed in the struggle. Possibly they had already surrendered. Who would be the next to fall? The silence was broken again by the faltering voice of another weak brother. He said:

"It's good fur snake bites."

The pilgrims now began to get interested. They crowded around the three brethren who had spoken so significantly of "camphor," "snake bites" and "bitters." The crisis was passed. The battle was lost to the saints. The devil's guns had swept the field.

The talking now became general. They all said it looked like foolishness to throw away several gallons of good "sperits" which they had paid for, when they all had to buy such stuff, much as they detested it as a beverage, for camphor, snake bites, bitters and other medical purposes. The ex-saloon-keeper and late convert had a full supply of jugs, bottles and kegs. Why not buy all the vessels he had on hand and divide the "sperits" among the brethren in proportion to the amount of money each one had paid? Of course that was the only wise thing to do under the circumstances, when it was suggested. It was commendable economy against shameful waste. It was also a part of their duty to the ex-saloon-keeper and late convert, to buy his stock of jugs, bottles, barrels and kegs, as well as his stock of liquor. What use could he have for such vessels after his saloon was closed? He could not sell them; he was not able to lose them.

The jugs, bottles and kegs were promptly bought, and the liquor was equitably divided among the brethren. Then came another pause in the proceedings. The convention again needed a leader, and for lack of one it collapsed. The silence of a Quaker meeting settled down upon the little band of halting pilgrims. What they needed now was a man to cry "make way for liberty," and throw himself upon the altar of his country, so to speak. That man was not present. There was not even one to say "give me liberty or give me death." They stood like sheep for the slaughter, and like lambs before the shearer, they were dumb. By this time it was night. Clearly, something must be done. It was time to adjourn, and yet the main business of the convention, as they all understood it now, had scarcely been touched. Finally the camphor man said:

"My old 'oman's mighty partic'lar about the kind of sperits she uses to make camphor out'n."

No one else spoke. The silence was painful. The pilgrims groaned in spirit. By and by the snake-bite man said:

"I would be afeared to resk anything but the best o' sperits fur a snake bite."

Only a sigh from the rest of the pilgrims. For several seconds no one else spoke. Everybody seemed embarrassed. The last speaker was clearly endorsed by the whole convention, but no one seemed disposed to put the question squarely before the house. At last the bitters man said:

"My old 'oman allus tells me to be shore'n' *taste* liquor before I bring it home fur bitters. It takes mighty good sperits to make bitters that's wo'th a cent."

This sounded like business. The pilgrims became interested again. They crowded around the speakers. The suggestion about tasting the "sperits" fairly electrified the crowd. Clearly that was the proper thing to do under the circumstances. The bitters man tasted the liquor in one of the jugs. He was somewhat doubtful as to the quality of the stuff. He wanted to know whether the other jugs contained a better quality of "sperits." He tried another jug and pronounced it better. One of the other brethren present openly expressed doubt as to the taster's judgment. The doubter tasted both jugs. They at once got into an animated argument and both men tasted both jugs again. They were further apart on the second ballot than the first. They put the main question again, including other jugs. Result, a "dead lock" on the third ballot and neither of the tasters could remember which jug he said was the best on the second ballot. Clearly they were both too drunk by this time to know anything about it. Each one of them appealed the question to the house. This made it necessary for everybody to taste the contents of all the jugs in dispute, and in less than an hour that little band of loving brothers was a howling mob of drunken backsliders. They whooped, they yelled, they embraced each other with maudlin affection and sang sketches of revival hymns. They preached, they exhorted, they prayed, they shouted, they quarreled, and finally they ended the carousal in a free fight and a general fisticuff.

CHAPTER X

BROADHORN BOYS AND STEAMBOAT BULLIES

FROM the pre-Homeric age of Mike Fink to the Iliadic and Odyssean epoch of Tom Sawyer and Huckleberry Finn and the Prince of Pilots, the Mississippi River was "the highway of humor." It was so for the main reason that it was the mile-wide tawny and slippery avenue upon which, for a long time, most of the people lived, along which they hauled and haggled, sold and stole most of their goods and chattels, up and down which they wandered and fought and gambled and made love and took their pleasure. It was the Midway of the longest and greatest World's Fair our country has boasted. In its own and its Arkansas, Ohio, and Missouri tributary cities it numbered a dozen Vanity Fairs. Every barge, broadhorn, and keel boat was a floating booth; every steamboat, a showboat. Sodom and Gomorrah and the ancient cities of the plain seem willing but ignorant hick towns of a twilight age in comparison with the lurid glare and boisterous mirth of Memphis, Natchez-under-the-Hill, and New Orleans. Memphis, grandly recalling the fame of an Old World river country, ballyhooed from its front its New World infamy. Natchez-under-the-Hill, says old Timothy Flint, was "full of boatmen, mulattoes, houses of ill fame, and their wretched tenants, the refuse of the world," where "The fiddle screaks jargon from these *faucibus orci,*" and "Where you see the unhappy beings dancing, and here they have what are called 'rows,' which often end in murder." The crown (quite properly near the mouth) was, to Mike Shouter, from Yazoo, Mississippi, and to his greenhorn gossips in a hundred other Yazoos, "that sitty of unhearn-of-wikkedness, frogs, katfish, and Frenchmen, called Orleans, of which so much has been hearn, spoke, and writ, and the half not told."

Most of our following sketches and yarns are pre-Homeric. To enlarge the picture of the age, the reader must go to Audubon and Alexander Wilson and Noah Ludlow for vignettes of Kentucky boatmen, with money in their pockets from their whisky, flour, and tobacco, trudging and roaring up the Natchez Trace to Mussel Shoals. He must turn to George H. Devol for long-distance gambling. But there is ample suggestion, below, of what could have been the human side of Banvard's canvas. Here is old Mike Fink, in at the kill under the bluffs at Natchez. Here is the "man-half-horse-half-alligator" emerging from the river slime to roar upon a barge. Here is that miniature treatise upon the boats of the pre-Fultonian Mississippi, and the following tense story, not unrelieved by humor, of the first steamboat voyage down the river. Here is Davy Crockett in a gorgeous "Row at Natchy-under-the-Hill." Here are chronicles of flatboat wars and Fool Rivers.

J. H. B. LATROBE

John Hazlehurst Boneval Latrobe (1803–1891) was a lawyer, an inventor, a railroad executive, a public servant, and a writer.[1] Resigning a third-year cadetship at West Point in 1821, he went to Baltimore, studied law, and was admitted to the bar. At first he eked out his income by writing for annuals, biographical dictionaries, and legal publishers. In 1827 he began a connection with the Baltimore and Ohio Railroad which lasted till his death. He wrote a history of that railroad (1868) and *Reminiscences of West Point* (1887). Among other public services, he founded the Maryland Historical Society and was almost life-president. He was on a committee which awarded a prize to Edgar Allan Poe's "MS. Found in a Bottle."

The Captain Nicholas J. Roosevelt who figures in the following story of the first steamboat that came to Natchez is, of course, one of the family of the present President of the United States.

The selection from Latrobe's narrative is placed first because it contains an excellent description of the early types of boats that plied the river.

[1] Data from *Dictionary of American Biography*.

THE FIRST STEAMBOAT ROUNDS TO AT NATCHEZ

By J. H. B. Latrobe [2]

WHEN reading to the Maryland Historical Society, on a former occasion, "A Lost Chapter in the History of the Steamboat," I had occasion to refer to the first voyage of a vessel of that description on the Western waters, calling it a Romance in itself. . . . I now propose to tell it. And, first, a word or two to explain how I come to be the narrator.

Mr. Nicholas J. Roosevelt, the hero of the Lost Chapter, married my eldest sister in the year 1809; and she made that voyage with her husband in 1811. Its events were the stories I listened to in my childhood. The impressions then made have never been effaced. They were deepened, when my father removed his family to Pittsburg, in 1813, having become interested with Livingston and Fulton in the steam navigation of the Ohio. . . .

Prior to the introduction of steamboats on the Western waters, the means of transportation thereon consisted of keel boats, barges and flat boats. Keel boats and barges ascended, as well as descended, the stream. The flat boat was an unwieldy box, and was broken up, for the lumber it contained, on its arrival at the place of destination. The keel boat was long and slender, sharp fore and aft, with a narrow gangway just within the gunwale, for the boatmen as they poled or warped up the stream, when not aided by the eddies that made their oars available. When the keel boat was covered with a low house, lengthwise, between the gangways, it was dignified with the name of "barge." The only claim of the flat boat, or "broad horn," to rank as a vessel was due to the fact that it floated upon the water and was used as a vehicle for transportation. Keel boats, barges, and flat boats had prodigious steering oars, and oars of the same dimensions were hung on fixed pivots on the sides of the last named, by which the shapeless and cumbrous contrivance was, in some sort, managed. Ignorant of anything better, the people of the West were satisfied with these appliances of trade in 1810.

Whether steam could be employed on the Western rivers was a question, that its success between New York and Albany was not regarded as having entirely solved: and after the idea had been suggested of building a boat at Pittsburg, to ply between Natchez and New Orleans, it was considered necessary that investigations should be made, as to the currents of the rivers to be navigated, in regard to the new system. These investigations Mr. Roosevelt undertook, with the under-

[2] "The First Steamboat Voyage on the Western Waters," *Fund Publication, No. 6,* the Maryland Historical Society, Baltimore, October, 1871.

standing, that if his report were favorable, Chancellor Livingston, Mr. Fulton and himself were to be equally interested in the undertaking. The Chancellor and Fulton were to supply the capital, and Roosevelt was to superintend the building of the boat and engine.

[Roosevelt deemed it first necessary to make an exploratory voyage down the rivers to New Orleans in the old manner. He built a flatboat and, with his wife, to whom he had been but recently married, he descended to Natchez and made the rest of the voyage on a rowboat. Reporting in New York in 1810, he was instructed to go ahead. He constructed the *New Orleans* in Pittsburg—116 feet long, 20 feet beam—at a cost of $38,000. In September, 1811, the voyage commenced; the "people of Pittsburg turned out in mass and lined the banks of the Monongahela to witness the departure of the Steamboat." Mrs. Roosevelt again accompanied him. Mr. Jack was the pilot. At Cincinnati people told him: "We see you for the last time. Your boat may go *down* the river; but as to coming up it, the very idea is an absurd one." At the Falls of the Ohio, the boat escaped from her anchor, but showed her power by bucking the current. Down the rising Ohio forged the boat. "Mrs. Roosevelt had, for the second time, become a mother. The events of the voyage were certainly multiplying."]

. . . But now were to come "days of horror." The comet of 1811 had disappeared, and was followed by the earthquake of that year . . . and the earthquake accompanied the *New Orleans* far on her way down the Mississippi.

The first shock that was observed was felt on board the *New Orleans* while she lay at anchor after passing the Falls. The effect was as though the vessel had been in motion and had suddenly grounded. The cable shook and trembled, and many on board experienced for the moment a nausea resembling sea sickness. . . .

. . . The bottom lands on either shore [of the Mississippi] were under water, and there was every sign of an unwonted flood. Canoes came and went among the boles of the trees. Sometimes, the Indians attempted to approach the steamboat; and, again, fled on its approach. The Chickasaws still occupied that part of the State of Tennessee lying below the mouth of the Ohio. On one occasion, a large canoe, fully manned, came out of the woods abreast of the steamboat. The Indians, outnumbering the crew of the vessel, paddled after it. There was at once a race, and for a time the contest was equal. The result, however, was what might have been anticipated. Steam had the advantage of endurance; and the Indians with wild shouts, which might have been shouts of defiance, gave up the pursuit, and turned into the forest from whence they had emerged.

. . . Mrs. Roosevelt and himself were still discussing the adventure when they retired to rest. They had scarcely fallen asleep, when they were aroused by shouts on deck, and the trampling of many feet. With the idea of Indians still predominant, Mr. Roosevelt sprang from his bed, and seizing a sword—the only weapon at hand—hurried from the cabin to join battle, as he thought, with the Chickasaws. It was a more alarming enemy that he encountered. The *New Orleans* was on fire; flame and smoke issued from the forward cabin. . . . By dint of great exertion . . . the fire was extinguished. . . .

. . . At New Madrid, a great portion of which had been engulphed, as the earth opened in vast chasms and swallowed up houses and their inhabitants, terror stricken people had begged to be taken on board, while others dreading the steamboat even more than the earthquake hid themselves as she approached. . . .

One of the peculiar characteristics of the voyage was the silence that prevailed on board. . . . Tiger, who appeared, alone, to be aware of the earthquake while the vessel was in motion, prowled about, moaning and groaning . . . Orders were given in low tones; and the usual cheerful "aye, aye, sir," of the sailors, was almost inaudible. . . . Sound, continuous sleep was apparently unknown . . . Flat boats and barges . . . uttered no word as the *New Orleans* went by . . . the travellers . . . fancied, as they looked at each other, that they had become haggard. Mrs. Roosevelt records "that she lived in a constant fright, unable to sleep or sew, or read."

Sometimes, Indians would join the wood choppers . . . From these it was learned that the steamboat was called the "Penelore," or "fire Canoe," and was supposed to have some affinity with the Comet that had preceded the earthquake,—the sparks from the chimney . . . being likened to the train of the celestial visitant. . . .

As the *New Orleans* descended the river it passed out of the region of the earthquake, and the principal inconvenience was the number of shoals and snags, and sawyers. These were all safely passed, however, and the vessel came in sight of Natchez, and rounded to opposite the landing place. Expecting to remain here a day or two, the engineer had allowed his fires to go down, so that when the boat turned its head up stream, it lost headway altogether, and was being carried down by the current far below the intended landing. Thousands were assembled on the bluff and at the foot of it; and for a moment it would have seemed that the *New Orleans* had achieved what she had done, so far, only that she might be overcome at last. Fresh fuel, however, was added,—the engine was stopped that steam might accumulate, presently the safety valve lifted—a few turns of the wheel steadied the boat,—a few more gave her headway; and, overcoming even the Mississippi, she gained the shore amid shouts of exultation and applause.

The Romance of the voyage ended at Natchez, where the same hospitalities were extended to Mr. and Mrs. Roosevelt, that had been enjoyed at Louisville. From thence to New Orleans, there was no occurrence worthy of note. . . .

Although forming no part of the story of the voyage proper, yet, as this has been called a Romance, and all romances end, or should end, in a marriage, the incident was not wanting here: for the Captain of the boat, falling in love with Mrs. Roosevelt's maid, prosecuted his suit so successfully as to find himself an accepted lover when the *New Orleans* reached Natchez; and a clergyman being sent for, a wedding marked the arrival of the boat at the chief city of the Mississippi.[3]

A BEAR STORY[4]

THE old saying, a rolling stone gathers no moss, may hold good in some instances, but in others it amounts to about three cents in the dollar. So much for the beginning—at least such is my experience; and in giving it as such, I hope the reader will pardon me for dealing in mysteries. I have an aversion to mysteries, &c., but when a rare chance offers, and a moral can be drawn therefrom, I may be excused for giving Jim Higgins' account of the Mysterious Pilot, which is true, to the best of my belief and knowledge.

"After the *steamboat* came in fashion," said Jim, "old Bill Reese and myself used to take at least one trip to Orleans once a year on a *flat,* carrying with us such articles as turkeys, tobacker, and the produce of our section of the State. We always went together, so that when one of us would git into a bad drive, we could whip ourselves out without trouble. We had been down with a load, and made considerable of spekulation on our purchases. And knowing the trade would keep up for mor'n a short season, we started back home to buy another cargo. We had *fifteen hundred miles to walk,* and knowing that, we sot our trotters to work, and in less than six days we reached home, and——"

"Guess you were a little tired about then?" interrupted one of the passengers.

"Tired! ha, ha, ha, out of it my darlin'! We commenced buyin' up produce, and at the eend o' ten days, we had two new boats built, and filled with such articles as we wanted, and boatin' down the river with

[3] This last paragraph is printed in the original as a footnote.
[4] *Spirit of the Times,* vol. 18 (April 15, 1848), p. 88.

colors histed! When we got to the Mississippi, we just let our flats smooth the surface of the water accordin' to their own action. I think we had been in the river two days, runnin' sometimes over twenty miles an hour, when my boat run aground on one o' them cursed sand-banks; and there I staid for mor'n' a week. I was out huntin' one day, jest for amusement, and I treed one o' the orfullest *bars* ever rised in Arkansaw! I saved him after a hard fight, got 'im aboard, and tied him to a big cable. I had a old fiddle aboard, and was givin' 'im lessons in dancin' a day or two afterwards, when I looked up the drink, and saw——"

"What?" chimed several voices, "saw what?"

"The fust *steam*boat that ever fluttered a wheel on the Massippi! and if you'll believe me——

"Why, sirs! I believe she was drivin' every fish and allygator in the river before her. My bar jumped overboard, and I was near follerin' as the *steam* fixin' rid by me; just then somethin' jerked my flat plum luse from the island, and she took rite arter the steam critter as fast as the nater of the occasion would let 'er! Well, sirs! we soon cotch her, and fer a hour or two, we had it interestingly—the steamboat was bilin'! and the flat! don't mention it! She darted before as easy as the wind, and the way the critter puffed and blowed after us, wasn't fast enough to ketch up! What was the matter with my craft I didn't know! She was ridin' like a dancin' fether and throwin' the water from one bank to the other. I began to get skeered, but knowin' I could cut the cable afore she could run to the Gulf of Mexico, I thought I'd let her rip! I jest sot back, tuned my fiddle, and played to kill time. It was the purtyest wether in the world, and I enjoyed it amazingly. The breezes stretched my colors beautifully, and the moon would peep down once in a while to see what I was drivin' at! I was alone, but had no use for company. The flat was now turning the most dangerous bend in all the river, whar I knowed she'd be apt to run agin one o' the free and independent snags, and sure enuff——"

"She did!" exclaimed several of the listeners.

"And sure enuff, afore I had time to say Jack Robinson, or draw my bow across my fiddle, I saw one snag and another just below it, and——"

"She busted herself agin 'em?" said one or two.

"When I got to 'em," continued Jim "they wasn't thar; I found 'em about as fur ahead as they was when I fust seed 'em. In the mornin' I looked out and thar they was just as far apart—a splittin' the water like a lightnin' pole. 'What was they?' I asked myself; but it's no use; that evenin' my boat was piloted to Orleans, and she ran up to the *levee* handsomely, bein' only a few hours out from the sand bar, and beatin' the *steam* boat a day and a half; and now, gentlemen, all said—after this beautiful instance of my mysteriously out running a steamboat—what power do you supposed carried it along?"

"The tide, forced by the fish and allygators," said a knowing Jake.

"Murder!" said Jim; "take down your sign."

"A sudden rise, then," roared another.

Some guessed one thing, some another, and so on, until Jim, recovering his strength, for he was feeble, rose to his full height, and said—

"Gentlemen, you may think as you please, but it was *nothing else but that bar that was tied to the cable!*"

"Mr. Higgins, have you got the papers?"

"Yes, sir, but I've left 'em in my pocket book at home. It's true, every word of it; for jest as soon as the bar jumped overboard, a thunderin' big catfish took after 'im, and then they had it from thar to Orleans—the bar beatin 'im about six feet and a half! I didn't know how fast the bar pulled the boat, but the fish swum so fast that he *jumped fifty seven feet out on the levee, and didn't stop floppin' his tail for a month!*"

Tennessee Telegraph.

ALLIGATOR: HALF MAN, HALF HORSE

(Natchez, 1808)

By Christian Schultz, Jr., Esq.[5]

THE evening preceding that of my departure from Natchez being beautiful and bright, I walked down to the Levee, in order to give some directions to my boatmen. In passing two boats next to mine, I heard some very warm words; which my men informed me proceeded from some drunken sailors, who had a dispute respecting a *Choctaw lady*. Although I might fill half a dozen pages with the curious slang made

[5] *Travels on an Inland Voyage,* vol. II, pp. 145-146. For note on Schultz, see p. 89.

In George Philip Krapp's *The English Language in America* (New York, 1925, vol. I, p. 300) there is an interesting discussion of the half man, half horse, and half alligator character:

"As early as the first decade of the nineteenth century the Kentuckian had taken his place in American folk-lore. . . .

"In the Salem Gazette for June 12, 1812, a correspondent from New Orleans says that 'half horse, half alligator has hitherto been the boast of our up-river countrymen when quarreling. The present season however has made a complete change. A few days ago two of them quarreled in a boat at Natchez, when one of them jumping ashore with a horrid oath declared that he was a *steamboat*. His opponent immediately followed him, swearing he was an *earthquake* and would shake him to pieces.'"

The reader will remember the account of the fight on the raft which Tom Sawyer and Huckleberry Finn heard and saw, in *Huckleberry Finn.*

use of on this occasion, yet I prefer selecting a few of the most brilliant expressions by way of sample.

One said, "I am a man; I am a horse; I am a team. I can whip any man *in all Kentucky*, by G—d."

The other replied, "I am an alligator; half man, half horse; can whip any *on the Mississippi*, by G—d."

The first one again, "I am a man; have the best horse, best dog, best gun, and handsomest wife in all Kentucky, by G—d."

The other, "I am a Mississippi snapping turtle: have bear's claws, alligator's teeth, and the devil's tail; can whip *any man*, by G—d."

This was too much for the first, and at it they went like two bulls, and continued for half an hour, when the alligator was fairly vanquished by the horse.

T. B. THORPE AND MIKE FINK

T. B. Thorpe was the creator of "The Big Bear of Arkansas," a Western frontier character whose whopping tall tales rivaled those of the Baron Münchausen. The character and the first yarns of that name first appeared in W. T. Porter's New York *Spirit of the Times*, on March 27, 1841. Others followed, and in 1854 Thorpe collected these in *The Hive of the Bee-Hunter* (1854). It is from the latter that the story of Mike Fink's fight with the Indian is extracted. This story is important for being one of the best printed sources of information about the epic hero of the old river days.

Mike Fink was "King of the Keelboatmen." [6] A hunter and a trapper in the early years of his century, Mike condescended to the demands of progress to the extent of taking a job on the old keelboats. But he wore his rue with a difference, as the following story will make clear.

Among his many distinctions, Mike hated Indians and was an expert rifle shot. On his first voyage into the lower river country, at Louisville he insulted an Indian by snatching a hawk's feather from the brave's scalp-lock. For showing resentment at this insult, Mike, lining him up against the sky background of the levee, shot off the scalp-lock. This taking of the scalp-lock without the life was the

[6] For a fine study of this river hero, see Walter Blair and Franklin J. Meine's *Mike Fink, King of Mississippi Keelboatmen*, New York (Henry Holt and Company), c. 1933.

deadliest of all insults to a brave. On the Indian's attempt to obtain revenge hangs the sequel of the story. The catastrophe comes under the bluffs at Natchez.

MIKE FINK'S RAPE OF THE LOCK

By T. B. Thorpe [7]

IN THE vicinity of Natchez rise a few abrupt hills, which tower above the surrounding lowlands of the Mississippi like monuments; they are not high, but from their loneliness and rarity, they create sensations of pleasure and awe.

Under the shadow of one of these bluffs, Mike and his associates made the customary preparations for passing the night. Mike's enthusiasm knew no bounds at the sight of land again; he said it was as pleasant as "cold water to a fresh wound"; and as his spirits rose, he went on making the region round about, according to his notions, an agreeable residence.

"The Choctaws live in these diggins," said Mike, "and a cursed time they must have of it. Now if I lived in these parts I'd declare war on 'em just to have something to keep me from growing dull; without some such business I'd be as musty as an old swamp moccason snake. I would build a cabin on that ar hill yonder, and could, from its location, with my rifle, repulse a whole tribe, if they dar'd to come after me.

"What a beautiful time I'd have of it! I never was particular about what's called a fair fight; I just ask half a chance, and the odds against me,—and if I then don't keep clear of snags and sawyers, let me spring a leak and go to the bottom. It's natur that a big fish should eat the little ones. I've seen trout swallow a perch, and a cat would come along and swallow the trout, and perhaps, on the Mississippi, the alligators use up the cat, and so on to the end of the row.

"Well, I will walk tall into varmint and Indian; it's a way I've got, and it comes as natural as grinning to a hyena. I'm a regular tornado—tough as hickory—and long-winded as a nor'-wester. I can strike a blow like a falling tree—and every lick makes a gap in the crowd that lets in acres of sunshine. Whew, boys!" shouted Mike, twirling his rifle like a walking-stick around his head, at the ideas suggested in his mind. "Whew, boys! if the Choctaw divils in them ar woods thar would give

[7] The *Hive of "The Bee-Hunter," Including Peculiar American Character, Scenery, and Rural Sports,* by T. B. Thorpe, Author of "Tom Owen, the Bee-Hunter"; "Mysteries of the Backwoods"; Etc. Etc., Illustrated by sketches from Nature, New York: D. Appleton and Company, M.DCCC.LIV.

us a brush, just as I feel now, I'd call them gentlemen. I must fight
something, or I'll catch the dry rot—burnt brandy won't save me."

As night wore on, one by one, the hardy boatmen fell asleep, some
in its confined interior, and others, protected by a light covering, in
the open air.

The moon arose in beautiful majesty; her silver light, behind the
highlands, gave them a power and theatrical effect as it ascended;
and as its silver rays grew perpendicular, they kissed gently the summit of the hills, and poured down their full light upon the boat, with
almost noonday brilliancy. The silence with which the beautiful
changes of darkness and light were produced, made it mysterious. It
seemed as if some creative power was at work, bringing form and life
out of darkness.

But in the midst of the witchery of this quiet scene, there sounded
forth the terrible rifle, and the more terrible war-whoop of the Indian.
One of the boatmen, asleep on deck, gave a stifled groan, turned upon
his face, and with a quivering motion, ceased to live.

Not so with his companions—they in an instant, as men accustomed
to danger and sudden attacks, sprang ready-armed to their feet; but
before they could discover their foes, seven sleek and horribly painted
savages leaped from the hill into the boat. The firing of the rifle was
useless, and each man singled out a foe, and met him with the drawn
knife.

The struggle was quick and fearful; and deadly blows were given,
amid screams and imprecations that rent the air. Yet the voice of
Mike Fink could be heard in encouraging shouts above the clamor.

"Give it to them, boys!" he cried, "cut their hearts out! Choke
the dogs! Here's hell a-fire and the river rising!" Then clenching with
the most powerful of the assailants, he rolled with him upon the deck
of the boat. Powerful as Mike was, the Indian seemed nearly a match
for him. The two twisted and writhed like serpents,—now one seeming to have an advantage, and then the other.

The general fight lasted less time than we have taken to describe it.
The white men gained the advantage; two of the Indians lay dead
upon the boat, and the living, escaping from their antagonists, leaped
ashore, and before the rifle could be brought to bear, they were out of
its reach.

While Mike was yet struggling with his adversary, one of his companions cut the boat loose from the shore, and, with powerful exertion,
managed to get its bows so far into the current, that it swung round

and floated; but before this was accomplished, and before any one interfered with Mike, he was on his feet, covered with blood, and blowing like a porpoise: by the time that he could get his breath, he commenced talking.

"Ain't been so busy in a long time," said he, turning his victim over with his foot; "that fellow fou't beautiful; if he's a specimen of the Choctaws that live in these parts, they are screamers; the infernal sarpents! the d—d possums!"

. . . Mike himself was a good deal cut up with the Indian's knife; but he called his wounds—blackberry scratches.

The master of the "broad horn" was a business man, and had often been down the Mississippi. This was the first attack he had received, or knew to have been made from the shores inhabited by the Choctaws, except by the white men; and he suggested the keeping of the dead Indians until daylight.

Not until after the rude breakfast was partaken of, and the funeral rites of the dead boatman were solemnly performed, did Mike and his companions disturb the corses of the red men.

Mike went about his business with alacrity. He stripped the bloody blanket from the Indian . . . He examined carefully the moccasons, pronouncing them at one time Chickasaws—at another time, Shawnese. He stared at the livid face, but could not recognize the style of paint.

. . . Mike was . . . about giving up his task as hopeless . . . the dead body . . . was turned upon its side. Mike's eyes distended . . . "like a choked cat's."

He drew himself up in a half serious, and half comic expression, and pointing at the back of the dead Indian's head, there was exhibited a dead warrior in his paint, destitute of his scalp-lock—the small stump which was only left, being stiffened with *red paint*. Those who could read Indian symbols learned a volume of deadly resolve in what they say . . . revenge [for] the fearful insult of destroying, *without the life*, the sacred scalp-lock.[8]

[8] *Op. cit.*, pp. 163-183.

DEACON SMITH'S BULL,
OR,
MIKE FINK IN A TIGHT PLACE

By Scroggins [9]

MIKE FINK, a notorious Buckeye hunter, was contemporary with the celebrated Davy Crockett, and his equal in all things appertaining to human prowess. It was even said that the animals in his neighborhood knew the crack of his rifle, and would take to their secret hiding places on the first intimation that Mike was about. Yet strange, though true, he was little known beyond his immediate settlement.

When *we* knew him, he was an old man; the blasts of seventy winters had silvered his head, and taken the elasticity from his limbs; yet, in the whole course of his life, Mike was never worsted, except upon one occasion.—To use his own language, he "never gin in, used up, to any thing that traveled on two legs or four," but once.

"That *once*, we want," said Bill Slasher, as some dozen of us sat in the bar-room of the only tavern in the "settlement."

"Gin it to us now, Mike—you've promised long enough, and you're old now, and you needn't care," continued Bill.

"Right! right! Bill," said Mike; "but we'll open with *licker* all round fust, it'll kind o' safe my feelin, I reckon."—

"Thar, that's good—better than t'other barrel, if anything!"

"Well, boys," continued Mike, "you may talk o' your scrimmages, tight places, and sich like, and subtract 'em altogether in one almighty big 'un, and then they haint no more to be compared to the one that I war in than a dead kitten to an old she bar! I've fout all kinds o' varmints, from an Ingin down to a rattlesnake! and never was wil'n to quit fust, but this once—and 'twas with a Bull!

"You see, boys, it war an awful hot day in August, and I war nigh runnin' off into pure *ile*, when I war thinkin' that a *dip* in the creek mout save me. Well, thar was a mighty nice place in old Deacon Smith's medder for that partic'lar bizziness. So I went down amongst the bushes to unharness. I jist hauled the old red shirt over my head, and war thinkin' how scrumptious a feller o' my size would feel a wollerin' round in that ar water, and was 'bout goin' in, when I seed the Deacon's Bull a makin' a B line to where I stood.

"I know'd the old cuss, he'd skar'd more people than all the parson's o' the 'settlements,' and cum mighty nigh killin' a few. Thinks I, Mike, you're in rather a tight place—get your fixins' on, for he'll be a

[9] Holly Springs *Mississippi Palladium*, June 6, 1851, p. [4].

drivin' them big horns o' his in yer bowels afore that time!—Well, you'll have to try the old varmint naked, I reck'n.

"The Bull war on one side o' the creek and I on t'other, and the way he made the 'sile' fly for a while, as if he war a diggin' my grave, was distressin'.

" 'Come on, ye bellerin' old heathen,' said I, 'and don't be standin' thar, for as the old deacon says o' the devil, "ye are not comely to look on." '

"This kind o' reached his understandin', and made him wishous; for he hoofed a little like, and made a dive.—As I don't like to stand in anybody's way, I gin him plenty o' sea room!—So he kind o' passed by me and cum out t'other side; and as the captain o' the Mud Swamp Rangers would say, ' 'bout face for 'nother charge.'

"Though I war ready for 'im this time, he cum mighty nigh runnin' a foul o' me. I made up my mind the next time he went out, he wouldn't be alone. So when he passed I grappled his tail, and he pulled me out on the sile, and as soon as we war both a top o' the bank, old brindle stopped and war about comin' round again, when I begun pullin' t'other way.

"Well, I reck'n this kind o' rild 'im, for he fust stood stock still, and looked at me for a spell, and then commenced pawin' and bellerin', and the way he made his hind gearin' play in the air, was beautiful!

"But it want no use, he could teach me; so he kind o' stopped to git wind for somethin' devilish, as I judged by the way he started. By this time I had made up my mind to stick to his tail as long as it stuck to his back-bone. I didn't like to holler fur help nuther, kase it war agin my principles; and then the Deacon had preachin' at his house, and it want fur off, nuther.

"I know'd if he hearn the noise, the hull congregation would cum down; and as I wasn't a married man, and had a kind o' hankerin' arter a gal just thar, I didn't feel as if I'd like to be seed in that predicament.

"So, says I, you old sarpent, do your cussedest! And so he did; for he drug me over every brier and stump in the field, until I war sweatin' and bleedin' like a fat bar with a pack o' hounds at his heels. And my name aint Mike Fink, if the old critter's tail and I didn't blow out sometimes a dead level with the varmint's back.

"So you kalk'late we made good time. Bimeby he slackened a little, and then I had 'im for a spell, for I jist drapped behind a stump and thar snubbed the critter! Now, says I, you'll up this 'ere white oak—break yer tail, or jist hold on a bit till I blow!

"Well, while I war settin' thar, an idee struck me that I had better be gettin' out o' this in some way. But how, adaxckly, was the *pint!* If I let go and run he'd be afoul o' me sure!

"So, lookin' at the matter in all its bearins', I cum to the conclusion that I'd better let somebody know whar I war. So I gin a *yell* louder than a locomotive whistle, and it want long afore I seed the Deacon's two dogs down like as if they war seein' which could git thar fust.

"I know'd who they war arter—they'd jine the Bull agin me, I war certain, for they were orful wenemous and had a spite agin me.

"So, says I, 'old Brindle, ridin' is as cheap as walkin' on this route; if you've no objection, I'll jist take deck passage on that ar back o' yourn!' So, I want long gittin' astride o' his back, and then you'd o' sworn thar want nothin' human in that ar mix! The sile flew so orfully as the critter an I rolled round the field—one dog one side and on t'other, tryin' to clinch my feet!

"I prayed and cussed and cussed and prayed, until I couldn't tell which I did last—and neither want any use, they war so orfully mixed up.

"Well, I reckon I rid about an hour in this way, when Old Brindle thot it war time to stop to take in a supply o' wind and cool off a little! So, when we got round to a tree that stood thar, he nat'rally halted!

"Now, says I, old boy, you'll lose one passenger, sartin. So I jist clum upon a branch, kalk'latin' to rest thar till I starved, before I'd be rid round in that way any longer.

"I war a makin' tracks for the top o' the tree, when I hearn somethin' makin' an orful buzzin' over head! I kinder looked up, and if thar want—well, thar's no use a swarin' now, but it war the biggest hornet's nest ever built!

"You'll gin in now, I reckon, Mike, kase thar's no help for you. But an idee struck me then, that I'd stand a heap better chance ridin' the old Bull than whar I war. Says I, old feller, if you'll hold on I'll ride to the next *station*, any how, let that be whar it will!

"So I jist drapped onto him agin, and looked aloft to see what I'd gain in changin' quarters; and, gentlemen, I'm a liar if thar want nigh half a bushel of the stingin' varmints ready to pitch onto me when the word 'go' was gin.

"Well, I reckon they got it, for 'all hands' started for our *company*. Some on 'em hit the dogs, about a *quart* struck me, and the rest charged on old Brindle.

"This time the dogs led off first, dead bent for the old Deacon's and as soon as old Brindle and I could get under way, we followed! And as I war only a deck passenger, and had nothin' to do with steerin' the craft, I swore if I had, we wouldn't a run that channel, any how!

"But, as I said afore, the dogs took the lead—Brindle and I next, and the hornets dreck'ly arter. The dogs yellin', Brindle bellerin', and the hornets buzzin' and stingin'! I didn't say nothin', for it want no use.

"Well, we'd got about two hundred yards from the house, and the Deacon hearn us and come out. I seed him hold up his hand and turn *white!* I reckon he war prayin', then, for he didn't expect to be called for so soon; and it want long, neither, afore the hull congregation, men, women and children, cum out, and then all hands went to yellin'.

"None of 'em had the fust notion that Brindle and I belonged to this world. I turned my head and passed the hull congregation! I seed the run would be up soon, for Brindle couldn't turn an inch from a fence that stood dead ahead!

"Well, we reach'd that fence, and I went ashore, over the old critter's head, landin' on t'other side, and lay thar stunned. It want long afore some on 'em who ware not so skeer'd cum round to see what I war! For all hands kalk'lated the Bull and I belonged together! But when Brindle walked off by himself, they seed how it war, and one of 'em said,—'*Mike Fink has got the wust of the scrimmage wunst in his life!*'

"Gentlemen, from that day I drapped the courtin' bizziness, and never spoke to a gal since! And when my hunt is up on this yearth, thar won't be any more Fink! and it's all owin' to Deacon Smith's Brindle Bull."

GO AHEAD READER

By Colonel Davy Crockett [10]

I was born in a cane brake, cradled in a sap trough, and clouted with coon skins; without being choked by the weeds of education, which do not grow *spontinaciously*—for all the time that I was troubled with *youngness,* my cornstealers were *na'*trally used for other purposes than holding a pen; and *rayly* when I try to write my elbow keeps coming round like a swingle-tree, and it is easier for me to tree a varmint, or swaller a nigger, than to write. Some persons tickle up their fancies to the scribbling point, and then their pen goes like a fiddler's elbow. Of books the divel of a one have I read, except Tom Toe and the Axes of the Apostles. And although my I*dears* run through me like an hour glass that never wants turning, if I only know'd how to scrawl the alphabet, I'd soon row some of the larned ones up Salt River—for

[10] *Go Ahead Almanack, 1838,* p. 2.

Honor and fame from no condition rise;
Axe well your part and down the tree soon lies.

For it's the grit of a fellow that makes the man; and I'm half chicken hawk and steel-trap. So I will just let you know, reader, what I think about gineral matters and things in particular.

A ROW AT "NATCHY UNDER THE HILL" [11]

ON MY return home from my tour "Down East," in 1835, whilst going down the Mississippi, our steamer came to, for a few hours, at Natchez. This city, which on the heights displays a beautiful appearance, is nevertheless more noted on the river here for the character of the lower town, or "Natchez under the hill," which the boatmen make a kind of rendezvous, and is the frequent theatre of a royal row. At the time of our stop there, over fifty boats of different descriptions were lying off in the river opposite this place. Close to the wharf, upon the deck of a broadhorn, stood a fellow of powerful muscular appearance, and every now and then he would swing around his arms and throw out a challenge to any one *"who dared to come and take the rust off of him,"* styling himself a *"roarer,"* and declaring that he hadn't had a fight in a month, and was getting lazy.

The men standing around seemed neither disposed to take much notice of this fellow, nor to accept his challenge and from this I imagined that he was a regular bruiser, and no one cared to oppose him.

Presently a little stubbed fellow came along, and hearing the challenger dare any one to rub the rust off of him, stepped up, and in a dry kind of style looked up in his face and inquired, "Who might ye be, my big chicken, eh?"

"I'm a high pressure steamer," roared the big bully.

"And I'm a snag," replied the little one, as he pitched into him, and before he had time to reflect, he was sprawling upon the deck. A general shout of applause burst from the spectators, and many now, who before had stood aloof from the braggadocia, jumped on board the boat and enjoyed the manner in which the little fellow pummeled him.

This scrape appeared to be the signal for several other fights, and in the evening a general row ensued, in which several houses were torn down. When we were ready to start again in the steamer Hunter, says I, "How's the water, Captain Stone?" "Why, Colonel, the river

[11] *Ibid.,* pp. 43-44.

is pretty considerable for a run, but the water is cool as Presbyterian charity. Clear off the coal-dust out of your wizzard, and give us a yarn about your tower." "Why, captain, may I be shot if you mightn't run with this same craft of your'n down, through and out of Symmes's lower hole, and back again, afore I could get thro' half what I've seen. I've been clean away amongst the Yankees, where they call your name *Stump*." "Well, colonel, here's to you; I'm sure you didn't get any thing better any where; and afore we quit, just tell me, did you see the sea sarpint?" "No, indeed, I did not, although I spoke for him not to be out of the way." "Well, Colonel, I wonder at those Yankee fellows, they are monstrous *cute;* but I suspect they don't know much about *Snaking.* I think with me in the Hunter here, you with your rifle, and one of these 'long shore Spaniards with his lasso, we'd give him a little of the hurricane tipt with thunder." "If we didn't catch him," says I, "we could scare him out of his skin, and that's all they want at the museum."

"IT'S ALL RIGHT, CAPTAIN" [12]

As THE fleet steamer R. was coming up the Mississippi, not long since, several way passengers came on board at Vicksburg, and among others, a giant-looking, middle-aged Kentuckian, who very soon became the subject of curiosity, wonder, and general remark. After traveling a short distance, the party, except our hero, made their way to the captain's office, and paid their fare to the place of destination. The next day, the clerk made bold to call on the delinquent passenger, who had taken no berth, but had passed the greater part of the time in sleeping in his chair, and with his usual urbanity of manner, asked the Kentuckian to give him his place of destination, as it would help him in making up his book, intending his question also as a gentle hint for him to pay his fare.

The giant rose from his lethargy, and replied:

"I'm going up the river a-piece. It's all right, Mr. Clerk."

The clerk not being much the wiser from this answer, again politely asked.

"At what point do you intend to land, sir?"

"Don't land at *no point*, Mr. Clerk. It's all *right*, though."

Here the clerk left our old hero and went to consult the captain, who at once lost his wonted good humor, as the clerk related the result of his interview with the delinquent customer. The captain proceeded

[12] Natchez *Daily Courier*, August 17, 1853, p. [2].

forthwith to bring the matter to a focus, and accosted the Kentuckian, saying:

"How far are you going to bear us company up the river, Uncle?"

"Oh! I'm going a-piece up with ye—but it's all *right*, Captain!"

"But, sir," said the captain, "you have neither paid your fare nor given the clerk your place of destination, and you are old enough to know the custom of steamboat men, that when a man refuses to pay his fare, or to give a good reason for not paying, we put him ashore immediately."

"We-l-l, captain, 'spose 'tis your custom, but it's *all right!*"

Here the captain lost his patience, and resolved to put him ashore forthwith, and accordingly ordered the pilot to land, and told him to make ready to go ashore, to which he very graciously replied:

"It's *all right*, captain."

The boat landed; and the plank put out, the giant was told to walk, to which he readily assented, saying:

"It's all right."

After getting on terra firma, the captain gave him a short blessing for giving him the trouble to land, and threatened him a top-dressing if he ever saw him again, &c. To which the old man responded again, with an air of triumph, pointing to a fine-looking cottage just above him on the bank:

"It's all right, captain, that's my house. It's *all right!*"

H. S. FULKERSON

By his own account, H. S. Fulkerson, author of *Random Recollections of Early Days in Mississippi*,[13] was a native of Kentucky and came to Rodney, Jefferson County, Mississippi, in 1836, at the age of nineteen. He lived there, at Port Gibson, at Natchez, at Vicksburg, and at various other places in the state, holding office as deputy United States marshal for the Southern District of Mississippi, as deputy clerk in the circuit court of Claiborne County, and as a political party man, and engaging in various kinds of business. His work and his associations were such as to throw him into contact with the interesting events and personalities of the great financial crash of 1837–1840 and of bond repudiation in Mississippi. Many of his sketches, he says, were first published in the Vicks-

[13] Vicksburg, Miss. (Vicksburg Printing and Publishing Company), 1885.

burg *Evening Post* and in the directory of the same city. They tell of such worthies as Shocco Jones and Seargent S. Prentiss, of yellow fever epidemics, of hanging gamblers, and of flatboat wars.

I. STEAMBOATS AND STEAMBOATMEN ON THE LOWER MISSISSIPPI IN EARLY DAYS

By H. S. Fulkerson [14]

POSSIBLY the earliest venture in the way of a local packet was that of the steamer Mississippi, a sea-going vessel, brought out from New York to New Orleans as early as 1820, to run between the latter point and Natchez. She was put into the trade, but in her build and equipments she was poorly adapted to river navigation, so poorly that she occupied a week's time in making the trip from one point to the other.

No serious attempt was made at a regular packet business, however, until some fifteen or twenty years later; the through boats doing all of the business both in freight and passengers. These through boats were often commanded by men of marked individuality, great force of character and courage, though as a rule, they were men without cultivation or early education. Such men were best adapted to the business, as it was a wild and hazardous life in those days, they having to deal often with desperate characters, both on board of their boats and on shore. One of these striking characters was Capt. John W. Russell, who ran the river in command of different boats for a number of years. He was a man of stalwart build and great strength, and marvelous stories were told of his lifting power; too marvelous to tell in a work that eschews extravagance. But a short story of his daring and determination may be told. On one of his trips up from New Orleans, he took on board his boat, at Baton Rouge, a number of Methodist preachers from a Conference at that place, just adjourned, who were on the return to their homes. Upon reaching Natchez, where the boat was detained several hours, one of the unsophisticated younger preachers of the party, having a considerable sum of money on his person,—maybe as agent of one of their societies, as preachers rarely travel with large sums of money of their own, or for that matter stay at home with the like,—went ashore alone, and in strolling about "Under the Hill," was induced by curiosity or some other innocent influence to enter, without his knowledge, a den

---

[14] *Random Recollections of Early Days in Mississippi,* Vicksburg, Miss. (Vicksburg Printing and Publishing Company), 1885, pp. 17-19.

of gamblers and other loose characters, where he remained but a few minutes, but long enough to be dispossessed, in a skillful way and without violence, of his money. After leaving he missed his money and went to the boat and reported the fact to the Captain. Russell went immediately to the house, which was situated on the bank of the river, and resting in part on piling driven into the river, demanding the money of the inmates, which they denied having taken. He persisted in his demand and told them that if the money was not returned within an hour he would pull their house into the river. The hour expired and no money came. He then hitched on to the undergearing of the house, and commenced backing his boat. As soon as the cracking of the timbers was heard the gamblers called to him, shaking the money in their hands. He eased up, and they went aboard and delivered up all of the money!

II. THE FLATBOAT WAR AT VICKSBURG

(1838)

By H. S. Fulkerson [15]

AT THAT day, the flatboatman was an important factor in the business of the place as well as its social status. The later comers to our city will be surprised to learn that in those earlier times it was no uncommon thing to see in the Winter months as many as four or five hundred "broad horns" as the flatboats were called, tied up at our landing. They averaged about four men to the boat, giving a transient population of some fifteen hundred to two thousand souls, of this class alone. These flatboats were in active competition with the regular dealers in the city, and no good feeling at the time existed between them.

In the Winter of 1838, when McGinty was Mayor, and Schofney was Chief of Police, this hostility came near culminating in a bloody war between the flatboatmen and citizens. The City Council had levied a tax of $1 per month on all flatboats, which was promptly paid. Subsequently the tax, or wharfage, was raised to $2.00 per day, which was also promptly paid. But this heavy tax failed to run the flatboats off, and at a later meeting of the Council an ordinance was adopted raising the tax to $50.00 per day. At this, flatboatmen rebelled and determined upon resistance by force, if necessary, if enforcement of collection were attempted before adjudication in court could be had. To this end they armed themselves with the one or more rifles or shotguns on each boat and with heavy bludgeons cut from a

[15] *Random Recollections,* pp. 97-99.

boat load of hickory hoop-poles lying at the landing. There were four hundred boats at the landing, and in two hours time the sum of $2000 was raised to test the matter in court. But before the proceedings could be instituted the day for enforcement of the new ordinance arrived, when two companies of military, in full uniform, with muskets and fixed bayonets, and a piece of ordnance in front—perhaps the four pounder piece with which Captain Miller "brought to" the suspected boat twenty years afterwards—the whole preceded by the Mayor and the Chief of Police, took up the line of march for the levee. A breastwork of cotton bales had been made opposite the wharfboat owned by Hall and Eddie, who were in the rebellion and who had a cannon loaded for the expected conflict. The flatboatmen assembled at the landing with their clubs—the guns being near at hand—mingled freely and fearlessly with the soldiers, and it is said, spiked their cannon. After much quarreling and threatening, and some feeble attempts at casting off the lines of some boats, disgust at the situation suddenly seized the citizens and soldiers, and they "marched up the hill again," concluding it was best to let the courts decide the question. Finally the Circuit Court decided against the city, and my informant, an intelligent gentleman who was an active party on the side of the resisters, says, taxed Guion and Prentiss, the owners of the landing, and for whose benefits the suits were instituted, with the costs. The distinguished lawyer, Joseph Holt, who later acquired a national reputation, was attorney for the flatboatmen. And this ended what at one time threatened to be a bloody conflict. The story is related more to illustrate the character of the times and of the people than for any intrinsic merit in it.

ANOTHER STORY "UNCLE JOHNNY" [16]

Dear P.—I was busily engaged the other night over at BUNTIN's (Natchez,) when the hours, like the late commercial affairs in England, had seen their lowest and were slowly improving, watching a game of billiards between A. L. B., Jr., and another one of the b'hoys, when simultaneously with a tap on the shoulder, I was greeted with—

"Howdy, Obe?"

Looking around, Uncle Johnny became apparent. "Less take sumthin, boy, you look sleepy?" I was glad to see him, and of course touched transparencies with him.

"Ah!" said he, putting down his glass, "this is whar towns beats the woods—better licker, and eny sort of d—— thing to put in it,

[16] *Spirit of the Times*, vol. 18 (March 18, 1848), p. 43.

at that; but as regards licker, I'm like CHUNKEY—thar is good and better licker. I don't 'stand the comparison, good or bad. I ain't never seen no *bad* yit; but drinkin licker with the fixins, jest makes a man *thirsty;* 'taint like takin' it out a chunk bottle away in the woods; thar he'll take three or four good mouthfuls afore he takes her down, and that'll git all over him in a minit."

"Well," said I, "that'll do about liquor, now. Where have you been all this while?"

"Been? Why all over the 'Swamp,' mostly, tho', at Gabe's, thar, at the mouth of Fool River, on Tensas. Bless your soul, boy, I don't bleeve I've seen you sence that new Captain tuck his boat up Fool River. No? In course, then, not sence we run that other new boat out in the trade?"

"I'm behind the times, certainly; but you know, Uncle Johnny, I live in *White* Settlement."

"Yes—mity fur back in it, though. Well, you see, ginerally the Tensas ain't more'n about two hundred yards wide, at common water, but jest whar Gabe lives it widens out to about half a mile or so, spang up to the mouth of the Naçon; they call this wide place Tensas Lake; well jest whar it begins to widen, Fool River comes in to it right squar from the West—"

"What river is *that?*" enquired I.

"Ruther a strange name ain't it? Lissen about the Cap'm and you'll see 'taint nuthin else—it's got one of the prettiest mouths *for* a river you ever seen. Smooth, slopin banks, kivered with sand, mussel shells, and beautiful trees down to the very water's edge; water's as clear as a sun shiney day, and it's so deep that the water at the bottom's as cold as Buntin's ice—we git it a purpose to mix it, sometimes. Well, this Cap'm came along late one evenin; 'twas his first trip in them branches—me and Gabe was off huntin, and when he got thar and see sich awful spreadin out of the waters, I recon he, too, thot he'd tuck the wrong shute sumwhar, and got out into the ocean; after knockin about awhile, he see the other river off to his left, so up that he puts. Gabe's niggers was workin up Fool River, and when they heard a steamboat up thar, *they* knowed sumthin was wrong, so they drops hoes and plows and puts off to head it;—they all got thar on the bank in a lump, and began to holler. 'Hello, master!—hello de boat! You's wrong!—dat ain't de road.' 'Yah, yah! des lissen at de fool Henson, callin de river de road!—git away, nigger! Hello! you's wrong; dat ain't de *river* you's in!—dat's Fool River!—*it* don't run no whars, it stops—' 'Golly, now, des hear Uncle Danel! It do run out in Sandy bio!' Sich like was gwine on mong the niggers, and the Cap'm seein the commotion, stopt steam, and told 'em he was only gwine up a piece to put out frate. 'Da ain't nuffin up dar to git it, den, but bars and allergaters!' Well, he kept on; they all come home and sot on the bank watin for the boat to come back.

"Well, me and Gabe got back bout dark; the niggers told us of the boat, and had their laff over agin. I'd killed a fat, barren doe, and knowin the boat would be back by supper, we had a nice lot ready for the fellers. 'Bout nine o'clock here she come. *We* was busy at Buckshot Poker. Gabe had jest went 3; I seen it, and was gwine 5 better, when the Cap'm opened. 'Good landin here?' 'Yes, massa, fus rate! Whar you put date frate?—we gwine take de skiff and git it, fore de wolf!'"

We jest turned our hands over on the table and left the bottle, nily half full, standin between 'em, and got out jest in time to keep the feller from wollapin sum of the darkies. He was very polite, and asked if he could *lay* at the landin all night? Gabe told him no, him and the balance of the fellers had better come up and *sleep* in the house; plenty er room, plenty licker, and a big supper a gettin, and so they must all come up.

" 'No,' says he, 'they'll stay aboard; I'd like to git sum infermation bout these rivers, fore I move.'

"After he got in the house, he looks all around, and seein the cards and the bottle, he turns round to Gabe, and says he, 'Stranger, whar do you *live?*' 'Right here,' says Gabe. 'Oh, I know,' says he, 'but whar *is* it?' 'Catahoula—mouth of Fool River.' 'Yes, I'm d—d ef it ain't Fool River, and I'm one of 'em, too!' says the Cap'm. 'One uther piece of infermation, ef you please. How fur is it to the head of that river?' 'Jest three miles,' says Gabe, 'and navigable plum up to its head!' 'I'm lost—turned round: when I was comin' out of it, it seemed to me we was gwine to the upper end, and I stopped two or three times to find out; at last I hearn them infernal niggers; but *they* seemed to be at the wrong end.' 'Well,' says Gabe, 'we'll straten you by mornin'; less take sumthin' for supper.' That Cap'm was a fair drinkin' man, and between that poker and that licker we sot up twill about this time. Obe, talkin' so much makes me mity dry!"

"Certainly, let's take a sweetner and go to bed."

"Oh no, we'll git that over at McDonell's; less set a while—I see Lewis is beatin' that feller."

"Well, what became of the Captain?"

"After tightenin' his hide with licker and supper, he bid us good evenin', and put for his boat; but he was lost yit, and dident know the way, so we tuck him down; he roused up the whole crew, and had somethin' for us to take. Just then Gabe says, 'Cap'm, will you be so good as to tell me where it is that a steam boat Cap'm ain't a man?' 'Raly, sir,' says he, 'I'm so bad lost I don't know nothin'; ef you'll be so good as to give the information.' 'Oh, certny,' says Gabe, 'it's when he's *a board!*' Incourse we had to drink agin. We left the Cap'm 'bout sun rise, and then he tuck the back track down Tensas, and ain't never bin hearn of sence."

Yours, in the trade,   OBE OILSTONE.

STEAMBOAT RACING [17]

IT IS said that immense sums of money have been bet on the result of the Eclipse's trip to Louisville—it being understood that she was to make the "best time" this season. We consider the best time, in this instance, the worst time. We are heartily sick of railroad disasters —deliberate massacres—and ruinous "accidents," which are the consequence of foolish bravado or insane avarice. The business of the country—its commercial affairs—can be conducted at a moderate speed, with as satisfactory a result as if it were transacted by lightning.

Steamboat racing may be very exciting and pleasurable to idiots— but in the face of recent facts—stern, solemn, implacable witnesses against it—we cannot give it our unqualified approval, and must use towards it, instead, a deliberate condemnation. Human life should not be thrown into one scale and dollars and dimes into another. The existence of a vagrant, even, is of more value in the sight of God than the accumulation of golden millions. Yet, of late, Life has frequently been weighed against money, the former kicking the beam!

The parties who encourage this system, and speculate on disasters, by extravagant wages, are almost as criminal as the employers who enter upon it for the realization of a little capital, in ready money, or notoriety. Public opinion must be with this racing madness, or it could not exist. It must have backers, or it could not stand a day. We are resolved—as far as our poor influence goes—that it shall be scouted as an insanity, or punished as a crime.

It is very probable that the Eclipse will not blow up or burn, but reach her destination in safety, and be greeted with unanimous applause by the reckless multitude. But that probability does not justify the officers who started, with malice prepense, on a racing tour, and made

[17] Natchez *Daily Courier*, May 19, 1853.

the lives of their passengers dependent on the ultimate capacities of the machinery. Neither does it justify the individuals who, safe on dry land, urge on the recklessness of the directors by their desperate gambling on blood.

We trust that public indignation, aroused at last, will brand this racing business as a crime against the community.

CHAPTER XI

CAPTAINS, COLONELS, AND PRIVATES

LOUISIANIANS from the France of the Louis, and Alabamians and Mississippians from Virginia and South Carolina, all alike, inherited from older lands and ages the soldierly tradition. With it, too, they inherited Gallic and Cavalier capacity to laugh at the comicalities of the military character and the absurdities of the calling of arms.

They have fought and laughed their way through many wars—notably, the War of 1812 (with its climactic Battle of New Orleans, still celebrated in the old fiddle piece "Eighth of January"), the Mexican War (recalled by the children's play-party game "Had a Big Fight in Mexico"), and the Civil War (abundantly remembered in humorous folk-songs, also, like "I'll Eat When I'm Hungry," "Open Your Cupboard to Me," and "I'm a Good Old Rebel"). Their stories about all of them are even better than their songs. The best of these have never been printed. We have such things as Longstreet's and Reuben Davis's descriptions of "milishy" muster and drill; the anonymous "Great Pop-Gun Practice," which caught the eye of Frank Moore and was saved in the *Rebellion Record* (a title that must have made "high private" Toby turn over in his unmarked Shiloh or Vicksburg grave and wish for his pop-gun again); the Mississippi jokes for *Southern Punch;* and droll yarns by "Private" John, embalmed in (of all things!) the *Congressional Record*. But most of the kind that Mark Twain heard on steamboats and verandahs ("Lawzee, miss, dat moon ain't near so pu'ty as 'twuz befo' de wa' ") have been lost or, if preserved at all, retained in the fading memories of second- or third-generation Southerners living to-day.

The early frontier soldiers were perhaps the most versatile. They could exterminate a canoe full of Indian warriors or marry a young couple with equal despatch, reclaim a "widow woman's" property from plundering Indians or catch a horse-thief on an *"ognum torum writ"* with the same rough and ready ingenuity.

A. B. LONGSTREET

In deference to the fact that Augustus Baldwin Longstreet (1790–1870), dean of ante-bellum Southern humorists, was for seven years (1849–1856) president of the University of Mississippi, died at Oxford, Mississippi, and sleeps there in St. Peter's Cemetery, near his more famous son-in-law, L. Q. C. Lamar, the following sketch from the *Georgia Scenes* is included in this book. It was first published in *The Magnolia*, a Charleston literary magazine, in 1843, and is here reprinted from a photostatic copy.

Longstreet was a graduate of Yale. He studied law at Litchfield, Connecticut, took up residence at Greensboro, Georgia, began the practice of law, married, was elected to the state legislature, and became a judge of the state supreme court. In 1833 he published anonymously, in the Milledgeville *Southern Recorder*, the first of the *Georgia Scenes*. Subsequent sketches were collected and published in book form, again anonymously, in 1835. His major interests were politics, religion, and education. In 1838 he became a Methodist minister, and from 1839 to 1848 he was president of Emory College, Oxford, Georgia, an institution of that denomination. Before his death in 1870 he had been president of three other institutions of learning—Centenary College, in Louisiana; the University of Mississippi; and the University of South Carolina. In 1865 he returned to Oxford, Mississippi, and lived with his son-in-law, L. Q. C. Lamar, until his death in 1870.

The best critical biography of Longstreet is Professor John Donald Wade's (1924), elsewhere cited in this book.

Both the scenes and the materials of Longstreet's imaginative writings belong to Georgia. The following somewhat sentimental and idyllic sketch of two old soldiers, with their tall tale of reminiscence and recognition, may serve, however, to suggest the kinds of stories that veterans of the Revolution once told in Alabama, Mississippi, and Louisiana.

THE OLD SOLDIERS

By A. B. Longstreet [1]

ON A calm summer's afternoon, at the door of an humble but comfortable log dwelling, sat the venerable John Chavers. He had done much service in the war that won our liberty; but liberty was nearly all that he gained by it. A private in the ranks, he retired from the field with no other worldly estate than a little continental money, and a small farm, but poorly improved. His first wife died soon after the war; and he married a second, fifteen years younger than himself. By both he had children, but some had died, and all the rest had married and left him, at the time of which I am speaking. While his strength remained, he exerted in honest industry, and thus managed to keep his family above want; and now that it had deserted him, a small pension from the government, and the labor of two servants, supplied the demands of his waning life. Some of his sons had served in the war of 1812, but the old man gave them little credit for it; "because," as he used to say, "that was mere child's play compared with the old war. No tories in your day, boys—no prison ships. March out with your bright muskets and bayonets all furnished to your hand —wagons following loaded with good fat rations—canteens full, good clothes on, march where you please without danger, sleep soundly all night in your tents, without fear of being waked by bullet or tomahawk—pshaw! A mere frolic! You ought to have lived in the parched-corn and tory times, when bare-footed and in rags, we *bogued* thro' thickets and cane-brakes, and mud and swamps, wet or dry, hot or cold, with an old Indian-trader or rusty shot guns in our hands, that made three snaps and one flash to a fire. Then go to sleep on a bed of grass or dirt to the music of wolves and owls; sometimes in sight of your own house, which you dare not enter for fear that you'd never get out again till the traitors flung you out. Polly, there, can tell you— no, she was 'most too young to recollect much about it; but Nancy could have told you something of those days. Look at the spoon-handle in the little pine box on the top of the *beaufat;* that'll tell you a story about hard times. Polly won't believe that story about the spoon-handle; but, there it is, and it speaks for itself. If it wasn't so, what did I make the box to put it in for?—And what do I take it down and look at it every fourth of July for?—Bill Darden was there, and John Taylor was there, and Arch. Martin was there; but, poor fellows, they've all gone and left me, long ago, I reckon."

---

[1] *Georgia Scenes,* New Series, from *The Magnolia,* New Series, Volume II (January-June, 1843, Charleston, 1843), pp. 160-161.

But the old man had for years ceased to talk thus, and for the best of reasons, namely, that he found no body to talk to. The young seldom visited him, and the old of his neighborhood—alas, compared with him, there were none. His iron constitution had struggled manfully with Time; but the conqueror of all had overpowered him, and doomed him to perpetual confinement to his dwelling and its enclosure. There is one from whom time cannot banish us, from whose presence prisons cannot seclude us. This one lingered with the old soldier in his solitude, and made calm and peaceful the twilight of his life. He had just been tottering round his little garden, when he took his seat at the door where I introduced him to the reader. The sun was just setting, when on the highway that led by his house, he observed an aged foot-passenger approaching. Slow and trembling were the footsteps of the stranger. When within about twenty rods of the house, he stopt, leaned for a moment upon his walking stick, then lifting his hat, drew from it a handkerchief, or what served its purpose, and wiped the perspiration from his brow.

"Poor old man!" said Chavers, as he looked on the bending form, and snow-crowned head of the traveller. "Where can he be going? Begging, I suppose!"

The stranger advanced, and seating himself on the step of the door, drew a deep sigh and said—"Can an old revolutionary soldier, who has nothing to pay, get supper and lodging——"

"Yes, old man," interrupted Chavers. "That's a countersign that passes any man to my table, bed and heart. Get up old man, get up—that's no place for an old *seventy-sixer*—give me your hand, and I'll help you in as well as I can, though I'm but poor help. Polly, hand the old man a chair, for he seems almost done over."

"And, indeed, so I am," said the guest; "these sandy roads don't suit such old limbs as mine."

"And what makes you take the road at your age, old man? Old folks, like we, ought to stay in doors, lest death find us where friends can't."

"That's true, friend, but we can't always do what we ought to do, or wish to. I have been living with my son for many years, but he has lately died, leaving a large family and nothing to feed them on; for though he worked hard, and I helped him all I could, yet he died very poor. His wife's kinsfolks sent for her away West somewhere, and I concluded to try and get to my grand-daughter's, who is married and settled about thirty miles below here; but, it seems to me, I shall hardly ever get there, at the rate I get along. My strength's gone—my strength's gone, friend; I can't travel now as I once could——"

"I know very well how to believe that. But how do you get along without money in these closefisted times."

"Oh, mighty well, mighty well. I generally tell the people, where I stop, beforehand, that I've no money, but that I am an old soldier, and this, with my white head, always gets kind treatment. I haven't found but one man that turned me off; and I didn't mind that much, as I hadn't far to go before I found a better; but he called me an impostor, and that was the hardest saying I've had to bear for these thirty years——"

"The rascal! Why didn't you give him your stick?"

"Oh, God bless your soul, I had better use for my stick. It doesn't become old men like us to use sticks except to walk with. Besides, I am trying to get to a country where none but the peaceable can go."

"You're right, old man—you're right, and I'm wrong," said Chavers, as he drew his sleeve across his eyes.——"And you say that you are a revolutionary soldier;—who did you serve under!"

"Well, now, I can't say that I was much in the regular army, though I did some little there too. My service was mostly against the tories, and it doesn't seem much thought of in these days, yet it ought to be, for, I tell you, I have seen some as tough times as any in the regular army ever saw; and made some as narrow escapes as any made during the war."

"Well, suppose you tell us one, for its a long time since I've heard any one talk about the old war, that was in it."

"Well, I'll tell you one of the narrowest I ever made. There were some forty or fifty of us once in pursuit of a gang of tories, and a little before sunset we came within a few miles of where we heard that they had encamped. We stopt at a branch, and our captain told us to fix up our guns, and refresh ourselves as well as we could, (for we had precious little to refresh with, beside water,) and that about the time of sound sleep, we would march down upon them and give them rations. While we were here there came a man to us and told Capt. Ryan——"

"Told who?"

"Told Captain Ryan, Captain John Ryan, we were under him— that the tories were to have a great dancing frolic, at Smith's tavern that night, and that if we'd come upon them, before they broke up, we might take or kill the whole of them. Well, soon after dark we pushed forward, and as we neared the tavern, sure enough, we heard them fiddling and dancing in high glee. 'Boys,' said Capt. Ryan, 'we've got 'em safe enough.' He divided us into two parties, and told us to march in a body to within about a hundred yards of the house, and then separate, and one party take the back door, and the other the front door, at the same time. On we pushed, very softly and briskly, fiddle playing and feet thumping, until we got within five steps of the doors, when all of sudden out went the lights, and pop, pop, pop, we were fired upon on all sides. Bless your soul, friend, such slaughter as they made of us, you never saw. They wounded Captain Ryan badly in the shoulder, and killed or took prisoners nearly every one of us——"

"And how did you get out of the scrape?"

"I, and three or four more, were taken prisoners, and put on board a prison-ship; and there we saw tough times, I tell you."

"Did any thing—did any thing uncommon happen, while you were on board that ship?"

"Why, yes, friend, one of the strangest things that I reckon ever did happen, but I'm a'most afraid to tell it, for fear you will not believe me; but it's just as true as that you sit in this chair, and since you've brought it up, I'll tell it to you——"

"Polly, give me a drink of water, if you please—no, sit still!"

"One day, while we prisoners were all seated round a tray of mush, (for that was about all we got to eat,) a thunder cloud passed over us, and just as the man opposite to me was raising his spoon to his mouth, there came a flash of lightning, and cut the handle right off at the bowl, and didn't hurt any of us."

"The Lord help my soul!" exclaimed Polly.

"I know it's hard to believe, ma'am, but it's every word true, as sure as you live."

"I believe——"

"Hush, Polly!" interrupted Chavers. "Stranger, do you remember the name of the man that held that spoon."

"Why I'm not so sure I can call it now—but I think it was *Shivers* or *Chivers*, or some such name——"

"Was it Chavers?"

"That's the very name!" said the stranger, slapping his thigh with a force disproportioned to his strength.

"Why—why—Taylor!" exclaimed Chavers rising—"Is that you?"

"Chavers!——"

"Taylor!——"

The old men embraced, but their emotions were too powerful for their strength, and they sunk together to the floor. When they rose, Polly was standing by them with the pine box in her hand, and her apron to her eyes.

QUEUE PENDANT

By Minnie Walter Myers [2]

IN 1798 the first United States troops that came down the Mississippi were quartered at Fort Adams. General Wilkinson, Colonel Hamtramck, Major Butler, Captain Green, and other officers were making merry over their punch one night, and the general by some accident got his queue singed off. Next day he issued an order forbidding any officer to appear with a queue. Major Butler refused to obey, and was put under arrest. Soon after, he was very sick and when he knew he could not live he made his will, and gave instructions for his burial, which he knew would be attended by the whole command.

"Bore a hole," said he, "through the bottom of my coffin, right under my head, and let my queue come through it, that the damned old rascal may see that even when dead I refuse to obey his order."

These directions were literally complied with.

"THE BEST MARRIED PEOPLE"

By Albert James Pickett [3]

UPON the Tombigby and Lake Tensaw, the people still [in 1800] lived without laws, and without the rite of matrimony. For years, the sexes had been in the habit of pairing off, and living together, with the mutual promise of regular marriage, when ministers or magistrates should make their appearance in the country. An amusing incident will here be related, in which a young couple were united by a functionary not hitherto known as participating in such sacred rites.

The house of Samuel Mims, a wealthy Indian countryman, was the most spacious in the country, and hither the young and the gay flocked to parties, and danced to the music furnished by the Creoles of Mobile and others, for the country abounded in fiddlers, of high and low degree. Daniel Johnson and Miss Elizabeth Linder had, for some time, loved each other. She was rich and he was poor, and, of course, the parents of the former objected to a *pairing*.

On Chirstmas night, a large party was assembled at "Old Sam Mims'," and the very forests resounded with music and merry peals of laughter. In the midst of the enjoyment, the lovers, in company

---

[2] *Romance and Realism of the Southern Gulf Coast*, Cincinnati (The Robert Clarke Co.), 1898, p. 51, quoted from Claiborne's *Mississippi As a Province, Territory, and State.*

[3] *History of Alabama and Incidentally of Georgia and Mississippi, from the Earliest Period*, c. 1851; T. M. Owen reprint, Birmingham (The Webb Book Company, Publishers), 1900, pp. 464-465.

with several young people, of both sexes, secretly left the house, entered some canoes, paddled down Lake Tensaw, into the Alabama, and arrived at Fort Stoddart, an hour before daylight. Captain Shaumberg, who had risen early to make his egg-nog, was implored to join the lovers in the bonds of matrimony.

The proposition astounded the good-natured old German, who protested his ignorance of all such matters, and assured them that he was only a military commandant, having no authority whatever to make people man and wife. They entreated, telling him with truth, that the Federal Government had placed him there as a general protector and regulator of affairs, and that the case before him demanded his sanction and adjustment.

After the egg-nog had circulated pretty freely, the commandant placed the lovers before him, and, in a stentorian voice, pronounced the following marital speech: "I, Captain Shaumberg, of the 2d Regiment of the United States Army, and commandant of Fort Stoddart, do hereby pronounce you man and wife. Go home! behave yourselves—multiply and replenish the Tensaw country!"

The happy pair entered their canoes, rowed back to the Boat Yard, and were pronounced, by the whole settlement, "the *best* married people they had known in a long time."

"NOW FOR IT, BIG SAM!"

(Canoe Fight on the Alabama River, 1813)

By Albert James Pickett [4]

IN THE meantime, Austill had reached Randon's plantation, with the canoes, a quarter of an hour in advance of the main party. When they came up Dale ordered them to cross to the western side, as it was found impracticable to continue the route on the eastern, on account of the cane and thick vines. While the company of Captain Jones or Lieutenant Montgomery was being ferried over, Captain Dale, Jere Austill, Lieutenant Creagh, James Smith, John Elliott, a half-breed, Brady and six others occupied a position in a small field, between a sand bluff and the river, where, kindling a fire, they began to boil some beef and roast a few potatoes for their morning repast.

When all the command had passed the river except these men, and immediately after the negro, Caesar, had returned, with the smaller canoe, the men from the western side gave the alarm that the Indians were rapidly descending upon those who occupied the little field.

[4] *Ibid.*, pp. 563-566.

They sprang up from their hasty meal, retreated to the river side, and were partially screened from the enemy's fire by a small bank. While in this perilous situation, hemmed in by the Indians and the river, their attention was directed to a large flat-bottomed canoe, containing eleven warriors. Naked, and painted in a variety of fantastic colors, while a panther-skin encircled the head of the Chief, and extended down his back, these Indians presented a picturesque and imposing appearance.

For some reason, those in the rear now retired, leaving Dale and his little party free to attack those in the canoe. The red voyagers, apparently unapprised of their danger, glided gently down the river, sitting erect, with their guns before them. Dale and his party immediately opened fire upon them, which they promptly returned. Several rounds were afterwards exchanged, resulting, however, in but little injury, as the Indians now lay flat in the canoe, exposing nothing but their heads. At length, two of the latter, cautiously getting into the water, swam for the shore, above the field, holding their guns dry above their heads. They swam near the land, above the mouth of a stream, over whose muddy bottom Austill and Smith crossed with difficulty to pursue them. When near the Indians, the buckskin leggins of Austill, suspended by a band around his waist, fell about his feet from the weight of water in them, causing him to slip and be precipitated down the bluff. At that moment, a ball from Smith's unerring rifle perforated the head of one of the Indians, who immediately turned over upon his back and then sunk. The other gained the bank and ascended it, keeping Smith off with his gun, which he pretended was charged. Austill, who had now gained the top of the bluff, pursued the Indian up the stream, when a gun was fired, the contents of which passed just over his head. Imagining himself among the enemy, and hesitating for a moment, the savage escaped. The fire proved to be from Lieutenant Creagh's gun, who, in the thick cane, supposed Austill to be the warrior, in whose pursuit he was likewise engaged.

While these things were rapidly transpiring, Dale ordered the large canoe to be manned on the opposite shore, and to be brought over to capture the Indians who were still in their canoe. Eight men sprang into it, but having approached near enough to see the number of fierce warriors still alive and ready to defend themselves to desperation, this cautious party rapidly paddled back to the western side. The exasperated Dale now proposed that some of his men should follow him in the small canoe, which was immediately acquiesced in.

Dale leaped down the bank into the boat, and was followed by Smith and Austill. All the others were anxious to go, but it afforded room for no more. The noble Caesar paddled towards the Indians' canoe, and, when within twenty yards of it, the three resolute Americans rose to give them a broadside; but only the gun of Smith fired, for the other two had unfortunately wet their priming. Caesar was ordered to paddle up, and to place his boat side by side with that of the warriors.

Approaching within ten feet, the Chief, recognizing Dale, exclaimed, "NOW FOR IT, BIG SAM!" At the same time, he presented his gun at Austill's breast. That brave youth struck at him with an oar, which he dodged, and in return he brought down his rifle upon Austill's head, just as the canoes came together. At that moment, the powerful arms of Smith and Dale raised their long rifles, which came down with deadly force, and felled the Chief to the bottom of the canoe— his blood and brains spattering its sides. Such was the force of the blow inflicted by Dale, that his gun was broken near the lock. Seizing the heavy barrel, still left, he did great execution with it to the end of the combat. Austill, in a moment, engaged with the second warrior, and then with a third, both of whom he despatched with his clubbed rifle. Smith, too, was equally active, having knocked down two Indians. Caesar had by this time got the canoes close together, and held them with a mighty grasp, which enabled Dale, who was in the advance, and the others to maintain a firm footing by keeping their feet in both canoes. These brave men now mowed down the savages, amid the encouraging shouts of the men on both sides of the river, who had a full view of the deadly conflict. In the midst of this unparalleled strife, a lusty Indian struck Austill with a war-club, which felled him across the sides of the two boats, and, while prostrate, another had raised his club to dash out his brains, when Dale, by a timely blow, buried his heavy rifle barrel deep in the warrior's skull. In the meantime, Austill recovered his feet, and, in a desperate scuffle with another savage, knocked him into the river with the club which he had wrested from him.

The only word spoken during the fight was the exclamation of the Chief upon recognizing Dale, and the request of Caesar for Dale to make use of his bayonet and musket, which he handed to him. Having laid all the warriors low, these undaunted Americans began casting them into the bright waters of the Alabama, their native stream, now to be their grave. Every time a savage was raised up from the bottom of the canoe by the head and heels and slung into the water, the Americans sent up shouts, loud and long, as some slight revenge for the tragedy of Fort Mims.

ORIGINAL ANECDOTE OF GEN. JACKSON [5]

THE old General had with others been engaged in holding a treaty within the present limits of Mississippi; the result of which was the purchase of Territory and removal of the Choctaw Indians from that large and interesting portion of the State, known as the "New Purchase."

On his route homeward accompanied by one or two friends and a servant, it was necessary for him to camp out or lodge at the *"stands"* on the route,—usually kept by the Choctaws and half breeds.

On one occasion, in order to make a forced march, the party started at an early hour, aiming for a particular house at which to procure breakfast; they arrived, ordered breakfast, and while eating, heard a good deal of noise, bustle, &c., in another room of the house. It did not at first attract their attention; finishing their breakfast they were about proceeding, when they heard calling to them a voice *"for God's sake, white men, come and help me";* (the old man was always quick on the trigger, he jumped forward, opened the door, and out marched a woman of advanced age, or rather, beyond the meridian.

She complained bitterly of the conduct of the host—of her arrival there two days previous, with her small *carriole* and two negroes, clothing, &c., on her way from Tennessee to Lower Mississippi, or as she called it the "Natchey Country."

Her negroes had disappeared, her horses strayed, and she barely left in the house by sufferance of her host, who threatened to drive her off.

The old General's horse was standing ready saddled, and his friends already mounted—he heard her story, and told them they might ride slowly forward, and that he would overtake them. They declined, knowing there was a "breeze brewing." He was known, either personally or by some free masonry, to *every* Indian that ever met him after the Creek war. He called to his host and ordered him to come out before the cabin; and in hot haste, warm language and earnest manner, told the Choctaw, in mixed English and vernacular, to unsaddle his horse —*"hobble him, take him to your trough, water him, and give him fodder."* "Now, sir, lay my saddle *here,"* pointing to the shady side of a spreading blackjack.—When these arrangements were completed at double quick step, by the Indian, the old man very deliberately laid himself down, using the saddle for a pillow.

Taking out his watch, looking at the time, and reflecting a moment —the Indian standing like a statue, with folded arms, before him, awe struck: "Now sir, I'll give you until dinner time to get this good woman's negroes and horses; you have stolen them and run them off. *Begone!* it is now eight; you have until twelve—if they are not here by that time, *your ears come off*. In the meantime, before leaving, order a good dinner for all of us."

Twelve o'clock came—the Indian, negroes and horses, in good order and well conditioned, made their appearance, and were transferred to the widow, who went on her way rejoicing and blessing him for the good deed. She knew not his name, and asked the Choctaw. *"Ugh! Big Mingo heap; kill Ingin plenty; General Jackson. Ugh! Ingin no fool him!"*   *Concordia Intelligencer.*

THE *OGNUM TORUM* WRIT [6]

In 1826, when North Mississippi was cleared of the Indians partially, the whole of this country was then called Yazoo County, extending over one hundred and fifty miles square. The law had not taken effect for the want of organization, except in the militia. One Colonel Cassou commanded in his regiment the whole country, and he was all the officer, civil or military, that lived in that large tract of country. The country, as was to be expected, was filled up with a horde of trifling fellows, and thieves, and the like. About this time there were missing two horses in the neighborhood, and Col. Cassou called a meeting of the citizens generally, to consult upon the best measures to adopt in relation to it. Accordingly, a large collection met at the house of the Colonel on Big Black, (where Holmes county now is,) and called the Colonel to the chair. Suspicion soon fell upon a young man by the name of Dobson, who was not present. After consulting, and discussing the subject, pro and con, it was agreed that Dobson should be brought forward for trial. An old gentleman, rather more intelligent than some of his contemporaries, asked how the meeting could get hold of him? Col. Cassou drew down his eye-brows in a dignified manner, as if casting about in his mind previous to giving "the opinion of the Court," and said, "Gentlemen, I will issue an *Ognum Torum* Writ, and have him corpurally before me." "But what kind of a writ is that, Colonel?" said an old gentleman, with caution. "It is a writ," said the Colonel, gravely, "to take him as well where he ain't, as where he is, and have him corpurally before us." This was satisfactory to the meeting, and six men were despatched with this awful writ, who returned in about an hour with the renowned Dobson in strings. He was arraigned—witnesses sworn—but no evidence of even a secondary nature could be obtained; yet, after taking the vote, a majority found him *guilty*. The Colonel then put on an awful solemn visage, and said, "Isaac Dobson! by authority of the ninth section of laws in these cases, I pass sentence of death upon you, to be hung by the neck till you are dead, *dead*, DEAD; not for stealing horses, but that horses may *not be* stolen."

That evening Dobson was led to a blackjack, and hung according to the sentence of "the Court," admitting that he had stolen the horses, and that he intended to have taken them to Red River Raft, and acknowledged the justice of his sentence. This country is now well settled, and divided into twenty counties, but the old Colonel was heard the other day to say, "These are shocking times; a man must be tried three or four days for stealing and the like, then get clear by some quirk of the law, when he stole the horse as plain as the nose on my face—I will go to Texas, and git among civilized folks."—*Boston Post*.

PERFORMANCES IN EXCESS OF THE GENERAL'S EXPECTATIONS

By Reuben Davis [7]

SOME time before [the summer of 1842], I had been elected brigadier of militia, and Major-General Bradford now sent me an order to call out for review the militia in the six counties which composed my brigade. At that time there was some talk of a war with Mexico, which increased our military ardor. I issued the order, and in August we began our review in the county of Tippah, four miles from the courthouse. The county had two regiments, and the ground selected was common to both. General Bradford had provided himself with a uniform so gorgeous as to smite the eyes of all beholders. His glittering chapeau was crowned with long white plumes, and the gilt scabbard of his sword was girt around him with a magnificent yellow sash. He was a tall and handsome man, and in his dazzling array looked, and felt, every inch a hero. He left Pontotoc two days before the review, and being clad in full martial attire, with sword dangling by his side, and mounted upon a gallant charger, he rode on to Ripley, a joy to all beholders.

In the meanwhile, I, with my chief of staff, Captain Joel M. Acker, left Aberdeen in a buggy, drawn by two horses, which were to serve our purposes on occasions of parade as well as by the road. Although

[7] *Recollections of Mississippi and Mississippians*, pp. 137-141.

we travelled in the plain garb of peaceful citizens, I promise you we were not unprovided with the paraphernalia of magnificent regimentals. We might not carry it off as grandly as the major-general, but our little trunk contained accoutrements not to be sneezed at.

We reached Pontotoc, where we expected to find our chief and to proceed in company, but found him already off the field. When we got to Ripley, we were greeted with immense enthusiasm, passed a merry night, and were roused all too soon on the next morning by the strains of martial music and all the preparations for a field day. Captain Acker and I had soon finished breakfast, and started off, attended by a crowd, to the parade ground, about three miles away. We soon discovered that the people were disgusted by our appearance in citizens' clothes, and considered themselves defrauded of part of the show. We hastened to repair this injustice, and soon appeared disguised in splendors that might have startled a Comanche Indian. This appeased the multitude, and we were greeted with thunders of applause.

Still no sign of our commander. The crowd grew weary, and I ordered the colonels to form their regiments. Just as this was accomplished, our superior appeared, gallant and glorious. There was a cloud upon his manly brow. We had been too precipitate. It would have been more seemly to await his arrival. I made a deep obeisance and asked pardon for my indiscretion. "It is granted, sir; but you will hereafter observe a more decorous delay." "Most certainly, sir; but you will appreciate the ardor of a young officer, eager to make his first display before an army panting for action." The chief was mollified, and as I observed he had no aide, I tendered the services of Captain Acker. This offer was graciously accepted. The parade went on, and it was a sight to behold. Our men acquitted themselves with so much credit that our hearts swelled with pride, and a sweet complacency stole into each bosom. Alas, it is in moments of overweening security that our downfall awaits us! Why, oh, why could not the major-general have left well-enough alone?

In an evil hour he directed me to advance and inform the colonels that he would himself assume command, and direct certain evolutions upon which he prided himself. I ventured to intimate a doubt as to the expediency of tempting fate by any new manoeuvres, but was ordered to "obey orders promptly or quit the field." I rushed off. "Colonels, I am instructed, etc.,—now obey orders or quit the field."

My chief then ordered me to take my post, promising that I should now witness some splendid evolutions which could not fail to give me great pleasure. He even turned back yet once more to inform me that these evolutions had been much in favor with the great Napoleon.

He then moved forward and gave the command, "Battalions, prepare to form into columns of attack by companies. Battalions, form columns of attack on your rear—on your right—into line—wheel!"

Unfortunately the troops had not been faced to the rear. They hesitated. The general shouted again, and the evolutions began. In a few seconds, each separate company seemed to march straight into every other company. Some struggled in one direction, some in another, and confusion reigned supreme.

In this emergency, the chief appealed to me, and I could only suggest that he might send me to make a short address of thanks and dismissal. He hastily ordered me to do so as quickly as possible. Having called the troops into line, I said, as nearly as I can recollect: "Soldiers, your performances to-day have exceeded all the expectations of your general. He bids me thank you for the manner in which you have performed your duty, and for the soldierly bearing which you have displayed on this brilliant occasion. Should the bloody banners of war be unfurled, and our soldiers called upon to march into Mexico, he can point with pride to your regiments as fitted for service on any field. Soldiers, you are dismissed with three cheers for your gallant general." The cheers made the woods ring, and we left the troops well pleased. It may be mentioned, however, that in all our subsequent journey Captain Acker and I carefully abstained from any reference to the favorite evolutions of the great Napoleon!

HO! HO! FOR TEXAS AND THE WARS

(For the *Free Trader*) [8]

> I have no one to keep me here,
>   No cherished wife to love me,
> No dear sweet girl to shed a tear
>   When clouds grow dark above me.
>
> Then for the Texas ranks I go,
>   To honor and to glory,
> To fight the dusky "Mustang" foe
>   And place my name in story.
>
> *Brave* may I be in battle field,
>   As was of old the Roman,
> And *strong* the heavy sword to wield
>   Against my country's foemen.

[8] *Mississippi Free Trader and Natchez Gazette,* vol. XI (June 3, 1846), p. 4.

Yet may I have a heart still kind—
For the vanquished feel true sorrow,
And when a "Mustang's" widow find,
To do a kind deed for her.

May 22d, 1846   S.

GREAT "POP-GUN" PRACTICE[9]

TOBY is a high private in the First Regiment of the Mississippi army. His company is armed with the breech-loading Maynard rifle, "warranted to shoot twelve times a minute, and carry a ball effectually 1,600 yards." Men who fought at Monterey and Buena Vista call the new fangled thing a "pop-gun." To test its efficacy, Toby's Captain told the men they must "try their guns." In obedience to command, Toby procured the necessary munitions of war, and started with his "pop-gun" for the woods. Saw a squirrel up a very high tree—took aim—fired. Effects of shot immediate and wonderful. Tree effectually stripped, and nothing of the squirrel to be found, except three broken hairs. "Pop-gun" rose in value—equal to a four-pounder. But Toby wouldn't shoot toward any more trees—afraid of being arrested for cutting down other people's timber. Walked a mile and a quarter to get sight of a hill. By aid of a small telescope, saw hill in distance; saw large rock on hill; put in big load; shut both eyes—fired. As soon as breath returned, opened both eyes; could see, just could, but couldn't hear—at least, couldn't distinguish any sounds; thought Niagara had broke loose, or all out-doors gone to drum-beating. Determined to see if shot hit. Borrowed horse, and started toward hill. After travelling two days and nights, reached place; saw setting sun shining through hill. Knew right away that was where his shot hit. Went closer—stumbled over rocky fragments scattered for half a mile in line of bullet. Came to hole—knew the bullet hit there, because saw lead on the edges; walked in, and walked through; saw teamster on the other side, "indulging in profane language"—in fact, "cussin' considerable," because lightning had killed his team. Looked as finger directed—saw six dead oxen in line with hole through mountain; knew that was the bullet's work, but didn't say so to angry teamster. Thought best to be leaving; in consequence, didn't explore path of bullet any further; therefore, don't know where it stopped;

---

[9] *The Intelligencer* (Oxford, Mississippi); reprinted in *The Rebellion Record: A Diary of American Events, with Documents, Narratives, Illustrative Incidents, Poetry, Etc.* Edited by Frank W. Moore. New York: G. P. Putnam. 1861. Vol. I, "Poetry, Rumors and Incidents," p. 99.

don't know whether it stopped at all; in fact, rather think it didn't. Mounted horse; rode back through the hole made by the bullet, but never told Captain a word about it; to tell the truth, was rather afraid he'd think it a hoax.

"It's a right big story, boys," said Toby, in conclusion; "but it's true, sure as shooting. Nothing to do with a Maynard rifle but load her up, turn her North, and pull trigger. If twenty of them don't clean out all Yankeedom, then I'm a liar, that's all."

JOHN ALLEN WYETH

John Allen Wyeth, born in Marshall County, Alabama, May 26, 1845, was famous during the latter decades of the nineteenth century as a surgeon and a writer of learned articles on his science. As a private soldier in the Confederate army, though not in Nathan Bedford Forrest's command, he qualified himself partly by experience for his fine biography of the great cavalry leader. His experiences as a prisoner at Camp Martin likewise provided him the material for an article in the *Century Magazine* for April, 1890, on the treatment of prisoners. His *Life of General Nathan Bedford Forrest* is the result of immense research into war archives and hundreds of communications, oral and written, from Forrest's men, plus a fine talent for graphic, vigorous expression It is one of the most readable books about the Civil War. Few things of the sort are better than his story of how Emma Sanson, the North Alabama girl, helped Forrest's hard-ridden little band over a secret ford to the overthrow of the Yankees, or the two anecdotes, included in the present work, of how Mrs. Forrest senior got her basket of chickens safely home, pant'er or no pant'er, and how she got her sack of meal to mill, soldier or no soldier.

"SOLDIER OR NO SOLDIER"

By John Allen Wyeth [10]

SEVERAL years after the death of William Forrest, in 1837, his widow married Mr. Joseph Luxton, and when the Civil War broke out, in

[10] *Life of General Nathan Bedford Forrest*, New York and London (Harper & Brothers), 1899, pp. 11-12.

1861, she resided upon her plantation some few miles out from Memphis on the Raleigh Road. The oldest son by this second marriage was then eighteen years of age, and had for some months been employed as a clerk in one of the stores in Memphis, and had enlisted in the Confederate army in one of the companies organized in that city. On a Friday afternoon he appeared at his home clad in a neat-fitting new suit of Confederate gray, trimmed with gold lace and other fancy trappings, so much in fashion at the beginning of the war. His mother had some ideas of her own which the younger generation deemed old-fashioned, but to which, despite criticism, she tenaciously adhered. Some of her neighbors said "she was set in her ways." Among other eccentricities she maintained that no meal was so good as that which was ground from corn raised on her own farm and shelled under her personal supervision, where she could see that none of the faulty small grains near the point of the ear were used. Every Saturday morning, bright and early, she would send one of her boys to mill with a sack of this corn to be ground. As her son retired to his room that night she said, "Joseph, I want you to get up early in the morning and go to mill with that sack of corn." She did not seem to take into consideration that he was living "away from home," and was now a Confederate soldier. The young man did not respond to his mother's command, but went silently to bed none the less determined not to soil his new soldier clothes by riding on a sack of meal. The mother belonged to that robust and enterprising type of housewife who believed in getting up before daylight and having everything ready for work by the time it was light enough to see. On week-days everybody on her farm had breakfast by candlelight. The next morning, as usual, every one was called early, and all appeared at the table except the devotee of Mars. The old lady said to the negro servant who was waiting upon the table, "Tell Mr. Joseph to come to breakfast right away"; and continued, as the servant went on the errand, "I am not going to put up with any city airs on this place." She then occupied herself in pouring out the coffee for those at the table, and, while so doing, the negro returned with a message from her impertinent offspring, that "he did not intend to go to mill; she might as well send some of the niggers with the corn." . . . She was just in the act of pouring out a cup of coffee, with the cup and saucer in one hand and the pot in the other, lifted several inches from the table. For a moment she seemed dumfounded at such impertinence on the part of her son, and then, setting the half-filled cup and the coffee-pot down, she arose from the table. . . . She marched out into the yard, broke off three or four long peachtree switches, and went directly upstairs, pulled that eighteen-year-old warrior of hers out of bed, and gave him such a thrashing as to justify a remembrance of it for the remainder of his life. She made him get up and put on an old suit of farm clothes which he had left at home when he became a "city chap." The horse was already at the gate, and, accompanied by the prodigal son that far, she picked up the two-bushel sack of corn, put it on the horse, and made him get up on top of it, and away he went to the mill. As she came back into the house, her eyes flashing and her face red with anger and the exertion which the chastisement had called for, she said, "Soldier or no soldier, my children will mind me as long as I live."

THE IRISHMAN AND THE "TIGER"

By Frazar Kirkland [11]

THE dogged, obstinate, and bitter character of the Gulf troops was one of the familiar facts of the war, as the following incident, which happened near Martinsburg, Virginia, will show.

A son of Erin captured one of the famous "Mississippi Tigers," but while bringing him to the Union camp, the "Tiger," an immense fellow, managed to free himself and run. The plucky Hibernian disdained to use his musket, but chased him with the wildest speed. At last, seizing him, at it they went, in the most logical style of rough-and-tumble. The "Tiger," maddened by the stinging whacks which the lusty Hibernian dealt, basely bit him, nearly severing his thumb. The Celt dropped the soldier then, and retaliated in the same way. Finally he conquered him after a tremendous whaling, which dislocated his shoulder.

The next day he visited the son of the "Repudiation State" in the hospital, went up to him, and shaking his well arm with a hearty grip, observed, with his rich Irish brogue, "I haven't a bit of a grudge agin ye; be jabers! ye're almost as good as meself."

A BIG KETTLE OF PRESERVES

By Frazar Kirkland [12]

THE committee appointed to collect metal for cannon for the rebel army—the scarcity of ordnance in the Confederacy having at that time become a serious matter—applied to a planter in Adams County,

[11] The Pictorial Book of Anecdotes and Incidents of the War of the Rebellion . . . , Hartford, Connecticut (Hartford Publishing Company), 1866, p. 33.
[12] Ibid., p. 346.

Mississippi, for his bell. Not having such an article, he mentioned it to his wife, and she very patriotically offered her brass kettle.

The little ones rather demurred to the sacrifice, and one of them with a sweet tooth, said, "Lor, pa, what will we do for preserves?"

"My daughter," said the wag of a father, "our whole duty now is to *preserve* our country."

NOT IN THE BOOK

By Frazar Kirkland [13]

WHILE on a forced march in some of the movements in Mississippi, General Hardee, of the rebel army, came up with a straggler who had fallen some distance in the rear of his command. The General ordered him forward. The old soldier replied that he was weak and broken down, not having had even half rations for several days.

"That's hard," replied the General, "but you must push forward, my good fellow, and join your command, or the Provost Guard will take you in hand."

The soldier halted, and, looking up at the General, asked, "Are you General Hardee?"

"Yes," replied the General.

"Didn't you write Hardee's Tackticks?"

"Yes."

"Well, General, I have studied them tackticks, and know 'em by heart. You've got a order to double column at half distance, ain't you?"

"Well," asked the General, "what has that to do with your case?"

"I'm a good soldier, General, and obey all that is possible to be obeyed; but if your orders can show me a order in your tackticks to double distance on half rations, then I'll give in."

The General, with a hearty laugh, admitted that there were no tactics to meet the case, and putting spurs to his horse, rode forward.

[13] *Ibid.*, p. 427.
My own grandfather, who campaigned with Stonewall Jackson, told an analogous anecdote concerning that hero. During one of his celebrated Valley marches, Stonewall spied one of his straggling foot-cavalrymen up a persimmon tree. "What the devil are you doing up a persimmon tree?" asked the general. "Eatin' 'simmons, Gen'l," the private replied. "What, eating persimmons in July!" exclaimed Stonewall. "Why, man don't you know they'll draw your stomach into a hard knot?" "Waal, Gen'l, I figgered on that. I 'lowed to swink up my belly to fit my rations."

JOKES FOR *SOUTHERN PUNCH* [14]

Editor Southern Punch:

Sir:—It is known throughout General Lee's veteran army that all North Carolinians go by the name of "Tar heels," and are called so by troops from other States.

During the march from the Peninsula, a Regiment of Virginians chanced to meet a Regiment of North Carolinians; one of the Virginians feeling disposed to be witty, says, "Hallo! Mr. North Carolina, have you got the tar off your heels?"

North Carolinian.—"Yes, Jeff. Davis took all the tar from our heels to stick you Virginians in a fight."

When we arrived into Maryland, I saw around a "Yankee" lady a large crowd of Dixie soldiers. She was telling them that she expected to see the finest men of the South, clothed most magnificently, but she was disappointed; she found them a set of ragamuffins, and asked why we did not wear good clothes. One of our Lieutenant Colonels says, "Madam, we do not put on our best clothes to kill dogs in, but," he continued, "madam, we expected to find the greater portion of your state to be secessionists, but I find them Yankees." The lady replied, "Yes! there are plenty of Yankees in Virginia, too." An old, dirty looking wagoner, getting upon his mule, says, "Yes, marm, I know it, kase I see'd 'em dar; but dey are dead uns, tho."

The lady retired.   A MISSISSIPPIAN.

FINE SPIRITS [15]

A CORRESPONDENT of the *Memphis Argus*, writing from Lynchburgh, Va., says:—"We have two regiments from Mississippi and one from Tennessee with us, numbering one thousand each. All are well quartered, and in fine *spirits*—and they shall not want for the latter so long as our 'mountain dew' holds out. You could not find a more cheerful set of fellows in a week's travel; they play the fiddle, banjo, dance, and sing Dixie. One fellow told me his old mammy cried the the glasses clean out of her spectacles the morning he left, but on giving her *two bits* to buy another pair, she bid him go, and return to her covered all over with glory. Another said he didn't like these 'breeches' with a stripe down the leg, they pinched him; but just give him his old copperas-colored trowsers, and his own rifle, and he'd bore a hole *thru* Linkin's nose, through which to put a ring, and lead him about for a show."

[14] *Southern Punch*, Published by Overall, Campbell, Hughes & Co., Richmond, Va., vol. 1, No. 3 (August 29, 1863), p. 5 under column heading "Correspondence."
[15] *New York Tribune*, May 20, 1861; reprinted in Moore's Rebellion Record, Vol. I, "Poetry, Rumors and Incidents," p. 113.

CHAPTER XII

PIRATES AND PICAROONS

IF THE old South West was the Happy Hunting Ground on this earth, it was also the Paradise of pirates and picaroons. It was perhaps even better than the later Southwest or the Old West. The motto was the same for all—"Be shifty in a new land." But the swag and the getaway were probably superior in the lower South of 1800–1860. There was, it is true, no gold dust. But, besides rich new lands to grab and gamble over, there were niggers easy to drive, steal, or seduce; horses, cattle, and hogs as complacent as any; cotton fairly portable by wagon, flat- or steam-boat. There were swamps and forests that made Sherwood look like a gentleman's park, vast uninhabited or sparsely inhabited areas, for refuge and rendezvous. Headquarters of the Murrell gang was in an Arkansas swamp as impenetrable by ordinary methods as it was when De Soto floundered around it in 1541. For those that knew them, the maze of rivers, bayous, and creeks proved safe highways of exit or ingress. For pursuers, there were no highways or railroads, no trains or automobiles, no telephone or radio. All that the Reverend Mr. McGrath had to do, after he had "gone among the brethren" and his confederates had cleaned them out, was to ride, in his new bombazine on his new gift horse, to the next state and once more set up shop under the camp meeting arbor. No "parties" had been "notified to look out for and apprehend him." No highway patrols or city police had his "mug" and his "prints."

If the Mississippi was the "highway of humor" it was partly so because it was the pike of poker, the river of roulette, and the king's highway of keno. A voyage from New Orleans to Baton Rouge, Natchez, or Vicksburg, or from Mobile to Montgomery, was usually ample to shear the Coast or Delta or Canebrake planter of the golden fleece he had received for his cotton fleece. If the victim was a Yankee sport, he might go as far as St. Louis or Cincinnati and thus provide for real long-distance gambling. In any case, there were sure to be black-clad gentry aboard who would know how to trim anybody with anything sticking out or hidden. George H. Devol knew how to take on all comers and catch all goers.

The booming and crashing thirties and the roaring and exploding forties were the golden age of con and greengoods men. Besides more or less harmless "agents of the U. S. Treasury" wining and dining up and down the land on the strength of mysterious portmanteaus, there were "professors of appropriation" plying the various trades of preacher, doctor, lawyer, and professional colonel.

Then, in all other decades as in these, there were more obscure fellows, like "the old Dutch cuss" and the peddler of the Judgment Trumpet, to take in the yokels and hillbillies.

The various games were so easy for everybody who played them that the players were quite good humored about it all. Those who were articulate took that pride in their work that Gil Blas and Jonathan Wild the Great did. The victims and the spectators, the biographers and the chroniclers of great deeds, were likewise complaisant.

MURRELL, THE GREAT WESTERN LAND PIRATE

(1830's)

The most comprehensive source of information about John A. Murrell is *The History of Virgil A. Stewart, and His Adventure in Capturing and Exposing the Great "Western Land Pirate" and His Gang, in Connexion with the Evidence; also of the Trials, Confessions, and Execution of a Number of Murrell's Associates in the State of Mississippi During the Summer of 1835, and the Execution of Five Professional Gamblers by the Citizens of Vicksburg, on the 6th July, 1835*, Compiled by H. R. Howard, New York (Harper & Brothers), 1836.

Stewart, born in Georgia, was taken when a baby to Amite County, Mississippi, but, after the death of his father, his mother returned with him to Georgia, where he was educated. In 1830 he moved to Madison County, Tennessee. There he made the acquaintance of a preacher named Henning. Moving to Chocchuma, Mississippi, in the Choctaw Purchase, in 1833, he kept store for a man named Clanton. On a visit to his former home in Madison County, Tennessee, he was requested by Henning to search for two negro men slaves suspected to have been stolen by one John A. Murrell, a resident of the county. Setting out westerly on horseback, and making inquiries along the way, Stewart fell in with Murrell at the toll-house over the Hatchee river at Estanaula. By playing upon Murrell's vanity and loquacity, he soon ingratiated himself with his quarry and learned complete particulars about one of the most fantastic conspiracies ever formed against property and life in a frontier civilization. The catalogue of "the mystic clan" gives the surnames, and in many cases the christian names or initials, of 438 members scattered over Tennessee, Mississippi, Arkansas, Kentucky, Missouri, Alabama, Georgia, South Carolina, North Carolina, Virginia, Maryland, Florida, Louisiana, and of "Transient Members who travel from place to place." The headquarters seem to have been in the heart of an almost inaccessible swamp and cane-brake over the Mississippi in Arkansas. Among other particulars, Stewart obtained evidence sufficient to convict Murrell of negro-stealing and sentence him to the penitentiary of Tennessee for ten years. From that time on Stewart was a marked man, as to both character and life. On a business trip in Mississippi he was pursued by members of the gang, and was badly wounded in an ambush. In the meantime, his *Western Land Pirate* exposé of the Murrell gang had aroused the whole Mississippi Valley, and arrests, prosecutions, and convictions followed in swift order.

The selections from the *History of Virgil A. Stewart* will give some idea of Murrell and the operations of his "mystic clan." They will illustrate also the stiffly formal style of the compiler. The first is an adventure told to Stewart by Murrell as the two rode under the sleet-encased trees of Poplar Creek, west Tennessee, in January, 1834. The hero of the story is really Murrell himself (he had not yet reached the point of confiding his identity to his companion). The scene in which Brother Nobs' preacher "raised his hands in the most solemn manner, as though he was just going to open the windows of heaven, and select its richest blessings for Brother Nobs, his wife, and latest posterity," will inevitably remind the reader of Chaucer's equally rascally Pardoner, who boasts:

> Thanne peyne I me to strecche forth the nekke,
> And est and west upon the peple I bekke,
> As dooth a dowve, sittyng on a berne,
> Myne handes and my tonge goon so yerne.

I. THE PREACHER AND BROTHER NOBS' JACKASS

By H. R. Howard [1]

Murrell. "Come, sir, ride up; the night is cold, and we have far to go;—let us pass the time as pleasantly as possible:—come up, and I will tell you of another feat of this elder brother of whom I have been speaking."

Stewart. "Yes, sir, with all my heart, if it is as good as the last."

Murrell. "He is a likely fellow, tall, and well proportioned, and dresses rather in the Methodist order; and when he is off on his scouts, directing his men how to proceed (for he never carries off property himself, he always has men for that purpose), he frequently makes appointments, and preaches. He is well versed in the Scriptures, and preaches some splendid sermons. He has frequently preached at a place, and before he commenced pointed out some fine horse for his friend to steal; and while he was preaching and praying for them, his friend would save the horse for him. He always gives his residence some other course than the correct direction.

"In one of those jaunts he called at the house of one Nobs, a Methodist, on Elk river, in Middle Tennessee. Nobs had heard him preach a year before that in the neighbourhood, and was much taken with him as a preacher. He had given his residence in South Alabama, and had spoken a great deal of his negroes and farm; and of the perplexity he had in getting an overseer that would do his duty, and not abuse his slaves, and all such stuff as this, and Brother Nobs drank it all down. Supper came on, and he got them all around the table on their feet; he raised his hands in the most solemn manner, as though he was just going to open the windows of heaven, and select its richest blessings for Brother Nobs, his wife, and latest posterity. He was lengthy in his supplications at the table; but when he came to use the books, and go to duty, he was eloquent. The same service was rendered the next morning.

[1] *Op. cit.*, pp. 30-33.

"When about to start, he wanted to pay Brother Nobs; but Brother Nobs was almost hurt to think that he would suppose he would charge him. 'Well, Brother Nobs, will you be so good as to give me change for a twenty-dollar bill? I am out of change, and I dislike to offer a bill of that size to be changed where I stay all night, for the world will say he is a preacher, and does not like to pay for staying all night at a tavern—see, he has presented a twenty-dollar bill to be changed. This is the way of the world—and I hope God, in his mercies, will enable me to live in such a manner as never to dishonour the cause of the Gospel, or degrade the ministry.'

"Brother Nobs, anxious to render the preacher, and, as he thought, a very rich man, a favour, answered him—'Yes, brother, with pleasure.' He ran to his wife and got the keys, took out the purse, and counted out seventeen dollars and fifty cents, when his change gave out. Brother Nobs was in a peck of misery. 'Stay a little; I will run over to Brother Parker's and borrow the balance.'—'Do, if you please, and I will stay with Sister Nobs until you return.' Brother Nobs was not long gone, when he returned with as much pride of being able to accommodate his preacher as an East India merchant would show at the arrival of a rich cargo of goods. The preacher's bill is changed, and all is right.

"*Preacher.* 'Well, Brother Nobs, you have a fine young jack—did you raise him?'

"*Brother Nobs.* 'He was foaled mine, and I have raised him.'

"*Preacher.* 'Will you trade him, Brother Nobs?'

"*Brother Nobs.* 'I have raised him for that purpose; but I cannot get the worth of him in this country; I have never been offered more than one hundred and fifty dollars for him, and he is worth two hundred and fifty.'

"*Preacher.* 'Yes, Brother Nobs, he is cheap at that price; and, if I had the money with me, I would rid you of any farther trouble with him.'

"*Brother Nobs.* 'Well, brother, you can take him. You say that you will be at our camp-meeting. Bring me the money then—that is as soon as I will need it.'

"*Preacher.* 'Well, Brother Nobs, I will take him—I need him very much; I want him for my own mares; I am a domestic fellow; I raise my own mules for my farm.'

"The trade being completed, the preacher got ready to start; all the family gathered around him to receive his parting blessing.

"*Preacher.* 'Brother Nobs, may the Lord bless you, and save you in heaven; farewell. Sister Nobs, may the grace of our Lord and Saviour

Jesus Christ rest and remain upon you; farewell. May the Lord bless
your little children: farewell, my dear babies.'

"The preacher was soon gone from Brother Nobs; but not to South
Alabama, but to the western district of Tennessee. That day and night
put the preacher a long way off, as slow as his jack travelled; though
he was an uncommon fine travelling jack. The preacher sold his jack
for four hundred dollars, and passed a twenty-dollar counterfeit bill
on Brother Nobs. Poor Brother Nobs can never hear of his rich young
preacher since; but I have no doubt he is on a voyage of soul-saving,
and will visit Brother Nobs when he returns."

II. THE LAW IS AN ASS

By H. R. Howard [2]

Murrell. "He is about thirty, I suppose, and his brother just grown
up, and as smart a fellow as the elder brother, but not half the experience. I will tell you of one of his routs on a speculation a few months
past, and you can judge for yourself whether he is possessed of talents
or not.

"There was a negro man by the name of Sam, that had been sold
out of the neighbourhood of those two young men to a man by the
name of Eason, near Florence, Alabama. The elder brother was passing
that way on one of his scouts, and happening to see Sam, inquired of
him how he liked his new home and master? 'Bad enough,' said Sam.
'Well,' said he, 'Sam, you know me; and you know how to leave
the rascal; run away and get back to your old range, and all things
are safe.'

"It was not long before Sam was at his house. He harboured him
until Eason advertised him as a runaway, and offered a reward for him.
That was what he wanted to see. He procured a copy of the advertisement, and put it and the negro into the hands of his brother and a
fellow by the name of Forsyth, and told them to push and make hay
while the sun shone. They were gone about seven weeks, and his
brother returned with about fourteen hundred dollars in cash, seven
hundred dollars worth of ready-made clothing, and a draught on
Thomas Hudnold, of Madison county, State of Mississippi, for seven
hundred dollars, which is as good as gold-dust, though he has to sue
for the draught; but the recovery is sure—for they can never get the
negro, and without him they can never prove that he was Eason's
negro, and he will recover the draught in spite of them.

"Hudnold became suspicious that they got the negro again, and

[2] *Op. cit.*, pp. 23-25.

wrote to the house on which the draught was drawn to protest it. They did not act in that matter as the elder brother, the old fox, would have done: though, for young hands, they made a fine drag. They did not go immediately on and draw the cash, as one of them should have done; but delayed, trying to make more sales, and delayed too long before the draught was presented.

"That is twenty-eight hundred dollars he sold Eason's negro for, and now has the negro in Texas in the hands of friends: they did not make the disposition of Sam which they generally do with negroes on such occasions; he is too fine a fellow: and I think they will make more money on him when things get a little still. Sam is keen and artful, and is up to anything that was ever wrapped in that much negro hide. If Eason had got on his track and caught him, he could not have done anything with him."

Stewart. "I cannot see how he could have evaded the law in that instance."

Murrell. "It is a plain case, sir, when the law is examined by a man who understands it. In the first place, the negro had run away, and had escaped from Eason's possession; and, in the second place, Eason had offered a reward for his negro to any man who would catch him. This advertisement amounts to the same, in virtue, as a power of attorney, to take his property, and act for him to a certain extent; so you see the advertisement is a commission to take the property into possession; now, if the holder of the property chooses to make a breach of the trust which the advertisement confides in him, and, instead of carrying the negro to his owner, converts him to his own use—this is not stealing, and the owner can only have redress in a civil action for the amount of his property: and as for a civil action, they care nothing for that, for they will not keep property. Their funds are deposited in a bank that belongs to the clan. This is the way his ingenuity perplexes them. He has sifted the criminal laws until they are no more in his hands than an old almanack, and he dreads them no more. But what is it that he cannot do with as many friends as he has, who are willing to be subject to him and his views in all things? There lies his power: his great talent in governing his clan. He is universally beloved by his followers."

A SOUTH CAROLINA GIL BLAS IN THE DEEP SOUTH[3]

"A desire to do justice to the reputation and opinions of the writer, has led the present publishers to give no heed to suggestions which, while they would have operated against the evident desires of the author, would have deprived the public of a large amount of enjoyment, and of that species of edification which is needed to protect them from the 'assessments' of those *chevaliers d'industrie,* whose researches and appropriations extend to all communities and to every variety of movables." Thus much we learn, from the "Publisher's Advertisement," concerning the motives for publishing *The Life, Adventures, and Opinions of David Theo. Hines . . . in a Series of Letters to His Friends.* Most of the letters, written from various prisons where the hero was taking enforced rest from his adventures, are addressed to James Gordon Bennett, editor of the New York *Herald.*

By his own account, the "professor of appropriation" was born near Pineville, St. Stephen's Parish, South Carolina, about 1810. " 'I walked not in the ways of other' boys, as little as my Lord Byron, whom, by the way, it is said that I closely resemble, both in my personal appearance and the warmth and inveteracy of my passions. Perhaps had I not chosen the more difficult paths of action, I should have turned my attention, as well as himself, to poetry and the Turks. . . . I have, I must acknowledge, been very successful among women. I sometimes reproach myself, however, for my frequent treacheries to these fair ministers, and in this respect Lord Byron resembled me also." [4] Of his education, Hines says: "My books, in my boyish days, were few but exceedingly select. . . . There were . . . The Life of Jonathan Wild the Great, by Fielding; A Glimpse into the Domestic History of King Solomon, by a wonderful but unknown writer; . . . The Lives of Famous Housebreakers; Lives of the Martyrs; Newgate Calendar; Baxter's Saint's Rest; Joe Miller." [5]

[3] *The Life, Adventures and Opinions of David Theo. Hines, of South Carolina;—Master of Arts, and, Sometimes, Doctor of Medicine;—Alias, Dr. Hamilton, Col. Hamilton, Dr. Haynes, Col. Hayne, Dr. Porcher, Col. Singleton, Rev. Mr. Beman, Rev. Dr. Baker, Col. Allston, Maj. Parker, Col. Benton, Maj. Middleton, Lieut. Pringle, Capt. Rutledge, Col. Pinckney, Dr. Brandreth, Major Moore, &c &c &c. In a Series of Letters to His Friends. Written by Himself.* New York: Published by Bradley & Clark. 1840.

[4] *Ibid.,* p. 23.

[5] *Ibid.,* p. 25.

Putting a period to certain unhappy adventures on his native heath, he writes:

"With the 'hundred' at my heels, there was no longer refuge for me in St. Stephen's; and I took a hurried leave of my venerable parent.

" 'Git money, Dave!' she exclaimed in the simple, energetic idiom of the country—'Git the dollars; them's all we want now to make the pot bile. You haint tried to do much, no how; and Dave, my son, it's high time. Don't you think of the gals—they'll be your death yet. Look to the main chance—scratch in the dollars. I've hearn there's a mighty smart chance on 'em to be picked up in Alabam, and fudder down on to Mississipp.' [6]

". . . I became, therefore, a doctor for the nonce. Had I been murderously inclined, I should have invented some quack medicine also, and adopted Brandreth as my father for the states of Alabama, Mississippi, and Louisiana.

"To use a felicitous technical phrase, which admirably suited my adopted profession, I *operated* with great success upon the country through which I traveled. People sickened to my hands in every direction. The old women got all sorts of disorders, for which I had one unvarying remedy, in pills made of pine gum rolled in clay. Providence, fortunately for the country and the profession I had chosen, had bestowed upon the former a never failing supply of these excellent medicines; and I had the satisfaction of knowing, that while there was every prospect that a new physician must often effect great good with an imaginary disorder, there was no possible case in which medicines such as I administered could do evil. My conscience, which, as you may suppose, was always very tenacious of what performances I took in hand, was perfectly well satisfied with this conviction.[7]

"But I soon grew tired of a practice which afforded me so few chances of distinction. To feel pulses is a smaller business than to feel purses; and, though my successes were very great, and in every department to which I thought proper to direct my attention, still, the doctoring of an old woman's cough, cholic, or rheumatism, scarcely agreed with the dignity of my desires, or the majesty of my genius. Besides, my heart yearned once more to see my venerable

[6] *Ibid.*, pp. 78-79.
[7] *Ibid.*, pp. 80-81.

mother,—to return to that home, that soil, which was not less dear to me because it had wronged me. . . ."

He was aided in this laudable resolve to return home by three fellow-South Carolinians, also repatriating themselves *via* Georgia, who betrayed him to the authorities, and he was carried in chains to Charleston. Delivered by the trickery of his lawyers, he resumed his adventures, this time in New York.[8]

TURNS UP HIS NOSE AT THE GREAT "LAND PIRATE"

Impatient, at length, for new adventures, and in a new field, I set out for the west, and resumed the practice of medicine, in the states of Georgia, Alabama, and Mississippi. Many a worthy old rheumatic of those states, will remember with gratitude the skill and success of Dr. Hamilton, during the period of my progress through those parts. But the ambition is a small one. . . . I resolved upon giving up the practice. . . . When, therefore, I was not a colonel, I was a doctor, and when neither, I simply made a slight digression into other departments of art, for which nature had not less bountifully endowed me.

While passing from Montgomery, in Alabama, towards Mobile, I was joined one day by a stranger, whose look, manner, and deportment, at once fixed my attention and provoked my curiosity. He was evidently no ordinary man, and the instinct which prompted me to regard him with respect, assured me that he must be one after my own heart. This man was the celebrated Murrell, otherwise known as the famous "land pirate" of the west. This secret my ingenuity enabled me to find out after we had travelled half a day together. I had kept my secret from him, however, and believing me to be one of those subordinate spirits whom he could send hither and thither at pleasure, he made me certain overtures of alliance, which, I need not tell you, were instantly rejected. I disliked his mode of operations. There was a want of manliness in it and self reliance. He required numerous assistants, while it was my pride to succeed through the strength of my own unaided genius. He was something of a blackguard also—spoke bawdy—swore like a trooper, and to sum up all in little, he was no gentleman. To one, like myself, who was something of an aristocrat in bearing, feeling and language, his familiarity and mode of speech were sometimes inexpressibly offensive. He took the liberty, at one time, as we rode together, of putting his arm about my neck, by way of showing his affection, and I could scarce forbear returning the impertinence by hoisting him suddenly from the saddle.

[8] *Ibid.*, pp. 81-99.

. . . In addition to these defects of breeding, I soon discovered that Murrell was a brutal and blood thirsty creature; that he was fond of shedding blood, and preferred to obtain his objects summarily by a resort to his weapon, rather than to await the more slow, but far more beautiful and equally certain results of elaborate art.

The most common appropriators may obtain the purse of the traveller, by shooting him down upon the highway, or as he rides unsuspectingly through the woods; it requires neither skill nor adroitness for such a performance, and is work only fit for a monster and a botch. But to succeed in drawing from the enemy the secret of his soul, the watch from his fob, the purse from his pocket, not only without hurting his person, but without inflicting pain or annoyance;—nay, to do this when, forewarned and forearmed, he has all his eyes on the watch, all his defences manned, all his guards in readiness, and every suspicion roused; that is the perfection of art,—that is the triumph which only true genius can attain, and which only true genius should desire to attain.

More than this I did not seek,—less than this I was determined not to deserve; and the propositions, therefore, of Mr. John A. Murrell, I did not ask for the delay of a single instant unhesitatingly to reject. My rejection of his overtures, which he no doubt regarded as liberal enough, filled him with astonishment.

"What! not join us!" he exclaimed.

"No!"

His astonishment was now changed into something like anger.

"Ay, but by G—d, you shall," said he, "or we don't part so readily. You know too much to go off without leaving a pledge behind you; and you don't budge from this spot, my good fellow, without swallowing the oath or the bullet."

He soon found himself mistaken in his man; and the representative of South Carolina, on that day, obtained a signal triumph over him of Tennessee. While he spoke, I acted. Before he could obey the counsel of Hamlet, and suit the action to the word, my pistol flared in his face, while the click of its lock came with unpleasant and startling suddenness upon his ear. He sank back aghast.

"You call yourself lord of the south west, Mr. Murrell;" was my cool remark, as, having effected my object, I lowered my pistol; "know from this hour, that the lord has a master. Your boast that you have made a conquest of these plains, and fields, and villages, is surely idle now; and were I harsh enough to impose upon you the usual terms of the victor—*vae victis*—your empire would instantly pass away. But all in good season. You are still the professor of an art,—which, as it is—though with many qualifications—something kindred to my own, leads me to overlook your error and forgive your rudeness. There will be time enough in other days, and by other means, for me to assert my claim to a region over which you vainly imagine yourself to have sway. Let us part in peace, therefore, and not anticipate the future. Sufficient for the day is the triumph thereof, as well as the evil; but beware how you again offend me. I never forgive a second offense."

"Why, who are you?" he demanded with no little astonishment. When I revealed to him my name, he sank back with awe. He then felt how greatly he had offended. . . . He now changed the character of his proposition. He offered me equal command over his people with himself; but did not succeed in changing the nature of my objections. I disliked the man. He was possessed of no refinements, whether in society or in art—spoke like a vulgar ploughman—wanted grace—was equally deficient in all gentility; and so poorly versed in poetry, that I doubt whether he would not have taken Homer to have been a sort of Epidaurian outlaw, and Lord Byron to have been quite as much a pirate in the east as ever was his and my friend, Mr. Trelawney. Long and earnestly did my companion plead for my conjunction with him, and bitter must have been his disappointment when he found me resolute in my refusal.

At parting, I gave him an insight into some of my objections, while counselling him to a few alterations in his own practices.

I am afraid that my counsel was wasted upon this man. . . . I heard of him not a week after we had parted, in connection with some of the dirtiest deeds which had ever been perpetrated by himself or any of his gang before; and from that moment I resolved, that we were not only of different but antagonistic schools of art, and that it was a moral duty with me, whenever it came within my power, to arrest the progress of his, and put a final extinguisher upon pretensions which were no less evil than insolent.[9]

From Louisiana I passed to Mississippi state, and hearing that Murrell had been operating on the Yazoo with great success, and a notoriety rather unenviable, I was curious to see the scene of his performances, and to judge for myself how far his judgment deserved credit for his choice of region. I visited the several leading towns of Mississippi,—Natchez, Monticello, Jackson, Manchester and Vicksburg; and at the latter place, moved thereto by a sense of public duty, I gave the clue to the secret haunts of certain confederates of Murrell, though I failed in a plan to capture that dangerous and immoral

[9] *Ibid.*, pp. 101-105.

operator himself. He eluded me, though his escape was sufficiently narrow to let him see the danger of continuing in a sphere in which had risen a planet so superior. The miserable underlings, whom he deserted, were summarily hung up, under the solemn decision of Judge Lynch, to certain neighboring hickories, and died, as these atrocious ruffians usually do, by professing their innocence to the last. But I was vindictive in urging the claims of justice against them. It is such scoundrels as these that bring discredit upon the true lovers of art; who make the professional appropriator odious by associating his idea with that of the savage; and by foolishly overpassing the boundaries of good policy, defeat the designs and baffle the desires of the amateur. I must confess that I saw these miserable creatures perish without suffering much if any annoyance. It was a subject of regret, however, when I afterwards heard that a young man who was innocent, a member of the Smith family, was hung by mistake. The Smiths are always in danger.[10]

A BRUSH WITH OLD HICKORY

From Mississippi I passed into Tennessee, and operated with success upon the natives wherever I went. . . .

I took occasion, while in Tennessee, to visit General Jackson at the Hermitage. I have a profound admiration for the old man. His rugged and inflexible genius has always commanded the grateful admiration of mine. When the General understood, as he soon did from my conversation, that I had been a nullifier, he exclaimed, with a good humored smile,—

"Ah, you nullifiers!—it is well for you that I was not compelled to hang you."

There was nothing in this speech to offend me. "Surely," I said to myself, reflecting upon it afterwards,—"surely, my neck was never made for a halter." Still, I replied to the old man with a spirit that, while it staggered, did not seem to offend him:

"You are mistaken, General," was my answer. "It is you who would have been hung if any. We had made our arrangements to this effect, and more than fifty of us had volunteered to perform the honored duties of John Ketch, Esq." [11]

[10] *Ibid.*, pp. 119-20.
[11] *Ibid.*, p. 120.

INCIDENTS IN THE LIFE OF DAVID HINES

From the New Orleans *Sun* of June 7 [12]

PURSUANT to promise, we this morning published some incidents in the life of (Dr.) David Hines, a villain who has long gone "unwhipt of justice," but who is now on a charge of negro stealing, confined in the parish prison of Orleans. To bring individual character before the public through the press, is, in ordinary circumstances, and even though necessity urge it, always a source of pain; but the character which we are now about to trace, in lines too faint, is so blackened by the very worst dye of villany, that it is no less a pleasure than it is certainly an imperative duty, imposed upon every conservator of the public morals, to lay it bare to the execration of the world.

David Hines was born of respectable parents in St. Stevens parish, Charleston district, South Carolina. He was respectably educated, and in the course of his approach to manhood, was remarkable for his quickness of perception, great plausibility and firmness of purpose. In 1827, he was tried in Charleston for forging a draft and obtaining the money thereon from a mercantile house there, but for want of sufficient proof, was acquitted. He left that city immediately after his acquittal, and went into Georgia, and passed himself as Dr. Hamilton, and borrowed from and swindled every person at whom he could get a chance. He was arrested and lodged in jail at Augusta, on a charge of horse stealing, but was acquitted on the plea of having hired the horse. In the year 1833, he was again tried in Charleston on a charge of negro stealing and was acquitted, the evidence only showing that he had the negro in his possession and that he had called on several persons offering to sell them a negro answering the description of the one which he had stolen. In 1834 he visited New Orleans, and during the same year returned to Charleston, where he was tried for assault and battery on a female, with intent to kill. Upon this charge he was sentenced to and served two years imprisonment in jail.

Having done this service, he, in the year 1837, returned to New Orleans, and after staying a short time, took passage in a steam-packet for Texas. During his trip, he insinuated himself into the confidence of a Mr. White, a fellow passenger, and although Mr. White had been cautioned in regard to him by some of the other passengers who knew Dr. Hines, yet he would not believe their assertions; the consequence was, that they travelled together over Texas, and before they parted at Galveston, Hines had swindled White out of nearly

[12] *Mississippi Free Trader and Natchez Weekly Gazette*, Natchez, June 18, 1840, p. [1].

every farthing he had. It was for this cause that White published him in one of the New Orleans papers, as a swindler and a villain.

This man's infirmities have been so numerous, that he may well be dubbed the modern Robert McCaire. In the spring of 1838, we recognize him in Mobile, with a number of drafts to large amounts on Gen. Hamilton, in his pocket. From thence he came to New Orleans, and swindled a gentleman from Texas, named Cozzens, to the tune of five or six thousand dollars. This business being neatly performed, he determined upon going north, and accordingly, shortly afterwards, he took passage on a steamboat bound for Louisville. On his way up, he was detected robbing a fellow passenger, and put on shore. During this trip, he induced a negro boy on board the boat, to take a carpet bag and to secrete it. The bag was missed, search made, and Dr. Hines accused of having stolen it. He promised to deliver up the bag, provided they would not prosecute him, which they agreed to, and he gave up the bag. Arrriving at Nashville, he paid Gen. Jackson a visit, told the General he was a staunch friend of his, and that his character had been traduced by a set of scoundrels who were opposed to him in politics, and that he intended to commence an action against them for damages for injuring his character—that he was short of funds—asked the favor of the General to endorse his note for three hundred dollars. The General told him he could not endorse his note—that he was old and wished to bring his business to a close and not to make any more transactions.

Not being able to operate on the old General, he took passage for Louisville, and upon his arrival there, put up at the 'Galt House.' For some degradation, he had to leave that house in a hurry, and he concluded to take the mail boat for Cincinnati, where he selected the 'Broadway House' as the most fashionable and the most favorable for his operations. In Cincinnati he passed as Dr. Hayne, the nephew of Gen. Hayne of South Carolina—spoke largely of his cotton plantations in Mississippi, his cotton bags and negroes. Here he was for a time all the go. He was waited upon by the aristocracy, ogled by the ladies and adored by the bloods, who considered it "glory enough for one day," to drive him to Brighton or the Appolonian Springs.

He got the facsimiles of the signatures of some of the largest houses in the city, and came it pretty extensively over some of his masonic friends, he "put" for Pittsburg—took the canal from that place to Philadelphia, upon his arrival at which place, he put up at Sanderson's, had his trunk placed in the bar, and borrowed forty dollars from the landlord to settle his passage. Here, for some misdemeanor, he was arrested, and a number of forged drafts were found on his person, purporting to have been drawn by different houses in Cincinnati upon the banks of Philadelphia. From some legal flaw or deficiency of testimony, he was acquitted.

The Dr. is next discovered in Baltimore; here he passed himself off as Col. Benton of Hinds county, Mississippi, and nephew to Thomas H. Benton, representing himself as a planter, and wishing to purchase slaves: he engaged of Col. Slatter 15, and of Maj. Bailey 5, and promised to pay for them as soon as he negociated some bills he had on the United States Bank. In the mean time he succeeded in borrowing a little money, and getting a suit of clothes from a tailor, without paying for them, was arrested at the suit of the tailor, and lodged in jail. While in confinement, he writes to a reverend gentleman who pays him a visit. He told the preacher, that he was of a very respectable family, had been wild, and much of a spendthrift, that his parents were very old and very religious, and that he was imprisoned for the sum of $60, and without some person would have him released he would put an end to his existence. The preacher told him that he was sorry for him, and would try and raise money enough to have him released. On leaving the prison he inquired of the keeper the character of Hines, and was informed of his real character. Failing in this scheme, he was not long in trying another,—a German was put in prison under some criminal charge; he had $60 in money and a silver watch. Hines told the German, if he would give him the money and watch, he would get him out of prison, to which the German agreed; he sends for the tailor, pays him, gets discharged, and leaves the other prisoner to get out the best way he could. He then goes to New-York, passes himself as Mr. Alston, of S. C., marries a respectable girl, was arrested for swindling some merchant out of several hundred dollars worth of goods. He is again set at liberty, and is next heard of in Cincinnati, Ohio. In October 1839, he visited New-Orleans in company with a female as Dr. Haynes and lady, of S. C., and puts up at the St. Louis Hotel, leaves without paying his bill, and in November is arrested at Orangeburg Court House, S. C., having a servant, carriage and a pair of fine horses. He was released as there was no charge against him. A few hours after he was discharged from Orangeburg jail, the owner of the carriage and horses comes in pursuit of him.

At Montgomery, Ala., the Dr. arrived, and here he shone forth like a constellation. A public dinner was tendered him by the young men which he accepted, but on the morning of the appointed day he was detected stealing a watch. He again escaped and arrived at Mobile, where he dropped into a clothing store, tried on a suit of clothes and found they were a complete fit; told the clerk to call at his hotel at 11 o'clock, for the money. But when he called he found that the Doctor had just left for New-Orleans.

When he came to New-Orleans, he found it necessary to steal a negro, which in company with two persons named Johnson and Jones he took to Natchez and sold at auction at the store of Jacob Soria & Co. Coming back he thought it as well to steal a negress belonging to Noah Barlow, of the Natchez City Hotel, which, having brought here, he sold to a poor Dutchman, named Orgel H. Marits, for $380; about all the Dutchman was worth. He gave a bill of sale in the name of James Hagan, of Baton Rouge. The girl disappeared the same day she was paid for, and was found in possession of Hines, when he was arrested on a warrant from Natchez.

He displayed great science in trying to evade the officers and even after he was taken, wounded one of them. Before the Court, he pretended to be a very ill used young man indeed—asseverated that they had robbed him of his money, his watch, &c.; but it all would not do, and he now lies in the Parish Prison, under the paternal care of the Criminal Court, where every honest man hopes he will receive the sweet reward of his toils.

This is a mere skeleton of the character of Dr. Hines, but it is full enough to show what a pure disciple of honesty he is. It is reputed that he has, in different parts of the Union, no less than a dozen wives or mistresses, to whom, beyond question, this publication will be a source of inconsolable affliction. We pity those who are deluded by such a villain as much as we execrate their deluder.

It is understood that he has some accomplices at present in this city, but the police have a hawk's eye after them, and if any are taken, probably still more light will be thrown upon his recent acts of rascality.

In conclusion, Hines is a fine looking fellow, well set, middle height, of good address, and between 30 and 35 years of age; rather a young man to require so long, so sad, so sickening and revolting a history.

Dr. Hines still at large.—Our biographical sketch of the notorious David Hines in Sunday morning's paper, created an extraordinary excitement, and there is no doubt that while it will serve to guard those who read it against his continued rascalities it may also tend to deter the villain himself from such daring acts as we showed that he has hitherto been guilty of. There is only one regret in reference to him and his deeply stained life that we feel—a regret deep enough to destroy the best hopes of a virtuous people when they see barefaced blackguardism in its foulest form about to receive its deserts. It appears that in the opening and concluding parts of our sketch we were led into error in regard to the identification of individuals, and that altho' all the damning acts recorded by us were truly committed, still the individual who was arrested in this city, and who now lies in the parish prison, we have reason to believe, is not the leprous hearted wretch whose career we had traced.

From information received by us last evening, respecting the contrast in personal appearance between Dr. Hines and the person now in prison, and from the statements of respectable citizens who have seen both individuals, we are induced to make this brief notice, that public prejudice and feeling may not be kept in excitement against the individual for the faults of another. It is a fundamental principle in law, that every man is innocent until proved guilty, and upon this principle, every unbiassed person will, of course, consider the person now in the parish prison as *not* Dr. Hines, whom we now believe to be still at large. The sins of the person arrested may be great—probably they are, but there is no reason why he should answer for another's guilt.—*N. O. Sun, June* 9.

JAMES COPELAND

James Copeland, "the Southern land pirate, was born near Pascagoula river, in Jackson County, Miss., on the 18th day of January, 1823." [13] Under the tutelage of a wicked mother, he began his career of crime at the age of twelve, by stealing a knife which a woman had lent him to gather a sack of greens. Hog-stealing brought him and his brothers into their first collision with the law; a friend, who afterwards became the leader of the Wages-Copeland gang, engineered a way of escape, by burning down the court house containing the indictment. The first great exploit of the band was the sacking and firing of the business district of Mobile, in 1839, which netted twenty-five thousand dollars' worth of goods. With

[13] J. R. S. Pitts. *Life and Bloody Career of the Executed Criminal, James Copeland, the Great Southern Land Pirate, Leader of a Devastating Clan Ranging over a Great Portion of the Nation, Particularly the Gulf States, Spreading Terror and Insecurity Everywhere. Mystic Alphabet of the Clan, for Their Secret Correspondence, Giving a List of All the Members throughout the Union, with an Appendix of Profound Research, Bringing to Light More of Crime, Corruption and Dissimulation, Unveiling the Many Ways in Which Talent, Wealth and Influence Have Given Assistance.* [Second Edition.] Jackson, Miss.: Pilot Publishing Company, Printers and Binders. 1874.

these goods the good companions set out for Florida, peddling their stuff on the way. Copeland, while boarding with a rich old widow, seduced her mulatto girl, persuaded her, with an offer of marriage, to run away with him, and then cynically sold her to a Bayou Sara planter. One of the earliest acquisitions of the gang, which by now had taken on the organization and the mystic symbols and bloody oaths of a barbarous freemasonry, was an Irishman named McGrath. McGrath's rôle until his death was that of a roving Methodist preacher. The band operated in Louisiana, Texas, Mississippi, and Alabama. It did not suffer serious reverses until 1848, when, in the "famous Harvey battle," Wages and McGrath were killed. In the spring of 1849 Copeland was captured, taken to Mobile, requisitioned by the governor of Mississippi, and tried at Augusta, Perry County, for murder. He was found guilty, but by various maneuvers of his lawyers delayed expiation of his crimes until 1857, when he was hanged by the Sheriff of Perry County, the author of his history. This exposure, according to the author, completed the work of destroying the band, though some members remained bold enough to try to assassinate him, and did succeed in having him fined and jailed for libel in Mobile. This legal attack apparently interfered with the sale of the first edition, published in New Orleans, 1858, under the title *The Life and Career of James Copeland*.

The author of the *Life and Bloody Career*, Dr. J. R. S. Pitts, indicates that he was born about 1832 in Savannah, Georgia. In 1834 his parents removed with him to Rankin County, near Brandon, Mississippi. While still a schoolboy in Perry County, he became a candidate for sheriff, "left the schoolroom, and forthwith entered on the canvass, which resulted in his successful election by a handsome majority." "For some four years he continued in this office, during which time the painful duty devolved on him of executing James Copeland, the subject of the present work." He explains his title of Doctor in this sentence: "At a very early age, the author manifested a preference for the study of medicine, and in his capacity as Sheriff, his leisure hours, apart from the requirements of his office, were spent in making proficiency in his favorite science; and still more so after his trial—immediately following which he attended a medical college with ardor and assiduity."

The sheriff-doctor was doubtless a man of his hands in his dual profession, and, though his spelling, grammar, sentence structure, and diction do not always follow conventional modes, he makes a good story out of the *Life and Bloody Career*. When he writes of himself, he is copious in this wise:

Truth and justice, by oppression and by forces foul, may be held down for awhile, but the increasing and progressive powers of the spring will break and throw off the impediments—again bursting forth in vigor and strength not to be crushed nor repressed by sophistry nor by the influences of money and distinguished officials.[14]

But when he is quoting, or professing to quote, James Copeland, he is racy enough: "Our raise there was about four to five thousand dollars."[15] "The whiskey he had taken down made his coppers a little hot."[16] "We filled our flasks with whiskey, gave our negro a good horn."[17] "He had made a raise out of the religious brethren of about one thousand dollars."[18] "McGrath procured a bottle of whiskey, to which he added plenty of opium."[19] "They . . . made a conditional trade with him . . . if the negro could 'blow and strike.'"[20] "If you wish to bulk or fly back, take your seventeen hundred dollars and leave."[21] And he is crudely effective in describing scenes of terror, as that of the murder of an old Mexican rancher, and of the murderer's nightmare thereafter.[22] River navies and wagon caravans for hauling away the booty, midnight murders by torchlight, bandits shifting from hunting shirts and coonskin caps to clerical bombazine and beaver, sanguine oaths and secret conclaves, Mexican drovers and steamboat captains, green goggles and false whiskers, kegs of gold and sacks of jewelry, likely-looking sixteen-year-old mulatto mistresses dressed in boys' clothes and following their masters—these and a hundred other picturesque details make the *Life and Bloody Career* one of the best of the old thrillers. These merits and its advertised price of $1.50 stamp it as the Tamburlaine of Southern picaresque tales.

14 *Ibid.*, p. 9.
15 P. 29.
16 P. 49.
17 P. 51.
18 P. 55.
19 P. 58.
20 P. 75.
21 P. 84.
22 P. 44.

'REV. McGRATH WENT THAT EVENING AMONG THE BRETHREN' [23]

WE REACHED a settlement a little before night, on some of the waters of the Sabine River. It was the residence of some stock keepers; there were some three or four families, and some fifteen or twenty Mexican drovers, and horse thieves; they had just been to Natchitoches, and had a full supply of rum; a few of them could speak English. We quartered with them, and that night we opened the little remnant of our goods and jewelry, and had a general raffle. By the next day we had realized from our raffle sufficient to purchase each of us a good Spanish saddle and bridle, and a good Texas horse. We learned from one of these Mexicans the residence of the man who owned the negroes that we were after, and we also learned that he and his family were strict members of the Methodist Church. Now it was that one of us had to turn preacher, so as to reconnoiter the place. Wages and I put that on McGrath. We all mounted our horses and started, having procured plenty of lassoes, &c., McGrath being an Irishman and his tongue tipped with plenty of blarney.

We traveled for two days very moderately, and our chief employment was drilling McGrath, how to pray and sing, and give that long Methodist groan, and "Amen." He having made considerable progress, we went to Natchitoches. McGrath entered that town by one road, and Wages and myself by another. McGrath went among a few of his brethren that evening.

To our astonishment it was posted at every corner, that the "Rev. Mr. McGrath, from Charleston, South Carolina, would preach at the Methodist Church that evening, at half past seven."

We attended church. McGrath took his stand in the pulpit. He made a very genteel apology to his audience, saying he was very much fatigued from his travel; that he had caught cold and was very hoarse and could not sing; but he read out the hymn. It was "Hark from the tombs a doleful sound." One old brother pitched the tune to Old Hundred, and they all chimed in, Wages and myself among the rest; Wages sang bass and I tenor, and we all made that old church sound like distant thunder. After singing, McGrath made a very good but short prayer; he then took his text in the 16th chapter of St. Mark, at the verse where Mary the mother, and Mary Magdalene found the stone rolled from the door of the sepulchre. "And he said unto them, Be not affrighted; ye seek Jesus of Nazareth, who was crucified; he has risen; he is not here; behold the place where they laid him." He

[23] *Ibid.*, pp. 35-37.

read several verses in that chapter, and then made some very good explanations relative to the parables, and prophecies on the coming of the Messiah, and the mysterious way in which he disappeared, and wound up his discourse by telling the audience that he had been a great sinner in his young days, that it had been but a few years since the Lord had called him to preach, and he thanked his God that he was now willing and able to lay down his life upon the altar of God; he then raved, and exhorted all to repent and turn to God; and after having about half an hour called all his hearers that wished to be prayed for to come forward. The whole congregation kneeled down; he prayed for them all, and finally finished, sang another hymn and dismissed his congregation, and we all retired, Wages and myself to a gaming table, and McGrath with some of his brethren.

Next day the members of the church there waited on McGrath to know what was his pecuniary situation. He told them that he was very poor, was on his way to see a rich relation of his, about two hundred miles from there; that he carried his gun to keep off wild beasts, etc. They made up money to buy him a fine suit of black, a new saddle and saddle-bags and fifty dollars in cash. We remained there two days, when McGrath left.

Wages and I left by another road. We all met a short distance from the town and made the proper arrangement for our operations. McGrath was to go on to the house of this man that had the negroes, and there make what discoveries were necessary. He was to join Wages and myself at San Antonio on the first day of September following. Wages and I left in the direction for the Red Land on the Irish Bayou.

THE INDICTMENT THAT HANGED COPELAND [24]

STATE OF MISSISSIPPI, ⎫
Perry County.   ⎬

In the Circuit Court of Perry County—At March Term, 1857

THE Grand Jurors for the State of Mississippi, summoned, empanneled, sworn, and charged to inquire in and for the State of Mississippi, and in and for the body of the county of Perry, upon their oath, present, that James Copeland, late of said county, on the 15th day of July, Anno Domini, one thousand eight hundred and fifty-eight,[25] with force and arms in the county of Perry aforesaid, in upon one James

---

[24] *Ibid.*, pp. 110-112.

[25] This is evidently a misprint for 1848, since it is elsewhere specifically stated several times that "the famous Harvey battle" took place in that year.

A. Harvey, then and there being in the peace of God and the said State of Mississippi,[26] feloniously, wilfully and of his malice aforethought, did make an assault; and that the said James Copeland, a certain shot gun, then and there loaded and charged with gun powder and divers leaden shot, which shot gun, so loaded and charged he, the said James Copeland, did shoot off, and discharge; and that the said James Copeland, with the leaden aforesaid, out of the shot gun aforesaid, then and there by force of the gun powder, shot and sent forth as aforesaid, the said James A. Harvey, in and upon the left side of him the said James A. Harvey, then and there feloniously, wilfully and of the malice aforethought of him, the said James Copeland, did strike, penetrate and wound, giving to the said James A. Harvey, then and there, with the leaden shot so as aforesaid, discharged and sent forth, out of the shot gun aforesaid, by the said James Copeland, in and upon the left side of him, the said James A. Harvey, a little below the left shoulder of him the said James A. Harvey, divers mortal wounds of the depth of three inches, and of the breadth of one quarter of an inch, of which the said mortal wounds, the said James A. Harvey, from the fifteenth of July in the year aforesaid, until the twenty-fifth day of July in the year aforesaid, languished, and languishing did live; on which said twenty-fifth day of July in the year aforesaid, the said James A. Harvey in the county of Perry aforesaid, of the mortal wounds aforesaid, died; and the jurors aforesaid, upon their oaths aforesaid, do further present, that John Copeland, late of the county aforesaid, on the day and year first aforesaid, in the county of Perry aforesaid, feloniously, wilfully, and of his malice aforethought, was present, aiding, abetting and assisting the said James Copeland the felony and murder aforesaid to do and commit; and the jurors aforesaid upon their oath aforesaid do say, that the said James Copeland and John Copeland him the said James A. Harvey, in manner and form aforesaid, feloniously, wilfully and of their malice aforethought did kill and murder, against the peace and dignity of the State of Mississippi.

GEORGE WOOD, *District Attorney.*

GEORGE H. DEVOL

According to his own statement, Devol was born in 1829, at Marietta, Ohio, "the worst boy of my age west of the Allegheny

[26] As a matter of fact, Harvey was hardly "in the peace of God" or the State of Mississippi. He and the Copeland gang had quarreled bitterly over a "miserable forty dollar note" issued in partial settlement of a raid, and refused of payment, by Harvey.

Mountains that was born of good Christian parents." He ran away from home in 1839, shipping as cabin-boy on a steamboat. He was keno man, faro dealer, and rondo operator, all the way from Cincinnati to New Orleans and the Rio Grande, and most points between, working trains as well as steamboats.

The following selections from *Forty Years a Gambler on the Mississippi* are reprinted, with the kind permission of Henry Holt and Company, from the Holt reprint (1926).

I. LAY OFF A JUDGE[27]

I HAD beat a man out of $600 on the railroad from New Orleans to Jackson. I saw that if I got off he would put me to some trouble, so I kept on until I got to Canton, some twenty-five miles above. He followed me there and had me arrested. The trial was to come off in an hour, as it was meal-time with the Judge. We were all assembled in the court-room, and the Judge wanted him to tell how I had got his money. He said, "I could show you, Judge, if I had some cards." I pulled out some of the same cards I beat him with, and gave them to the Judge, and he wanted to know how they could bet money on three cards. I said, "Judge, I will show you so you can understand." I took the cards and mixed them over a few times, telling the Judge to watch the jack. He did watch it, and he could turn it over every time, as one of the corners of the jack was turned up, and he said it was as fair a game as he ever saw. I told him I had two chances to his one; so he dismissed the case. I came near giving it to the Judge for a few dollars, and then give them back; but I thought best not to do so.

When the fellows went out of the court-room, the Canton boys laughed at him and called him a fool. After he left, the Judge and I went over to a saloon and had some cigars. He said he dearly loved to play poker; but I did not want any of his game, as I thought I might need him again some time; and it proved I was right, for it was not long after that I was coming down on the train from Vicksburg, and beat five or six of the passengers out of a few hundred dollars. When we got to Canton we were behind time and missed connection, and

<hr />

[27] Devol, George H. *Forty Years a Gambler on the Mississippi. A cabin boy in 1839; could steal cards and cheat the boys at eleven; stack a deck at fourteen; bested soldiers on the Rio Grande during the Mexican War; won hundreds of thousands from paymasters, cotton buyers, defaulters and thieves; fought more rough-and-tumble fights than any man in America and was the most daring gambler in the world.* Cincinnati (Devol and Haines), 1887. New York (Henry Holt), 1926. Henry Holt & Co. reprint, pp. 66-67.

had to lay over until night. They had me arrested for the same trick, and taken before the same Judge; and you ought to have heard him after he found out how they had lost their money, for he just gave them a good old-fashioned turning over. He called them a lot of babies, and put the costs of the court on them. I got the Judge a box of fine cigars, and went down on the same train; but I was in the sleeper, and they did not see me until I got to New Orleans. I played poker in the sleeper all the way to the city, and did not lose very much, as the game was small, and we played on the square. I met some of them at the opera the same night, and they had their opera glasses pointed at me for some time. I guess they wondered how I got there so soon.

II. EVEN THE JUDGES DO IT [28]

THE love of gambling is confined to no class of people. Preachers and lawyers, doctors and men of business, are susceptible to the smiles of the fickle goddess of fortune as well as the roughest men.

George Hardy and myself were once going from Jackson, Mississippi, to Vicksburg, and, for want of something better to do, fell to talking over old times and tricks with cards. Near by sat a gentleman who seemed interested in our conversation, and I asked George who it was, as I had often seen him at Vicksburg. "Why, that's Judge So-and-so," and he introduced me. Pretty soon George remarked, "Devol, you ought to show the Judge the baby ticket," and as I had just played the trick for a joke, I said, "Yes, Judge, I have one of the best games for the drinks in the world; they play it out West altogether now instead of dice." Of course, he was anxious to see how it was done. Taking out some cards, the Judge was greatly amused, and at last George offered to bet me $50 that he could turn the card. I took him up, and he lost. Then the Judge, not at all discouraged by George's ill luck, said he could turn it up for $50; but I told him I did not want to bet with him, since he never had seen the game before. At last I consented to go him once. He turned the card and lost, and then I thought that George would die of laughter. This only riled the Judge, who was now bent on getting even; so he put up his gold watch and chain, and lost them. He was satisfied then, and the next day sent around a friend and redeemed them.

George remarked, "The Judge stands very high in this vicinity, so never say anything about this transaction"; and as I never did, I do not suppose George did. George had no idea that the Judge would

[28] Henry Holt & Co. reprint, pp. 164-165; with special permission.

bet. Both the parties are still living, and will, when they see this in cold type, heartily enjoy the story.[29]

III. THE QUADROON GIRL [30]

I GOT on the *Belle Key* one afternoon at Vicksburg; and as I claimed to be a planter from White River, I soon became acquainted with some planters that lived on the coast. There was a game of poker started, and I was invited to sit in. We played until supper was ready. I had played on the square, and had won a few hundred dollars. After supper they got up a dance, and that spoiled the game. I was sitting in the hall when one of the planters came up to me and said, "Don't you dance?" "No, I don't care to dance where I am not acquainted." "You are like me in that respect; I had rather play poker; but as those gentlemen who were playing in the game to-day have all got their families on board, they will not play, so what do you say to us having a game?" I said I did not care to play a while, but I would rather be a little more private, and that we might go up into the texas and play. We got the checks at the bar (and the bar-keeper did not forget a deck of my cards). We went up and had just got seated, when up came my partner and said, "Gentlemen, are you going to sport a little?" "We are; will you join us?" said the planter. "What are you going to play?" "Poker, of course." He sat in, and then it was a very nice, gentlemanly game. We played on the square for a while (that is, if the cards had been square). Finally I could put it off no longer, so I ran up two hands, giving the planter three eights, and then downed him for over $400. We played a little while longer, and then I ran up two more hands, and guarded them so that nothing could fall in that time. I gave my partner the best hand, and he took in about $600. The planter was then over $1,000 loser, so he excused himself for a few minutes, and I knew that he had gone after more money. He soon returned with $1,500, and that lasted him about one hour. He got up

[29] This old game is still going strong on the River. I saw it on the levee at Friars Point, Mississippi, in the summer of 1933. I was waiting for the ferry from that point to Helena, Arkansas. Two negroes were playing it on a bank by the side of the road leading down to the landing. They were apparently absorbed with each other. But when they saw from the corners of their eyes that I was watching them, they became very boisterous. When I approached, they went through the trick two or three times, changing quarters, without saying anything to me. Tired of waiting for me to speak, one of them asked me, respectfully, to try my luck. I requested them to explain how it was done. They went through the trick for my benefit, moving the cards slowly. Then one of them said, "W'ite folks, try yo' luck, jes' for fun, 'thout no stakes." I obliged, keeping close watch of the rather slowly moving cards, and called the right one. "Now, w'ite folks, you sees how it's did, 'n' how easy 'tis. Try a th'ow." I tossed him a quarter and told him to try another sucker.

[30] Henry Holt & Co. reprint, pp. 79-81; with special permission.

and said, "Boys, I must have some more money." My partner and I went down with him, as I did not think he could get any more. We were at the bar taking a drink, when he turned to me and said, "I would like to play some more, but I can't get any more money, unless you will loan me some on my negro, as I have one on board that I paid $1,500 for, and she is one of the most likely girls you ever saw." My partner loaned him $1,000, and got the clerk to draw up a bill of sale; then we resumed the game; but that did not last him but about half an hour, for I beat him out of nearly the whole amount on one hand, and that broke up the game. He had but seventy-five dollars left. We went down and took a drink, and then went to bed.

The next day he got the money and redeemed his girl; then he said to me, "I have got about $700, so let us go up and play single-handed." We went up, and I soon got that money. He said, "In all my poker-playing, I never played so unlucky in my life." He went to my partner and borrowed $1,000 more on the girl, and I took that in. He then went to Captain Keys, and tried to borrow the money to redeem his girl again, but the Captain would not loan it to him. He found a man that loaned him the money, and he redeemed her again. He was considerable loser, but he got some more wine in him, then he wanted more poker; but I told my partner not to have anything more to do with his negro, for it was making too much talk on the boat already. When he got to his landing, he and his negro left the boat, and I tell you she was *a dandy*.

SHOCCO JONES IN MISSISSIPPI

By H. S. Fulkerson [31]

THE successful cultivation of cotton and the profitableness of the pursuit, in Mississippi and Louisiana, in the years from 1834 to 1838, had led to so much speculation in wild lands, and such a rapid advance in them, that anybody with a little money had only to buy a tract of land, put a few negroes on it, and deaden the timber, to grow rich—*on paper*. The sales were all on credit; but the banks discounted paper freely and every man was ready to endorse every other man's paper.

The country was apparently so prosperous and everybody was growing rich so fast, that every little town had its bank, and the bigger ones two or more. Vicksburg had several of these "institutions," and Natchez, the oldest town in the State, had two, the Agricultural Bank and Planters' Bank, old banks, which had existed for a number of

[31] *Random Recollections of Early Days in Mississippi*, Vicksburg, Miss. (Vicksburg Printing and Publishing Company), 1885, pp. 66-70, 74-75. For note on Fulkerson, see p. 307.

years and had been very successful. The celebrated Union Bank was chartered in 1838, and was in operation the following year. The "boom" in every branch of business was immense, and everything was aglow with speculation.

It was just anterior to this period that General Jackson, as President of the United States, had his successful fight with the old United States Bank. The withdrawal of the public deposits from this bank had so deranged the finances of the country as to bring on a great financial crisis, which involved the Southern State banks in the ruin that followed.

It was at the height of the distress and anxiety growing out of this state of affairs, in the Fall of 1839, that the wonderful genius and Prince of Humbuggers, Shocco Jones, of North Carolina, burst upon the vision of the distressed Mississippians. He came unheralded, arriving in Jackson, the Capital of the State, by stage from Columbus, at which latter point he had created quite a flutter in the little coterie of bank officials and directors who controlled the fiscal institution of the city on the banks of the Tombigbee; making a soft place in the circle of its officers for an impecunious relative who dwelt in their midst, by sheer force of his unrivaled genius and unparalleled impudence, and strange to say only for the sake of a love of fun which was all-devouring with him and which he indulged alone for his personal gratification, for he never divulged to anyone of his boon companions, attracted by his captivating manners, that *fun* was his prime, and in fact his only, object. In his intense love of it he was unwilling to share it with others. He was a veritable hoarder of fun. Imperturbable impudence, a gracious manner, bright intelligence, and the business air of a monied man without solicitude for the future, made up his stock in trade, and were the tools with which he forged his fun. The gullible trait in human character was the field of his operations, and he had unbounded confidence in its resources, in its capacity to yield him an abundant harvest of fun under his skillful cultivation. A crisis in public affairs, a period of anxiety when everybody was on the *qui vive* for strange and startling things, was his fit occasion. His advent in Mississippi was opportune, and his knowledge of human nature and the condition of affairs told him so.

So soon after reaching Jackson as he made himself as presentable as becomes a man of affairs and a man of means, he got directions to the office of Dr. Wm. M. Gwin, who was then U. S. Marshal for the District of Mississippi, and proceeded thither, carrying under his arm a large bundle of papers carefully wrapped up, tied with red tape, and having on it seals done in red wax.

Arriving at the Marshal's office, he introduced himself as a confidential agent of the United States Treasury Department, and informed the Marshal that he had authority from the Secretary of the Treasury to enquire into the condition of the Southern banks in which Government funds had been deposited. This information was imparted in the quiet tone and with the mysterious air of one charged with valuable State secrets; the agent meantime carelessly turning about and thrumming upon the ominous looking package bound in red tape. The high functionary of the Marshal's office took in the situation promptly, and tendered his services to the agent. Dr. Gwin was himself a man of affairs and a man of parts, and he had a high place in the confidence of the Government.

The agent scanned the office of the Marshal in search of a strong box wherein to deposit his valuable papers, and seeing none, enquired of the Marshal if he knew of one. Certainly he did. The Receiver at the Land Office had the finest in the State. They went thither; the agent was introduced to the Receiver; the safe was carefully inspected by the agent; and the package locked up. Then the Receiver was taken into confidence and had the high State secret imparted to him. And it is said he had an armed watchman on duty all night over the safe containing the package.

Before separating, Shocco said he desired to consult them about a legal adviser; that besides the need of one in the affairs of Government, he thought it not unlikely that he would need one to examine land titles, as the cashier of the Cape Fear Bank of North Carolina had requested him, as he passed through on his way from Washington, to invest a large surplus of gold which the bank held, in Mississippi land mortgages, on one to three years; that the sum was great enough to meet the wants of many persons, and he would likely have to pass upon a number of titles. He had heard of a Mr. Prentiss, of Vicksburg, as being a very superior lawyer, and desired to know if he would be a proper person for so important a trust. The Marshal and Receiver agreed that he could do no better than to employ that distinguished gentleman, and the Marshal was requested to invite him to Jackson, by letter, which he did.

The great lawyer, promptly obeying the summons, repaired to the Capital and was presented to the great fiscal agent. A single look at each other and they were as firmly knit together as were Jonathan and David. "As face answereth to face in water," genius answers to genius when meeting. Until this moment the agent had not been seen to smile. The weight of great cares was upon him, and his bearing and expression were altogether such as became the occasion. But a magi-

cian was before him now with the rod of a Moses. One stroke—a single
flash of wit from the great lawyer—and the flinty face of the financier
broke into smiles, and a flash went back. The grave Marshal and Receiver heard explosion after explosion as the rockets of wit flashed thick
and fast, and the Treasury agent rose higher and higher in their estimation. What! a wit, a poet, a philosopher and an orator, as well as
an astute, sober-minded business man! What an acquisition to the
State! He must be held. And they went off, the lawyer on the agent's
arm, with his eloquent hobble—there was nothing about him that was
not eloquent—the Marshal and the Receiver following.

The boon and genial companions soon reached the point of in-
timacy which drops the formalities of social intercourse, and "Prent"
and "Shoc" became the terms in which their reciprocal endearment was
expressed. Prentiss for once had met his match, in some points—in *all*
points he was *matchless*. A trip to Vicksburg was arranged for; the
package with the dynamite load, which was to blow up the banks,
was withdrawn from the Receiver's strong box, and they started off
to storm Vicksburg, the stronghold of speculators in lands and negroes,
and shaky banks. The news of the contemplated visit by the Treasury
agent and money lender had preceded them. The bank officers were
shaking in their shoes, and the speculators were busy perfecting titles.
It must be remembered that at this early day the telegraph was
not in operation, and there were no fast mails. . . .

[The foregoing passage shows clearly Shocco's *modus operandi*.
He continued it, with slight variations of technique suited to particular localities, at Vicksburg, where there was a lordly banquet
and a wit contest between the North Carolina playboy and the Mississippi silver tongue, in which "Shakespeare and Byron and Scott
were freely quoted in illustration of the happier things said by the
champions"; at Natchez; and then for a short excursion to Grand
Gulf and Port Gibson. The grand climax developed on the return
to Natchez.]

The next packet came along. The agent was at the landing and as the
boat rounded to, the great lawyer emerged from the social hall, followed by boon companions. When Shocco was spied, the welkin rang
again with three cheers for the great deliverer. The scene on board,
as the boat wended her way to Natchez, is past describing. The gentle
reader must draw his own picture as best he can by the light of what
has been said already in that line. Shocco went to the barkeeper, after

greeting the party, and in his lordliest way ordered that functionary to let the little lame man (meaning Prentiss) have anything he called for, adding, "I will make it all right!" Arrived at Natchez, the banks were visited immediately by the prompt Treasury agent, and the great lawyer was taken charge of by his friends—the friends of his earliest Southern days. Natchez, at that day, was the seat of wealth and refinement and high aristocratic tendencies. It was the oldest city in the State, and had two banks, which were presided over by some of the wealthiest resident planters, and transacted a very large business. Shocco was not wanting in the needed resources of mind in meeting these magnates and notables. In their presence he rose to sublimest heights and discoursed eloquently of the noted citizen then at the head of the Treasury Department. The details of what tradition has handed down as having been said and done by him would weary the reader.

The red tape package with the broad seal was duly deposited in a bank, and the day after his arrival a dray backed up to the door of the bank, having on it boxes of specie, marked "S. Jones, U.S.T. Agent, care of bank." The boxes were deposited in the vault of the bank.

Numerous interviews of a private and confidential character were held with the bank officers, by the agent, and the attorney was besieged by parties with papers—in want of accommodations. A great dinner party was given the two distinguished visitors by one of the citizens.

But Shocco had an almanac, and a good memory besides, and these told him his time was nearly up. It was nearing the time when somebody might be receiving an answer to a letter which may have been mailed to Washington. A return to Vicksburg, to finish up business there, and then a return to Natchez, was determined on. The first boat up conveyed the two great men to Vicksburg, the specie having been left and the red tape package withdrawn and carried off. Arrived at Vicksburg, hurried business interviews followed the next day, and much high merriment the following night.

Late in the next forenoon, the revelers of the night before called at his lodgings, but Shocco was *gone!* and the country was *sold!* The red tape package was found on the table in his room. The seals were broken—contents, old *newspapers!*

The news flew to Natchez. The specie boxes were opened—contents, *scrap iron!*

BUT THEY NAMED A POST OFFICE FOR HIM

A NEW post office has been established at Shocco, Octibbeha County. The postmaster is Thomas J. Moore, Shocco, Octibbeha County.[32]

SHOCCO WITH SILVER STRANDS

By a Traveler on Foot [33]

I HAVE been engaged the last few hours in the indulgence of reminiscences of the past, seated, or rather stretched out at full length, beneath the shade of a little oasis of oaks in the prairie, not far from my Lodge, a cigar and my pet fawn my only companions. The cigar aids pleasant remembrances, and my fawn removes the idea of perfect solitude.

Among the persons and scenes of the by-gone years that revolve within the blue circles of cigar smoke that curl upward, to dissolve like memories, in the bluer air above me, the intelligent face of one appears vividly to present itself. Many years ago, not less than fifteen, as I was leisurely taking my dessert at the Astor, I noticed a gentleman opposite, whose fine dark face and intellectual and agreeable countenance would have attracted my attention anywhere. He was engaged in brilliant and witty conversation with three gentlemen on either side of him, and at the same time filling his wine glass of sherry with the brown kernels of pecans, which, when well-soaked with the richly-

[32] *Mississippi Free Trader and Natchez Weekly Gazette*, Thursday, April 9, 1840, p. [1].

[33] From "Pebbles: Picked Up in the Pathways of the World. By a Traveller on Foot. No. VII," Natchez *Daily Courier*, May 15, 1853, p. [5], and No. VIII, May 19, 1853, p. [2]. "Written for the *Natchez Courier*."

Fulkerson's account of "Shocco" Jones, above, and the two sketches "By a Traveler on Foot," with heading "From My Lodge on the Prairie," given herewith, are apparently founded on facts, whatever romantic liberties their writers may have taken with their subject. According to Marshall DeLancey Haywood (in S. A. Ashe's *Biographical History of North Carolina*, Greensboro, 1907, vol. VI), Jo. Seawell Jones was born at Shocco, Warren County, North Carolina, studied at the University of North Carolina and Harvard, and took an LL.B. from the latter in 1833. A man of brilliant but erratic genius, he was unable to control his personality, wasting his energies as a playboy, a frequenter of fashionable resorts in the East, and a practical joker. He was, however, the author of two serious books—*A Defence of the Revolutionary History of North Carolina from the Aspersions of Mr. Jefferson* (Boston and Raleigh, 1834) and *Memorials of North Carolina* (New York, 1838). The late Bishop Joseph B. Cheshire (*Nonnulla, Memories, Stories, Traditions, More or Less Authentic*, Chapel Hill, 1930, pp. 230-233) states that Jones played tricks on the Alabama legislature similar to those Fulkerson says he played on the bankers and politicians of Mississippi in the thirties. Reference by John W. Moore (*History of North Carolina*, Raleigh, 1880, vol. II, p. 107) to a work concerning Jones written about 1853 and entitled "My Log Cabin in the Prairie" at once suggests some connection with the "Pebbles" sketches included here, written for the Natchez *Daily Courier* in 1853 "From My Lodge in the Prairie." According to Haywood (*op. cit.*, p. 334), Jones died at Columbus, Mississippi, in 1855.

flavored wine, he would eat out with the point of a very delicate pearl-handled pen knife, all the while keeping his friends in the highest state of hilarity, with his stories and anecdotes, and masterly hits at character. This gentleman was afterwards introduced to me as Mr. Shocco Jones, of N. C. He was then putting through the press a history of North Carolina. But Mr. Jones' forte lay not so much in writing a book, as affording himself rare material for a book. A few days after my introduction to him, I found that I had become acquainted with the most "popular" man of the day, the greatest joker, the best wit, the most delightful conversationist, and one of the most polished and courtly gentlemen I had ever met with; a sort of Count D'Orsay, Beau Brummel, and the admirable Crichton combined.

It was some years after this meeting in New York, that I met this versatile North Carolinian again. It was in the aristocratic city of Natchez, where he was lionizing and being lionized in the most *recherché* style, by the nobility and the monied lords. He had, as was understood secretly, in his hands, the monetary destiny of the South, and when he would nod, the Union would nod! The adventures of "Mr. Jones, of Shocco," during his brief lionizing in Mississippi, would fill a volume most readable and instructive to financiers and bank gentlemen generally, and I shall therefore not anticipate the gentleman who may give the world a biography as racy, amusing, extraordinary, piquant and relishing, as was ever yet penned.

The next I heard of "The Marquis of Shocco," as he once introduced himself by card to the Brazilian Minister, was at Columbus, Mississippi, his predilections having somehow been in favor of the chivalry of the "Rifle State." In Columbus, he was also passing through a distinguished career of lionizing. He was feted, flattered, caressed, and dined, and balled, and it was a test of *ton* to know Mr. Jones! to dine Mr. Jones! to have Mr. Jones take an airing with one. The houses, the carriages, the albums, the pews of a Sunday, and the *purses* of the good people of this elegant city, were all at the service of Mr. Jones, of Shocco. It was deemed an honor to loan him money. If Mr. Jones had been Rothschild, and Rothschild the Emperor of Russia, and the Emperor of Russia the owner of all the world's mines, he (Mr. Rothschild) could not have been received with higher honors, had he paid that city a visit.

Eight years passed, and Mr. Jones, of Shocco, had ceased to appear before the public eye. He seemed suddenly to have sunk into oblivion. Whether he were gone down to "the vaults" of Death, or were touring in Europe as the agent of the United States Bank, or smoking a pipe with the Sultan, or doing pilgrimage, in sandal and sackcloth, to the

Holy Shrine of Jerusalem, or joining a caravan to that of Mecca, or
engaged in exploring for the northwest passage, or gone to establish a
bank in the Sandwich Islands, or become Prime Minister of the Emperor of Japan, or President of the Bank of China, I knew not. I only
knew that printers' boys, for eight years, had ceased to set up the odd
cognomination, "Shocco;" that editorial columns no longer were
familiar with it as whilom; that "types" had become "shadows," so far
as chronicling the movements of this distinguished North Carolinian.

But at length I once more met him in a very unexpected manner.
Last year, as I was traveling on horseback across the prairies east of
Columbus, and about twelve miles north of it, I came, at nightfall, to
a ford of the Tombigbee, which flows limpidly through the fertile region
of Northeastern Mississippi, watering the finest cotton country in the
world. Having achieved the passage of the river, though at some peril,
for my horse lost his footing, and had to swim for it with me upon
his back, I found, on inquiring of a negro on the bank, that I could
not reach Columbus until late that night. I therefore resolved to ride
to a house a mile distant, to which he directed me, and seek lodgings
for the night.

But I will leave for my next, the remainder of my narrative.
Yours,   W.

My last left me just after I had forded the Bigbee river, near
night-fall, upon the eastern bank. Like an experienced traveler, I measured the twelve miles which the next town (Columbus) was distant
from me, by the half hour of my watch that the sun was yet to measure to sundown. I am no lover of riding after dark, as my eyes are
none of the best, and my spectacles only bewilder my vision in a shad-
owy road. So I inquired for the nearest house, and set off to solicit the
hospitality of its proprietor.

The negro of whom I obtained my directions, was doubtless very
clear and graphic in his language. "You jiss go up dis road, massa, 'll
you come to big hickory, what has got struck wid thunder an split
open; den you goes to de leff, till you see a big gate. You leaves de
big gate on the right—no, on de *leff* han—and by'm by you comes to a
run. You crosses dem ar, and take de secun' turn to de right, (dis time
de right sartain,) and go through a lane half a mile, when you see de
chimneys o' de house top o' de trees, an den you find it easy nuff,
massa! Please, massa, got any bakky for poor old niggar?" I gave him
my last quid of Cavendish, with a dime under it, and with a dime and a
quid's worth of genuine hearty blessings, I rode off to follow the directions of my accurate informer. The evening air was delicious. Flowers

that bloomed on the Bigbee's banks filled the air with mingled perfumes. Scores of birds of gay plumage flitted about in the trees, now delighting my eyes with the splendor of their plumage, now with the sweetness of their songs. Ever and anon, the clear voice of a slave at work in a distant field beyond the river, would reach me and add to the varied harmony of the hour. The limpid surface of the river was enamelled with blue, orange, gold and purple tints, borrowed from the sunset sky; and occasionally dimpled into widening circles, by some silvery scaled fish cleaving it into the air, to fall back again with a splash into his native element. Tempted by the beauty of the scene, I let my horse walk with slacked rein, while I drew enjoyment from everything around me. A squirrel played bo-peep with me from behind a tall sycamore; and once I stopped to admire the splendor of the glittering scales of a gold and green snake that lay fearless and quiet directly in the road, a superb series of concentric bracelets, one within the other, that the Empress Eugenia might be proud to wear—if they were harmless! An Empress once wore such a one—the hapless Cleopatra!

So what with dallying and loitering, now letting my horse browse at the leaves, and now drink at a rivulet, I took little note of "Peter's" directions; and the sun set, finding me at least three miles beyond the ford where I had left Peter, and not a sign of other habitation than a deserted negro cabin in an old field. I drew rein and began to look about me. As to being guided by the marks which had been given me, was now out of the question; for the riven oak, the "old gate," the "lane," and other marks I was quite innocent of having had vision of. But a bewildered traveler, with a straight road before him, cannot go far without coming out somewhere. So I drew my bridle, touched the flank of my astonished steed sharply with the spur, and away we went upon a rapid canter along the woodland road before me. Birds, squirrels, flowers, snakes, golden skies and purple waters, I heeded not—I kept my eyes in search of a dwelling, hoping each moment to see one through the gathering twilight. I must have rode two miles at a very pretty pace, when I saw a light (it was already dark) to the right. I soon came to a lane into which, after passing through a gate at a spring, I turned. It conducted me in a few minutes into the very heart of a village of negro huts; and all the dogs, "Tray, Blanche and Sweetheart," came forth to bark at me.

Several slaves were returning from the field, and by them I was directed to a "long, low," whitewashed log mansion, enclosed by a paling, which was the the residence of the planter. It was surrounded by gardens, a lawn, and cotton-fields; and had that substantial air

which belongs to the plantation homes of thrifty planters in new coun-
tries; nothing was elegant or expensive, but everything substantial;
such as fine horses, sleek mules, fat negro children, plenty of turkeys,
ducks, geese, hens and chickens, and pigeon houses.

I alighted at the white gate, a hundred yards from the gallery of
the house, and one slave eagerly took my horse by the bit, while another began to remove my saddle-bags, before I drew my foot from
the stirrup.

As I walked towards the dwelling, I was met by a gentleman in a
linen roundabout and with a cigar in his mouth, who cordially shook
my hand and invited me in. As I have said, the house was built of logs,
but with many rooms, and being whitewashed, and a piazza running
along the front, it had an appearance of respectability that a North-
erner would never believe a log house could display.

At the tea table, which was profusely piled with good things, there
sat besides a dignified matron of the old school, her son, the young
host just named, and shortly came and seated himself a dark-complex-
ioned, thorough-bred looking gentleman, but evidently in premature
age. He was presented to me as "Mr. J——." He wore a long unshaven
grey and black beard, and his hair was streaked not thinly with silver
strands. I regarded him with some curiosity; for his suavity, his intelligence, his powers of pleasing in conversation, his finished courtesy
caused me to set him down as a man of society, and I marvelled to
find such a man in this seclusion; yet there was in his appearance a
something that made me perceive that he was but the splendid frag-
ment of what he had been.

After tea he hospitably invited me to go to "his castle," and led
me across a court in the rear of the mansion to a log-cabin of one room,
containing two beds, an enormous fire-place, garnished with a row of
long pipes, while tobacco, boxes and other appurtenances of a determined smoker, were stuck about in the crevices between the logs.
He offered me a pipe three feet long, and we commenced smoking, and
all the while I was puzzling my brain to know where I had seen this
gentleman—this Mr. Jones. He was full of anecdote! He knew Van
Buren, Jackson, both Adamses, Calhoun, Clay, Randolph, and every
man of note who had figured on the world's stage for thirty years past,
and had anecdotes to tell of each. He knew the private history of
every body who had any "private history," had danced with the belles
of two generations, had dined with all the foreign ministers of seven
administrations, and was *au fait* of all the political and domestic
scandal of Washington for as many reigns. He entertained me till past

the small hours, yet all the while I could not make out who he was. At length, at 2 o'clock in the morning, I put this question direct—

"In the name of all mystery, sir, tell me *which* of all the Mr. Jones' of the earth, *which* Mr. Jones you are?"

He laughed heartily and said:

"I know *you*, my dear friend. I recognized you at the first. We have dined together in New York years ago. I was waiting to see if you would recognize me. I am 'Mr. Jones of Shocco!' " This was said with a drollery inimitable. "I have for some years gone into retirement. This is the residence of my mother, where I have a home. Here I shall live till I have done with life's fitful fever. In this log-cabin, I smoke, I call up the past, I live Saratoga, Nahant, Washington over again. From between the crevices of my cabin, I can peep at the great world rolling by and laugh at it, as I did when I was in it. Take another pipe. It is only three o'clock in the morning."

And true enough, my old acquaintance Shocco, the world renowned, had turned up in a log-cabin on the borders of the prairies. There he had been living; forgotten by the world several years, smoking pipes all night, and dreaming of the world he had flown from and sleeping all day. He was very grey; he had the habits of a monk, in his love for solitude, for his cabin was his castle; and here he dwelt, though still so brilliant that not long ago he kept up by his fireside a certain venerable bishop till cock-crowing, forgetful of repose, listening to his fascinating "Reminiscences of the gay world he had lived in," yet he was now but half of himself as I formally knew him; for former conviviality had done its work upon his frame. To crown all, Shocco had become a devout Roman Catholic; and receives annual visits from a priest to absolve him from all his past offences. In more absolute obscurity a man could not live who had formerly been so prominent before the public eye. There in his log-cabin he still dwells, an anchorite. His venerable mother is since dead, but has effectually left him, whom she loved always, a small competence; and with his pipes and his rich memories, his penances and his prayers, his grey locks and his solitude, he will probably remain until the grave shall embrace all that was once the witty, the amusing, the financiering, the diplomatising, the fascinating, the accomplished and distinguished "Shocco Jones."   W.

PUSH-PIN

By William Russell Smith [34]

I HAD one encounter with Picher which I can never forget. It was after his house and his last acre of ground had passed out of his possession, when he had no place on which to lay his head excepting on a hired cot; nowhere to rest his hands excepting in the pockets of his butternut breeches.

I was at the time on a rampage through the country *expounding constitutions* in fence-corners and under spreading oaks to small or large audiences as the case might be.

It was a breezeless day in June, when the squeak of the jay bird indicated thirst; and when the yellowing wheat stood stiff and upright, scorching in the sun for want of a refreshing zephyr. Following the nose of my pony I found myself at a gate in front of a plank hut, on the roadside. There was a narrow piazza to this hut, propped up by a post at each end, in which was a long plank bench; sitting astraddle of which, and face to face, were two men, earnestly engaged in some absorbing pursuit. So absorbed indeed were they that they had not noted my advent, and I looked on, before hailing, a moment, to observe the scene and grasp the situation.

It was Charley Picher and Jack Vines, vigorously prosecuting a game of *"push-pin,"* rapping skillfully or not on the caved crown of a dilapidated hat, whose Sunday gloss had been washed out of it—possibly by the same rain that pattered on the shingles of the ark.

"Hello!"

"I gosh!" exclaimed Picher, "there's Judge S——"

"By darn," said Jack, "and so it is"; when both men jumped up and came in a fair run to the gate, with faces beaming exuberantly, one on either side of me, striving which should lift me from my pony.

"You're all right here, my boy!" exclaimed Picher, before I had dismounted. "Not a man in the beat will vote against you—is there, Jack?"

"Nary a one, as I knows on," replied Jack "There's one or two would like to, but they *daresn't,* they're *afeard of a massacree!"*

By this time we were on the porch of the cabin. I sat down on the bench near the flattened hat and saw the pins, these one-legged men of the impending battle, lying side by side, head and point together, but not *crossed;* significant that the game was not yet ended.

[34] *Reminiscences of a Long Life; Historical, Political, Personal, and Literary,* 2 vols., Washington, c. 1889, vol. I, pp. 111-114.

"Is the game up?" said I, quizzically.

"No," said Jack, *"there's licker in it."*

"Better than millions," said Charley, letting his eye fall on me an instant, little supposing that I perceived the languid but fierce glance of that eye of his, as it shot inwardly like an angry flash through the profitless past of his misspent life.

"Better than millions, Billy," he repeated, and his face fell into a tremulous glow of feverish, impatient languor, revealing a sadness of soul indescribable to the ear, but to the eye, oh! how visible!

The sturdy gamesters resumed the battle; now mainly for the amusement of the single spectator. "Tap, tap, tap!" so alternately went the skillful fingers of the competitors as the pins bounced about the cavernous crown of that antique sombrero, sometimes wider apart, now closer together, sometimes head to head, now point to point, then one pushing a charge, the other coyly retreating.

"Wait a minute!" said Jack. He saw that Charley's pin had got its head entangled in a tiny thread of wool and was thus in a state of quasi helplessness—*hors de combat*—so to speak, and Jack knew that the moment of victory for him had come! "Wait a minute; I must ketch that bird!" and he gobbled a gobble that would have enchanted the most coquettish turkey-hen in all those woods. Then, with his long, lean middle finger, he gave the hat a tap so light, so graceful, so magical that his pin bounded and fell, as if by a sort of sorcery, right across Charley's prostrate paynim! and the game was up—the brazen acrobats were still!

Jack rose up with a great horse-laugh, and Charley exhibited no less cheerfulness.

"Go to the spring, Jack," said Charley, "and come by the garden, and bring along a handful of mint. We've no *ice here*, Billy," he said, turning to me, "but the waters of yonder spring would freeze brother Jonathan's nose such weather as this." And so it would, for the weather was cold, and the julep was delicious.

VICKSBURG—THE HANGING OF THE GAMBLERS [35]

As OUR late article with respect to Vicksburg in the olden time seems to have attracted some attention, we feel encouraged to give the history of the transaction for which, previously to its late heroic resistance, it was most famous—we mean, of course, the execution of the gamblers by the citizens, or rather, by the military of the town,

[35] *Southern Illustrated News,* Richmond, Virginia, vol. I, No. 12 (Saturday, November 29, 1862), p. 2.

on Monday, the 6th day of July, 1835. Of course, great allowance is to be made for imperfect memory, at so great a distance of time.

The gamblers of Vicksburg, and of all the Mississippi towns at that day, were a very different description of persons from any ever known in Virginia. Here they are a quiet, well-behaved, orderly body of men. They keep themselves to themselves outside of their rooms, and interfere with nobody except those who come to bet at their banks. They are contented with winning a man's money, and seek no further commerce with him. It is very rarely that we hear of them in any manner, mixed up with scenes of violence and outrage. Demoralizing as their profession certainly is, its operations are silent, and screened sufficiently from public view to give but little umbrage and to cause but little scandal. Occasionally the police make a descent upon a faro-bank, and break up a gambler, and these occasions are almost the only ones upon which the affairs of the brotherhood are ever obtruded upon the public.

Very different was the gambler of the Mississippi at the time of which we are writing. He was generally a desperado and a bully. He was equally ready to cut a throat or a pack of cards. He belonged to a set that were almost numerous enough to form an army. They were to be found in swarms in all the towns on the river, and on all the steamboats that ploughed its waters. Their manners were insolent, truculent and overbearing, to an intolerable degree. They insisted on forcing themselves upon society, as it were, at the point of the bowie-knife. If any one resisted their claims, he ran the risk of his life. They occupied the streets in the day, in large bodies, and amused themselves by insolent remarks, loud enough to be heard, on everybody that passed, especially on ladies. To such a pitch of indecency had this practice been carried, at one time, in Vicksburg, that modest women were afraid to appear in the street, and shut themselves up in their houses altogether. They were afraid to tell their husbands and brothers, for they knew that the consequence would be bloodshed. In fact, the gamblers had made themselves the terror of the community. To offend them was to incur a serious risk. A party of them once went on a hunting expedition to the plantation of Governor McNutt, some miles above the city, in the neighborhood of the Lake. They got down, tied their horses, and proceeded on foot in search of game. The overseer coming by, and finding the horses, turned them loose, and the gamblers walked to town, swearing vengeance all the way. The next Saturday the man came to town. The gamblers becoming aware of the fact, went in pursuit of him, found him, and fired on him. He ran and they pursued, firing as they ran. He took refuge in a store on the wharf, and the proprietor, a man of great resolution, saved his life by snatching up a rifle and threatening to shoot dead the first man who advanced a foot nearer. As in the case of the Kangaroo, the law was altogether inoperative against this dangerous class of men.

On the 4th day of July, 1835, the Vicksburg volunteers had a company dinner after a parade, in a beautiful grove on the Walnut Hills. It was like all other dinners given by military companies; that is to say, nobody but the members and invited guests were expected to participate. Several gamblers came about the spot and endeavored to get in, but were all kept off by the guard except *one*, whose name at this distance of time, we cannot recollect. He, by some means, forced his way in, and became exceedingly troublesome, making a great noise, abusing the company, applying insulting epithets to individual members, and ending by jumping on the table and kicking off the glasses. This last feat was too much for the patience of the company. Lieutenant Brungard, who commanded it in the absence of John I. Guion, who was its Captain, ordered him to be seized. This was accomplished, after some difficulty, by Sergeant Alexander Fisher, formerly of this city, with the assistance of one or two of the men. The vote of the company was then taken upon the proper mode of dealing with him, and was unanimous for lynching. That punishment was accordingly administered with some severity, but not enough to cool down the recipient, who departed, bent upon a desperate revenge. The festivities having been thus rudely interrupted, were not renewed. The drum beat to arms, the company marched off to town, and summoned a public meeting by ringing the Court-house bell.

While the crowd was collecting, Alexander Fisher was informed that the gambler who had been arrested by him in his capacity of sergeant, and in obedience to orders, was on his way to the Court-house, armed to the teeth, and threatening to take his life. Knowing that he was a man of desperate character, he resolved to be beforehand with him. He stationed himself behind the door, and as the gambler entered, he sprang upon him, and seized both his arms, while some of his brother volunteers took from him an enormous bowie-knife, and we believe a pistol or two. He was a second time arraigned before Judge Lynch, and a second time punished—this time with considerable severity. He was then ordered to leave the town in twenty-four hours, which, to the best of our recollection, he did. The assembly of citizens then passed a resolution that the whole tribe should leave before Monday morning, and that the volunteers should see to the execution of the order. All accordingly left except a man named North, who kept a house on the street upon which the

Pinckard House was afterwards built, and four others, who lived with him. North was the great man of the fraternity. He was said to have been a person of a powerful understanding, and desperate courage. A strong will, and a great force of character, made him a leader, almost necessarily, among such men as he was associated with.

At an early hour on Monday, it having been ascertained that North and his immediate associates still remained in their house, the volunteers assembled. Their intention was to capture the gamblers, put them in a "dug-out," and turn them loose in the river, well knowing that they would float down the stream without any danger, until carried by the current to land, but to do them no farther harm. They accordingly took up the line of march. North's house having been built on a declivity of the hill, the front door was almost on a level with the street, while the back part of it was much higher. When the company reached the scene of operations, it was divided into two parts. One-half were drawn up in front of the house, and the other half in rear. The inmates were hailed and ordered to come forth on pain of having the door broken open. No answer was made in words, but by way of defiance, some one in the house fired off a pistol. The challenge was immediately accepted, and a party was detailed to break down the door, while the others stood under arms, ready to rush in. The door was soon broken open. The man that was nearest to it fell in the house as it gave way; and it was well that he did, for the fall saved his life.

The gamblers, to the number of five, had collected behind a bar which had been used by North for selling liquor (for he was a doggery keeper as well as a gambler). The door was in the centre of the room, and this bar in a corner. As soon as the door was wide open, all five of the gamblers fired their pistols at the man who broke it open. The bullets passed over him as he lay on the floor, but took effect on Dr. Hugh Bodley, who was standing under arms on the outside. One of them passed through his heart, and killed him instantly. He was a young man of considerable promise, and exceedingly popular. Without any orders, the body of troops stationed in front of the house immediately fired into it, mortally wounding one of the gamblers. Those in the rear, hearing the volley, by an uncontrollable impulse, also fired, their bullets passing entirely through the house, which was of wood, and one of them (a spent ball) striking a volunteer on the knee. The gamblers seemed to be instantly conscious that they had been guilty of a very rash action, which might draw down instant destruction upon them, and became struck with consternation. Two of them attempted to escape, and reached an upstairs room. Two stood as though petrified. One, as has been mentioned, was mortally wounded, and could make no attempt to escape, if thus disposed. The soldiers instantly rushed upon and secured them all.

A large crowd had assembled by this time. They, as well as the volunteers, were furious at the death of Bodley. It was debated, after the noisy fashion of crowds, what was to be done with them. Some person cried, "To the gallows with them." The cry was instantly taken up and repeated by a thousand tongues. It was impossible to resist the current, and they were hung.

Such, as well as we can recollect, is a true history of this famous transaction, upon which we shall make no remark whatever, except that the case was a desperate one, and apparently required a desperate remedy. If it be alleged that the gamblers acted in self-defence, still, it cannot be denied that the consequence of their act was well calculated to drive the people to frenzy.

LIFE IN MISSISSIPPI

GETTING A RAILROAD SUBSCRIPTION

By Thomas Chandler Haliburton [36]

HAVING seen nobody for thirty days, night overtook me at the center of Jones county. The road was only visible by the three "scores" on the trees, the grass growing on it rank and tall, like that in the adjacent woods. I was striking for the court house. I passed a small opening in which stood three rickety cabins, but they were untenanted. The road branched off into a dozen trails. Completely puzzled, I threw down the reins and left the matter to the instinct of my horse. He struck into one of the paths, and in fifteen minutes halted at a large farm house.

"Halloo!" cried I.

"It's halloo yourself," said the man in the gallery.

"How far to the court house?"

"Where are you from?" said the man.

"From Winchester."

"Then," said he, "the court house is behind, and you have come right by it there," pointing to the deserted cabins.

"Why, I saw nobody there."

"I reckon you didn't," said he. "There's a doggery and a tavern twice

[36] *The Americans at Home; or, Byeways, Backwoods, and Prairies,* Edited by the Author of "Sam Slick," in Three Volumes, London (Hurst and Blockett), 1854, vol. II, pp. 151 ff. For biographical note, see p. 178.

a year, two days at a time, but they come with the court and go with the court."

"And the clerk and sheriff," said I, "where do they live?"

"Oh, the sheriff is clerk, and the clerk is squire, assessor and tax collector in the bargain, and he lives away down on the Leaf."

"But the lots, my friend—who owns the lots?"

"The same individual that owns the best part of Jones county— the only landlord who never sues for rent—Uncle Sam."

"Well, sir, I am tired and hungry—can I stop with you tonight?"

"Light, stranger, light. Michael Anderson never shuts his door on man or beast."

Having carefully housed and fed my horse, I soon sat down to a substantial supper of fried chickens and stewed venison, corn cake, peach cobbler, milk, butter, and honey, served with a welcome and abundance peculiar to the pine woods. My host was a shrewd man, well to do in the world, preferring Jones county to any place this side of Paradise, having lived there twenty years without administering a dose of medicine, and had never been crossed but once during all that time. I was curious to know what had disturbed the serenity of such a life as his.

"Why, sir," said he, "I don't make a practice of talking about it, but being as you're a stranger, and I've taken a liking to you, I will narrate the circumstance. May be you've heard how the legislature chartered the Brandon Bank, to build a railway through the pine woods away down the seashore. In these parts, we go against the banks—but roads sort of shuck our prejudices. Before the bank could be set agoing, the law required so much of the coin to be planked up. The managers all lived about Brandon, but the metal was mighty scarce, and the folks about there didn't have it, or they wouldn't trust 'em.

"They strung what little they had around the babies' necks, to cut their teeth with. Well, it got wind that I had some of the genuine, and the managers kept sending to me for it, offering to put me in the board. But I always answered that my money was safer in the old woman's stocking than in the bank. I heard nothing more about it for three months, when one night a big, likely-looking man rode up, and asked me for a chunk of fire.

" 'Squire Anderson,' said he, 'my men have camped a quarter of a mile down there on the creek. We are surveying the railway to Mississippi City, but have come to a dead halt, because our line chucks up against your clearing, and we shall have to make a bend to get round to the court house.'

"The big man said this with so serious an air, and seemed so mystified at having to crook his line round my field, that his words went right through me. I invited him in. We talked it over, and emptied a bottle of liquor on the strength of it. Next morning we went down to camp. He took his compass and run the line right spang up again my smoke house, which I had just finished after six months' labour.

" 'Well,' says he, 'this is unlucky. The road will come out through your new smoke house; what's to be done?'

" 'You shall see,' said I; so calling my boys I ordered them to tear it down. Stranger, there lay the logs, the prettiest timber within fifty miles, all hewed by my own hand. I have never had the heart to put them up again. Well, the big man never changed countenance. He ran on with his line, and the next day he came back on his return to Brandon. I was mightily lifted with the notion of the railroad and a stopping place right before my door. I entered six hundred and forty acres of land. My neighbors said we'd get the state house here. The big man smiled and nodded; he pointed out where the cars would stop, and where the governor would like to have a summer seat—and when he went, he carried away three thousand dollars for me, all in two-bit pieces and picayunes."

"Well, squire," said I, "I suppose you got the value of it?"

"Stranger," solemnly replied the squire, "I never saw the big man afterwards; I heard no more of the road. Here's my smoke-house logs. My old woman's got the empty stockings. Here's what they sent me (a certificate on the Brandon bank stock) for the money, and if you've got a ten-dollar mint drop in your purse, I'm ready for a swap."

FREDERICK LAW OLMSTED

With eyes that saw nothing good, Frederick Law Olmsted traversed a wide area of Mississippi on the eve of the Civil War and subjected the people to his scrutiny. Already the author of two books unfavorable to the South, he traveled through the district below Natchez, proceeded thence overland to Memphis, and, journeying south again through northwest Mississippi, turned east after fifty or sixty miles and crossed to the Alabama line on his way to the Carolinas. The book which embodies the observations made on this journey completes Olmsted's trilogy against slavery,[37] and his

---

[37] *A Journey in the Seaboard Slave States, A Journey in Texas,* and *A Journey in the Back Country.* The title of the series is *Our Slave States.*

feelings on the subject of that evil no doubt colored his view of everything. But he was a good observer and wrote vividly and pungently of what he saw. Primarily an economist and a sociologist, he nevertheless has an eye for human comedy, and he informs most of his scenes with a sardonic humor.

I. THE PEDDLER OF THE JUDGMENT TRUMPET

By Frederick Law Olmsted [38]

WE WERE sitting at this time on the rail fence at the corner of a hog-pen and a large, half-cleared field. In that part of this field nearest the house, among the old stumps, twenty or thirty small fruit trees had been planted. I asked what sorts they were.

"I don't know—good kinds tho', I expect; I bought 'em for that at any rate."

"Where did you buy them?"

"I bought 'em of a feller that come a peddlin' round here last fall; he said I'd find 'em good."

"What did you pay for them?"

"A bit a piece."

"That's very cheap, if they're good for any thing; you are sure they're grafted, aren't you?"

"Only by what he said—he said they was grafted kinds. I've got a paper in the housen he gin me, tells about 'em; leastways, he said it did. They's the curosest kinds of trees printed into it you ever heerd on. But I did not buy none, only the fruit kinds."

Getting off the fence I began to pick about the roots of one of them with my pocket-knife. After exposing the trunk for five or six inches below the surface, I said, "You've planted these too deep, if they're all like this. You should have the ground dished about it or it won't grow." I tried another, and after picking some minutes without finding any signs of the "collar," I asked if they had been planted so deeply.

"I don't know—I told the boys to put 'em in about two feet, and I expect they did, for they fancied to have apple-trees growin'."

The catalogue of the tree-peddler, which afterwards came into my possession, quite justified the opinion my host expressed of the kinds of trees described in it. The reader shall judge for himself, and I assure him that the following is a literal transcript of it, omitting the sections headed "Ancebus new," "Camelias," "Rhododendrums," "Bubbs

[38] *A Journey in the Back Country*, New York (Mason Brothers), 1860, pp. 146-150. The scene is a farmhouse in northern Mississippi.

Paeony," "Rosiers," "Wind's flowers of the greatest scarcity," "Bulbous Roots, and of various kinds of graines."

SPECIAL CATALOGUE
OF THE PLANTS, FLOWERS, SHRUBS IMPORTED BY
ROUSSET
MEMBER OF SEVERAL SOCIETIES.

At PARIS (France), boulevard of Hopital, and at CHAMBERY, faubourg de Mache.

Mr. *Rousset* beg to inform they are arrived in this town, with a large assortment of the most rare vegetable plants, either flowered or fruit bearer, onion bulbous, seeds &c., &c. Price very moderate.

Their store is situated

CHOIX D'ARBRES A FRUIT
Choice of Fruit Trees

. . . .

APPLES

1 Violet Apples or of the 4 taste; the fruit may be preserved 2 years.
2 Princess Renette, of a gold yellow, spotted with red of a delicious taste.
3 White Renette from Canada, which the skin is lite scales strange by its size.

. . . .

6 Apple trees with double flowers. Blooms twice a year, Camelia's flowers like

. . . .

11 The Big Chinese Strawberry, weihing 16 to a pound, produce a fruit all year round, of the pineapple's taste.

PEACH TREES

. . . .

5 From Naples! said without stone.
13 The Prince's Peach, melting in the mouth.
14 The Prince's Peach from Africa, with large white fruit weighing pound and half each; hearly, new kind.
50 Others new kinds of Peach Trees.

. . . .

The Perpetual Rapsberry Tree, imported from Indies producing a fruit large as an egg, taste delicious; 3 kinds, red, violet and white.

PAULNOVIA IMPERIALIS. Magnificent hardy plant from 12 to 15 yards higth; its leave come to the size of 75 to 80 centimeter and its fine and larg flowers of a fine blue, gives when the spring comes, a soft and agréable perfume.

Besides these plants, the amateur will fine at M. ROUSSET, stores, a great number of other Plants and Fruit Trees of which would be to long to describe.

NOTICE.

The admirable and strange plant called *Trompette du Jugement* (The Judgment Trompette), of that name having not yet found its classification.

This marvelous plant was send to us from China by the cleuer and courageous botanist collector M. Fortune, from l'Himalaya, near the summit of the Chamalari Macon.

This splendid plant deserves the first rank among all kinds of plant wich the botanical science has produce till now in spite of all the new discoveries.

This bulbous plant give several stems on the same subject. It grow to the higth of 6 feet. It is furnished with flowers from bottom to top. The bud look by his from like a big cannon ball of a heavenly blue. The center is of an aurora yellewish colour. The vegetation of that plant is to fouitfull that when it is near to blossom it give a great heat when tassing it in hand and when the bud opens it produce a naite Similar to a pistole shot. Immediately the vegetation take fire and burn like alcohol about an hour and half. The flowers succeeding one to the other gives the satisfaction of having flowers 7 or 8 months.

The most intense cold cannot hurt this plant and can be cultivated in pots, in appartments or gpeen houses.

Wa call the public attention to this plant as a great curiosity.

Havre—Printed by F. HUE, rue de Paris, 89.

II. AN OLD DUTCH CUSS

By Frederick Law Olmsted [39]

At the ferry of the Homochitto I fell in with a German, originally from Dusseldorf, whence he came seventeen years ago, first to New York; afterward he had resided successively in Baltimore, Cincinnati, New Orleans, Pensacola, Mobile, and Natchez. By the time he reached the last place he had lost all his money. Going to work as a laborer in the town, he soon earned enough again to set him up as a trinket peddler; and a few months afterward he was able to buy "a leetle coach-

[39] *A Journey in the Back Country,* pp. 33–34.

dray." Then, he said, he made money fast; for he would go back into the country, among the poor people, and sell them trinkets, and calico, and handkerchiefs, and patent medicines. They never had any money.

"All poor folks," he said; "dam poor; got no money; oh no; but I say, dat too bad, I don't like to balk you, my friend; may be so, you got some egg, some fedder, some cheeken, some rag, some sass, or some skin vot you kill. I takes dem dings vot dey have, and ven I gets my load I cums to Natchez back and sells dem, alvays dwo or dree times so much as dey coss me; and den I buys some more goots. Not bad beesness—no. Oh, dese poor people dey deenk me is von fool ven I buy some dime deir rag vat dey bin vear; dey calls me de ole Dutch cuss. But dey don't know nottin' vot it is vorth. I deenk dey never see no money; may be so dey geev all de cheeken vot dey been got for a leetle breastpin vot cost me not so much as von beet. Sometime dey be dam crazy fool; dey know not how to make de count at all. Yees, I makes some money, a heap."

CHAPTER XIII

SCHOOLMASTERS AND COLLEGIANS

FOR a chapter on schoolmasters and collegians in the old river country between 1800 and 1860, the reader might expect something like the famous chapter "On the Snakes of Ireland" in a great *History of Ireland*—six words, "There are no snakes in Ireland." The contrary is mildly but interestingly true.

As early as September 15, 1725, Father Raphael, writing from Nouvelle-Orleans to the Abbé Raguet, announces that he has just made *"un etablissement pour un petit collége"* in that place.[1] This is believed to be "the earliest record of any sort of educational institution in the valley of the Mississippi." [2] From the same to the same, May 18, 1726, we learn that "the studies are progressing well." [3] Later in the century the Spanish tried unsuccessfully to found schools at New Orleans.[4]

It was not, however, until the establishment of a school at the Boat Yard, upon Lake Tensaw, by John Pierce, in 1799,[5] and the incorporation, by the Mississippi Territorial Legislature, of Jefferson College, at Washington, that education in any organized sense began in Alabama and Mississippi. Public land acts setting aside great tracts of the public domain for the support of schools laid, as early as 1803, some basis for a public school system, and the governor of Mississippi in 1821 urged that provisions be made for public education; but it was not until 1846, in Mississippi, and 1854 in Alabama, that anything comprehensive was undertaken, and these legislative acts were largely ineffective.

Meanwhile, private institutions and state institutions of higher

[1] *Mississippi Provincial Archives, 1701–1729*, p. 507.
[2] *Ibid.*, translator's note.
[3] *Ibid.*, p. 519.
[4] This and following facts about education in Mississippi from Rowland's *Mississippi, Heart of the South, passim.*
[5] This and following facts about Alabama from A. J. Pickett's *History of Alabama*, Owen ed., *passim.*

learning fared a little better. In 1818 the Methodists founded Elizabeth Female Academy, at Washington. In 1821 Franklin Academy was set up by the new little city of Columbus. By 1839 there were, as recognized by a legislative act, several score academies, male and female, in such places as Port Gibson, Fayette, Lexington, Kosciusko, Oxford, Pontotoc, Starkville, Holly Springs, Monticello, and Vicksburg. In Alabama Spring Hill College and LaGrange College (1830) and the University of Alabama (1831), and a large number of academies similar to those in Mississippi, began to receive students. Mississippi Academy (later to become Mississippi College), founded in 1826, Oakland College, in 1831, and the University of Mississippi, in 1844, complete the list of most notable ante-bellum colleges of Mississippi.

Most of the stories told by or about the old schoolmaster characters like the Reverend T. A. S. Adams, of the Kosciusko Academy, have undoubtedly been lost, or are preserved in the memories of people now growing old. But a few have been fished from oblivion. We have, for example, in our selections, Gideon Lincecum's unflattering opinion of "the highly lauded seminary" to which he sent his girls, at Columbus, and his account of an earlier school in the Creek country. As a sample of what audiences had to endure in the old days, a portion only of a series of accounts of commencement at Franklin Female Academy at Holly Springs is given. College pranks at the University of Alabama and the University of Mississippi, and a scrape at the University of Virginia, narrated by "Jo of Mississippi," illustrate the lighter moments of young gentlemen who took their dueling pistols, their racing stables, and their horse-boys to college with them. What the duels, the races, and the tournaments of love and beauty were like seems to have been unrecorded.

If, in the rougher, purely pioneer settlements, the schoolmaster was often regarded as one of the natural enemies of mankind, and every boy's hand was against him, in the older, more civilized places his lot must have been scarcely more enviable. Writing under the *nom de plume* of a "Northern Governess," in 1860, the Reverend J. H. Ingraham testifies that even a "young lady of great mental accomplishments and personal beauty, from the North, who was a governess . . . never came to the table when guests were present" and was "never invited at dinner parties." Furthermore, "even her pupils consider themselves her superior," and "she can never marry here; for the gentlemen would not address a teacher." Finally, "the gentlemen who teach in the South . . . are placed in exactly the same position as the governesses." [6] In the newer towns of Mississippi, however, where there was less feeling of caste, even in Columbus, the attitude of a boy toward his old teacher must have been more respectful and affectionate, as the following selection from R. C. Beckett will indicate.

THREE EARLY SCHOOLS

By Gideon Lincecum [7]

I. "COME, FIRST"

THERE came a man by the name of Young Gill, with his family, and made up a school, which was to be kept in a little old log cabin, a mile and a half from our home. Father entered my sister, brother and me as day scholars at the rate of $7.00 each per annum. We three started the next day and did not miss a day until father moved to the new purchase five months later. I was fourteen years old, and it was the first schoolhouse I had ever seen. I began in the alphabet. There were some very small boys, seven years old, who could read.

Whenever Mr. Gill would storm out, "Mind your books," the scholars would strike up a loud, blatant confusion of tongues, which surpassed anything I had ever heard before. There I sat in a sea of burning shame, while the clatter and glib clap of tongues rattled on. I soon accustomed myself to this method of studying aloud and felt myself very much at home. In accordance with the instructions of the master to come up and recite as soon as I was ready, I managed to say a lesson about every fifteen or twenty minutes during the first day. I was then spelling words of four letters. By hard study at night I was able to spell words of two syllables on the morning of the second day. I had one of Dillworth's spelling books at first, but there was so much talk about the new spelling book—Webster's—that father got me one. The teacher soon told me to bring paper and ink to school. He made me a pen and told me that after every lesson I must write two lines. He marked a place on the writing bench that was to be called mine, and said, "Here you are to keep your paper, ink, pens, books, etc., and no one shall interfere with them." I felt very proud

---

[6] *The Sunny South; or, The Southerner at Home, Embracing Five Years' Experience of a Northern Governess in the Land of Sugar and Cotton,* Edited by Professor J. H. Ingraham of Mississippi, Philadelphia, 1860, Letter XXXI.

[7] *Autobiography, Publications of the Mississippi Historical Society,* vol. VIII, pp. 455-456. For note on Lincecum, see p. 62, *supra.*

of my writing place, though it was nothing more than a wide two inch plank laid on some slanting pins or pegs, driven into two inch auger holes, in one of the pine logs that was a part of the wall of the house. The log above this had been cut out its whole length, leaving a long narrow window immediately above the writing bench. The seat consisted of another two inch plank, placed on top of some stakes driven in the ground—the house had a dirt floor—and this concludes the inventory of that seminary except some split timbers laid on blocks for seats.

The rule was that he who got to the schoolhouse first said his lesson first; and when the teacher came in—which was never later than an hour by the sun—he immediately took his seat and repeated, "Come, First." This meant that he who had got there first should come and recite his lesson. The school hours were from an hour by sun in the morning to an hour by sun in the evening.

At the end of five months I could read, the master said, "very well," could write a pretty fair hand by a copy, had progressed in the arithmetic to the double root of three, and had committed Webster's spelling book entirely to memory, besides many pieces of poetry which the teacher gave me for night lessons, many of which I remember yet.

II. A SCHOOL IN THE CREEK COUNTRY [8]

THE country near the Ocmulgee river was densely settled. At a little gathering one day I heard some of the men say that the boys had turned out and ducked and abused White, their school-master, so badly that he had quit the school. Some of the men remarked that their children were so bad that they feared they could never find a man that would be able to manage them. In reply to a remark which I inadvertently made one of the gentleman asked me if I could manage them, saying that if I would undertake it they would furnish me with forty pupils and give me ten dollars a piece to teach them until the first of December, which would be nine and a half months, and they would pay me cash when the term expired. It struck me at once that this would be a more profitable employment than hunting and fishing, and I told them to make out their articles, appoint a school committee, and tell me where and when to go and I would undertake it.

They immediately made out the school articles, requiring me to teach only reading, writing, and arithmetic. I signed them, and they told me to meet the scholars they would furnish me the ensuing Monday morning at the mineral springs, two miles from where I resided.

According to appointment, I was there at eight o'clock, and I was

[8] *Ibid.*, pp. 458-464.

astonished at the number of people I found there. The committee consisted of five men. There were forty-five pupils—fifteen grown men, five of them married, five grown young ladies, and boys and girls of all sizes and ages to make up the forty-five. All entered for the full term.

After sitting till I had examined their books and set the lessons, the committee rose up and remarked: "We feel well pleased at your method of setting classes to work, and, sir, you see what you have before you; we wish and believe that you will succeed." They bowed a good day and left.

These children had been born and raised to the age I found them among the cows and drunken cowdrivers on the outer borders of the State, and they were positively the coarsest specimens of the human family I had ever seen. I saw very distinctly that no civil or ordinary means would be applicable to their conditions.

In the course of the first day they had half a dozen fights in the house; talking and laughing went on incessantly; and at play time the cry of look what this one or that one is doing to me rang out from every part of the play ground. Those married and grown up young men participated in the devilment and seemed to enjoy it hugely. At the expiration of one hour, I called them to books, and one of the men as he came in at the door remarked, "You give but short play time, Mistofer." I replied good humoredly, as I should, "You will please recollect, my young friend, that this is my first day with you. I may learn to suit you better after a while." I further remarked to the young man that my intention was to make it the most pleasant and instructive school that had ever been instituted in that country, and that I should, when the proper time arrived, call upon him and his companions to aid me in the prosecution of a scheme I had arranged in my mind to make it so. "Hurrah for you! Boys, he is the fellow we ought to have had here all the time," was his reply.

They got their books and had a long talk about what I had said. They wondered what I could do to make the school more pleasant than it was.

I was bowed down over my desk, writing out my plans for the government of the school, which really consisted of the most outrageous ruffians, rollicking young women, and naughty children I had ever seen. I would occasionally, without looking up, cry out, "Mind your books," to which they did not seem to pay any attention. I called them up to say their lessons; and to this part of the exercise I paid strict attention, prompting and instructing them in the kindest and friendliest terms possible, and encouraging them to be good and get their lessons well. And so it went on with many curious and disgusting occurrences until twelve o'clock Friday. I had by that time completed a constitution and set of by-laws which were intended to teach the poor untutored marauders to govern themselves.

As soon as they had got through with their dinner Friday, they came rushing, and one of the men said good humoredly, "What's up now, hoss?" I replied: "It is Friday afternoon, and I am desirous of reading to you a set of rules for the school to go by. I have been engaged writing them all the week. Seeing the school is so large, it is necessary that there should be some systematic regulations to insure and control the equal rights of each individual. If you will all be seated I will read what I have written, that you may judge of its propriety and see what you think of it." They all took seats and became more and more attentive until I got through with the reading.

The constitution provided for a regularly organized court,—judge, clerk, jury, sheriff and a monitor. It made me the sheriff. It also specified the character and degrees of crime, terms of office, etc. The by-laws regulated the terms of court, duty of the officers, modes of drawing jurors, and the manner of conducting trials, punishments, etc., etc.

I read it very distinctly, and when I had finished it I enquired: "Well, gentlemen and ladies, what is your opinion of the documents?" They unanimously exclaimed, "It is the best thing in the world." "With your permission," I said, "I will take the vote of the school on the subject." "Yes, go it, hoss, it's a good thing," one of the married men said. And I put the question, "All of you who are in favor of this constitution and accompanying by-laws for the government and regulation of this school will make it known by saying 'Aye.'" The vote was unanimous in its favor.

I expressed my gratification at the result, and told them that I looked upon it as a very favorable indication to find them all of one mind on a subject of so great importance to them; and that I hoped to be able to convince them thoroughly before the school term had expired that the vote they had given was on the right side of the question. I added, "To certify your approbations, it is proper that you all put your names to the constitution. Let the married men sign first." Not more than half of the grown ones could write. They ordered me as sheriff to write their names. In the course of an hour all their names except those of the little ones who could not understand its nature, were on the paper.

One of the married men, whose name was Scatterwhite, exultingly remarked: "I tell you what, folks, this is a big thing. We never had such sort of doings afore in these diggings. What next, old hoss?" My reply was, "The constitution provides that officers of the court should be appointed by election." I then moved that an election be held for judge, clerk and monitor, the sheriff being already appointed by the constitution. "Name your candidates; and as it is a part of my duty to appoint managers and superintend elections, we can hold one immediately." After a good deal of telling and directing and much awkwardness, we succeeded in bungling out the officers.

I made out the monitor's list and after explaining it to him, I seated them and read the constitution and by-laws to them again. They were all so much pleased that they fairly shouted, and said they had heard how the "great folks done away far off, but none of them have ever come here afore."

After telling them that the constitution and rules were to be read every day at 12 m. and that Friday was regular court day, I dismissed them. They went off in great glee.

At an hour by sun Monday morning the whole number of pupils was present, and I thought I could discover a considerable change in their behavior. I concluded that it would be proper to read them the constitution to start with. I assured them that I felt confident that with such a healthy, smart set of pupils as I had, long before the nine months would expire, I would teach them and expand their minds to such a degree that it would excite the interest of their parents and other people to come and hear their court trials and their lawyers speak every Friday afternoon. To effectuate these great results the constitution and by-laws must be strictly adhered to, and they must pursue their studies industriously and earnestly. A number of them exclaimed that they believed what I said and were determined to do their best to follow my instructions. The effect of having put their names to the constitution on their general behavior was very visible. We got through the week without a fight, with but little talking in book time, and they got their lessons pretty well.

Friday came, and as soon as dinner was over they came into the house and demanded to have the court organized. I drew out a jury, and after some time got them to begin. The first case on the monitor's list was that of Stephen Herd, a grown man. The offense was throwing a little girl's bonnet into the branch. I appointed a lawyer for the defense, but being backward and awkward, he and the solicitor said but few words. The judge read the law in such cases, and put the case to the jury. They returned in a few minutes with the verdict of guilty. The judge sentenced him with three lashes, well laid on with a hickory. I had cut and trimmed a number of nice hickory switches and had them sitting handy. I selected a good one and said, "Come up, Stephen." Stephen came up smiling and looked as if he expected that as he was a grown man, I would just go through the motions with *him*. I laid the switch against his back to measure the distance, and then, with all the force that I possessed, inflicted the three lashes, cutting the homespun back of his waistcoat into three ribbands. It surprised him so badly that he burst out crying, and said that he knew of some things that were not on the monitor's list which he could tell if he was a mind to. I said, "Tell it to the court, Stephen, and whatever the decision of that body may direct me to do, you may rest assured that I will faithfully execute it. I am an instrument in your hands; you have the laws and regulations in your hands, and whatever in your deliberations you may order shall not fail on my part."

The next case was that of Elijah Scatterwhite, one of the jury. And drawing another to fill his place, I slipped in Stephen Herd, hoping that as he had just been punished he would be hard in the case and go for punishment. The crime was for wilfully running over a little boy. In this trial the lawyers were a little bolder, understood it better and spoke more to the point. The trial was a little more interesting, and the case being put to the jury, they went out. There being nothing but the wall between the seat I occupied and where they were sitting, I could distinctly hear their deliberations. They were highly elated at the prompt and vigorous manner in which I had discharged the mandate of the court, and were loud for finding Scatterwhite guilty of a good deal of offence. They seemed to rejoice at the opportunity and power they possessed, and were all in favor of putting it on to their criminal in good style, except Stephen Herd, who had not as yet expressed himself either way. "Well, Steve, what's your verdict in this case?" they asked. "Well, boys, I have been thinking about the matter very seriously. In the first place, I think we have an excellent chance with this man to learn a great deal, if we play our parts correctly. I also think that the regulations to which we signed our names is the best thing of the kind that could be made. It is liberal and just, placing the government of the school in our hands, with the teacher to prompt, instruct, and direct; and I am certain that if we perform our parts as well as I am now convinced he is sure to do, we shall all be proud of it. But if we all go for thrashing and punishment for every little offence, we shall soon all get up the spirit of spite among us and the school will go to nothing as all other schools in this settlement have done. I say, let us all try to do better, be more particular with the little ones, more respectful and polite to one another, and as lenient in inflicting penalty as the law will allow us. In this case of Scatterwhite's it was not clearly proven that the fact was willfully committed. The boy was not hurt, but made very angry and his clothes a little soiled. Mind you, I am not in favor of clearing Lige, but fine him. My verdict would be to find him guilty of running over the boy, without the *willful*, and fine him." Some of them said, "Make out your verdict and let's see how it looks." So Stephen wrote, "Guilty, but not willfully." They all agreed and brought it in. The judge sentenced him to pay three dozen good goose quills.

You will ask what they did with the fines. Well, the constitution recognized a treasury and an officer to take charge of and keep a regular book of all the receipts and disbursements. The treasury belonged to the school, the fines being all of a character suitable for school use. Any student could go with a lawful application and draw and receipt for anything he actually needed.

But Stephen Herd was the first and the last to receive corporal punishment. He was also the first to advocate its abolition. He afterwards became one of the most solid lawyers in my school. Green Wheeler and George Clayton were the other two. All three of them became distinguished lawyers of the State afterwards.

The school went on increasing in efficiency every day, and the interest that was excited among my employers filled the house every Friday afternoon with spectators. The boys borrowed law books and all of them were filled with the spirit of progress, and before the term was half out they were performing court action finely.

Several holidays occurred. At such times a very respectful position was drawn by a committee appointed for the purpose, specifying its object, and praying for a few days of vacation for the purpose of recreation. This was always granted in a manner that delighted not only the pupils but their parents and guardians.

They had all, males and females, become tame and quite polite, and on the last two days of the term had an examination. At the conclusion of it, my employers declared it to be a complete success. They paid every dollar that was due me and offered me $1,000.00 to teach another session of ten months. I declined most respectfully; for father had sold out and was ready to take the road again.

III. "THE HIGHLY LAUDED SEMINARY"

(Columbus, 1830's) [9]

IN NOVEMBER I concluded to go down and see how much the children had improved at the highly lauded seminary. I was so rejoiced at the

[9] *Ibid.,* pp. 491-493.

success I had met with in my little plan for providing the means for educating my offspring that I rode down in a perfect glee of delight. I pictured to myself the pleasure I should experience on hearing their polished answers to the questions I should put to them that night. I grew more and more anxious as I neared the place to see and hear their manifestations of progress. I knew they were all sprightly minded children and I knew at such a grand institution they would be greatly improved.

At length I reached the house they resided in. They were all glad and so was I, and they were so full of narrative, telling of what they had seen there, the shows, races, fights, shooting encounters, etc., etc., that I concluded not to interrupt their historical accounts by an examination that night.

Being anxious to ascertain how much they had learned, I did not wait long the next day before I began to interrogate them. I began by asking them what they were studying. They answered, "Geography and history."

"What kind of history?" I enquired.

"Well, it's just history," they said.

"History of what?" I asked.

"It's just history," was the reply.

"You say you are studying geography. Name the principal rivers in this State."

"Oh, we don't study that. We study geography."

"Well, then, tell me the names of the largest rivers in the United States, and tell me also where the United States is located."

"We don't study that. We just study geography and history."

I had strained every financial nerve I possessed in getting up a good house at Columbus for them to live in, and had exerted myself almost to the utmost to furnish provisions, clothing, etc., to keep them comfortable. And from the oft-repeated high reputation given the teachers in the newspapers, I had hoped much that I should experience the gratification of seeing some of the signs of it manifested in the progress of my children. But from their utter ignorance of the questions I put to them I began to fear that all my hopes would end in disappointment. As I could find nothing out from them by my questions, I directed them to question each other as they did in school.

At this proposition they brightened up, and said they would show me now that they had learned something and after deciding who should ask the first questions began:

Q. "Who was the first man?"

A. "Adam."

Q. "Who slew his brother?"

A. "Cain."

Q. "Who was the hairy man?"

A. "Esau."

A great many other questions equally as foolish were asked. I was overwhelmed with disappointment. I felt that the whole world was a sham. My children after six months' constant attendance on that highly praised institution could answer no question of use. But they *had been put on the road to salvation, and* could tell who was "the hairy man."

Now, I never cared who was "hairy"; nor did I believe that it would benefit my children any to learn such infernal foolishness. I was deeply wounded in my feelings and expectations and I decided at once to take them away from that hypocritical place. Before night of the same day, I had engaged a carriage and two wagons. Having loaded the wagons before I slept, I was on the road before nine o'clock in the morning.

I carried them back to the old settlement where my shop was. My friend Capt. Wall took eight or ten of his hands into the woods, cut and hewed out the timbers, and in the course of a month, with the assistance of the neighbors constructed a double log cabin, shop, smokehouse, kitchen and a stable on a forty acre tract of land he owned, in half a mile of his dwelling, and made me a present of it. It was a good, healthy home. I was proud of it, and went to work to improve it. I planted fruit trees, and made a three acre garden which in a short time yielded fine supplies for our table.

A BYE-LAW TOUGH ON LITTLE BOYS [10]

At a meeting of the subscribers to the Natchez Academy, agreeably to public notice on the 18th of March, 1829, the following resolutions were adopted, viz.:

. . . .

[Regulation] 6. None [of the boys] shall have liberty to retire oftener than once in the morning and once in the afternoon—at each time, not beyond five minutes.

[10] *Constitution and Bye-Laws of the Natchez Academy,* Natchez (Printed by William C. Grissam), 1829, p. 3.

JEFFERSON COLLEGE RIOT

(1859)

By Benjamin Leonard Covington Wailes [11]

[In May, 1859, the president of Jefferson College, the Reverend E. J. Cornish, had died. In the uneasy interregnum between this event and the arrival of his successor, W. F. V. Bartlett, the students had gone on a rampage in the little village of Washington. Because a groceryman refused to sell them liquor they broke into his store, helped themselves, and got uproariously drunk. On May 31, the new president complained to B. L. C. Wailes, president of the board of trustees, of a fresh outbreak, and asked for police protection. Wailes accordingly issued a call, and the planter trusteemen rode in next morning in their coaches and on horseback. They met in the large three-story brick main building of the college. This, in Wailes' language, was what greeted the honorable board:]

We were assailed by a wild outburst of horrid sounds from the Students from the upper rooms. Hooping and yelling accompanied by every infernal noise to be made with trumpets fiddles & pans rendered the building during nearly the whole time of the Session of the Board a perfect Pandemonium.

[The Board resolved and took measures, and apparently the new president reconsidered and took to the woods. It remained for a woman, the widow of the Reverend E. J. Cornish, to restore and maintain order. Thus developed what Wailes regarded as an unique and unprecedented situation—a woman presiding over a men's college. And the wise and harried Board left it at that.]

"OLD BULLET" ET PUERI [12]

One night in anno fifty one,
Hæc plan a pueris was begun,
Gaudenter.

[11] From the unpublished diary of B. L. C. Wailes, under date of June 1, 1859. The facts and the excerpt quoted were given me by Dr. Charles S. Sydnor, Professor of History in the University of Mississippi, who has in preparation a biography of Wailes, together with a study of the culture of the old Natchez region.

[12] *Mississippi Palladium*, Holly Springs, February 26, 1851, p. [3]. The scene of the anecdote is probably the University of Mississippi, at Oxford, about thirty miles south of Holly Springs.

Intentis was agere pell-mell
Some porcos into the College well
            Violenter.

Pueri Colligunt in a group
And sequunter porcos with a whoop,
            Multi sunt.

"Old Bullet" venit in a run,
"Habeam," inquit, "multum fun
            Dum ludunt."

Boys continue porcos agere
Intenti they some fun habere,
            Obliti "Bullet."

Adeunt the well many in numero
And catch a porcum by the tail O!
            Multum pull it.

"Old Bullet" jacet on the ground,
Cum ejus oculis he looks around
            Videre pueros.

Then one E pueris eum spies,
And "video old Judicem" loudly cries
            Observat nos.

Tunc M. exclamat, "give me a brick
Enim d—n him, he deserves a lick—
            Bullet look out!"

Sed "Bullet" capiens the alarum
From the well fugit harum scarum
            Omnes shout.

My tale nunc venit to an end,
Sed to the moral your attention lend,
            Benigne.

Quum in campum you take a spree,
Be sure to look behind every tree
            Studiose.
                    "UNIVERSITY."

INITIATING A GREENHORN

A COLLEGE SCRAPE

By M. C. A. [13]

You, Mr. Editor, and most of your readers, are probably aware of the course of *initiation,* which "green-horns" are "put through," at Colleges, and large male schools. Whether it is right thus to have fun at the expense of the unsophisticated "gentlemen from the interior," or the reverse, I shall not say, but leave each of the readers to judge for themselves. Whatever public opinion may be on this subject, I suppose these tricks will be carried on as long as Colleges are in operation, and fun-loving youths attend them.

The young gents of a certain College, which shall be nameless, a year or so since, had a case of this kind on hand, in the shape of a lively dare devil from M—— county, in the State of A——, named Ned Mathews. Ned had been in the service about a year, in the old 6th Alabama Regiment, having enlisted at sixteen. When the Conscript Act was passed, being under age, he was discharged; not, however, before he had had an opportunity of "fleshing his maiden sword" (or musket rather), at Seven Pines, and in the seven days battles, near Richmond.

In the ensuing Fall, in company with his cousin, Sam Mathews, about a year younger than himself, he became a student of the above mentioned College. Never having been off from home to school before, their manners and conversation produced the impression on their immediate room mates, Gus Taylor and Jim Carter, that they might have a little fun at their expense, before they became accustomed to the ways of the College; or, as they expressed it, "learned the ropes."

In discussing the various methods by which to accomplish their "initiation," they finally decided to "run" them, that is shoot at and scare them, and see what "grit" they were made of.

"Ned," said Gus Taylor, after they had decided on their plan, "don't you and Sam wish to have a little fun Friday night?"

"Yes! Yes!" said both, "we are in for anything to break this dull monotony."

"They are not keeping a first class table here," continued Gus, "and I want some potatoes. There is a big patch about a mile from here, with a goober patch adjoining. Suppose we give it a call? The owners will never miss a few."

[13] *Southern Field and Fireside,* New Series, vol. I, No. 36 (Augusta, Georgia, September 5, 1863), p. 223.

"Good as wheat," said Ned, visions of his old scrapes, "going out foraging," in the old 6th, crossing his mind. "Will Jim Carter go?"

"I guess not, I spoke to him about it, but he has a previous engagement," tipping a wink to Jim, who entered as he spoke, which Ned noticed, but said nothing then.

"We'll be ready to go with you Friday night then," said Sam.

"All right," said Gus, and the engagement was concluded.

Their plan of operation was as follows: Gus was to go with Ned and Sam to the potatoe patch, while Jim was to carry two or three others, and lie in ambush in a little clump of bushes on the edge of the field; each of these latter to have pistols, loaded with powder only. When arrived at a convenient distance, one was to shoot, when Gus should fall; expecting Sam and Ned to run, the others were to shoot then, and follow after them. How well they succeeded, let the sequel show.

"Sam," said Ned, as soon as they were alone, "we had better be on the look out for a trick. Let us watch pretty close, I saw a sly wink pass between Gus and Jim."

"Ah!" said Sam; "that must be the meaning of those whisperings I noticed this morning. I caught something about loading pistols with peas."

"We must try to give them as good as they send," said Ned; "we can make similar preparations."

Friday night came; but not before Ned and Sam had obtained a Colt's repeater apiece, which they charged with peas. About 8 o'clock, by which time Gus thought Jim had posted his ambuscade party, he proposed to Sam and Ned to set out on their expedition, which the latter, looking and acting as if they thought nothing on earth were going to happen, except perhaps that a few potatoes would be in their room next morning, assented to, and they were soon *en route* for the scene of operations.

There was no moon, but a clear star-light; "just the night for our fun," thought Gus. Having arrived at the patch, Gus carried them up to a place about thirty steps from the clump of bushes where the party were ambuscaded; all were seemingly intently engaged in grabbing potatoes, when they heard a stern voice issuing out of the bushes, crying:

"What are you doing on my premises at night, you scoundrels? Leave here!" Bang! bang! came a couple of balls or perhaps *peas*, when down fell Gus, groaning.

"Oh! mercy; I'm killed; take care of yourselves, boys; run for your lives," and then turned over with another groan; and from his side there was oozing out a liquid which Ned would have thought was blood, had he not seen him slip a little bottle of ink in his vest pocket before starting, and noticed something like the stopper in his hand.

"Lie down, 6th Alabama," exclaimed Ned, remembering the order issued to his old regiment whenever they were fired on. While they were lying down beside the potatoe ridges, a voice, which both recognized as Jim Carter's, cried out, as another pistol report saluted them.

"Shoot the other two; we've winged one of them!"

"Sam," said Ned, "you remain here and take care of the wounded, while I charge these bushes. I believe they are in there. Fire at them now though."

Bang! bang! went a volley from Sam and Ned, when Ned ran forward toward the concealed foe, firing again as he went. Before he reached the bushes, he saw three figure stooping and making tracks towards the fence, which they had nearly reached. He gave them another load, which one of them heard strike the fence; thinking it was a ball, said he: "Boys we must get from here quick; there's lead in that revolver."

"Charge them, boys! hurrah!" shouted Ned, firing again, just as two were on the fence, and another was climbing it, the latter of whom fell back, as the others jumped off on the other side.

"Give it to them again," cried Ned, still keeping up the idea of a mimic battle, as he fired his last load. He stepped on something, and picking it up, found it was a hat; and his attention was attracted by a little noise to his left, and he saw some one running down the fence, bare-headed.

"That must be Jim Carter, for this is his hat," said Ned to himself, "he's worse scared than any of them." He then made his way back to where Sam and Gus were; the latter of whom had become, or rather pretended to be, insensible. Sam had satisfied himself that Gus was unhurt, and was pretending to be trying to resuscitate him by bathing his forehead with water, which he brought from a ditch a few yards off; taking care in so doing to streak his face and neck well with mud, and fill his hair with sand.

"Ned," said Sam, as the former came up, "wet your handkerchief and bring it here; he has fainted."

"Here is a hat one of them left, I can bring water in." Going to the ditch, he scooped up a hatful of water, and with it plenty of mud; which, thought he, would give it anything but a decent appearance next morning.

"Open his vest and shirt bosom," said Ned, when he brought the water; and as Sam did so, poured the water in his face and bosom, saying, "I think that will bring him to."

"O, gracious," said Gus, unable to stand it any longer, and rightly expecting his trick was understood; "this is carrying a joke too far. Let us——"

"We must carry him home before he faints again," said Ned, breaking in before Gus had finished, and seemingly determined not to understand the true state of the case. Notwithstanding the remonstrances and kicks of their friend, Sam and Ned seized him, the one by the feet, and the other by the head; the last one contriving to let his head fall several times, *accidentally,* of course, while carrying him out of the patch. When they reached the fence, being unable to get him over, on account of his struggles, they let him loose, and made their journey back to the College in quiet, if we except the little sallies of our two friends at the expense of Gus, who, for the life of him, could not see the sense of carrying a joke too far.

When they reached their dormitories, the other boys tried, by all sorts of inducements, to prevail on Ned and Sam not to tell the joke, which, with seeming reluctance they agreed to. Whether or not they kept their engagement, I know not; but the secret got out, and was all over the College next day. The boys immediately concerned did not seem to care much for it; but whatever may have been its effect on them, I only know, that when the next term commenced, the old students did not try to "run" any of the "new boys."

MY FIRST FROLIC IN COLLEGE
By "*Jo of Mississippi*" [14]

A few nights before Christmas in 183– I was poring over the chapter on "personal identity" in Brown's philosophy; the fire was burning cheerily and but for Brown and the study I was in, I would have felt comfortable. I had just reached a portion where the Philosopher seemed confounded, when I was interrupted by a boy who delivered the following note—

Dear Sir:

We are to have a little egg-noggin' at our room, No. 19 Rowdy Row, on —— evening; come down and join us.

Yours,
Peter Patrick.

[14] *The Southern Literary Messenger: Devoted to Every Department of Literature and the Fine Arts*, vol. XI (February, 1845), pp. 109-112. The author, otherwise unknown, says of his contribution: "The sketch may be too frivolous for your dignified journal, but we have the high sanction of the great Longstreet in giving such chronicles of our youthful days." The editor "cannot compliment 'Jo of Mississippi' by saying that he yet 'equals the great Longstreet.'" *The Southern Literary Messenger* was the most distinguished ante-bellum Southern magazine. Edgar Allan Poe was its most famous editor.

Here was a new train to my ideas—the joys of Christmas! The question was, shall I go? And forthwith a silent but fierce debate ensued, in my *mental Congress,* between Prudence, Inclination and Conscience.

The negative had the argument, but Inclination still held me in suspense, until that night came, and it was a glorious one for a Christmas frolic. The moon hung high in the heavens, and the earth, covered with snow, so cold, so dead, gave a ghostly brightness to everything. Towering above the surrounding buildings, stood the modern Pantheon of science, while far off in the distance loomed the mountain-tomb of Jefferson. . . . In such a night. . . . I forthwith pronounced Conscience "out of order," and decided to devote this night to fun and frolic.

The room where the guests were to assemble was of small dimensions, and had two beds, one deal table, two closets, (which in the sequel proved important), and a book-shelf ornamented with Dunglison's Physiology, and one of the works of Dewees. On the mantel was a stray novel of Bulwer, accompanied by the poems of Coleridge, Shelley and Keats. It was evidently a studio, not luxurious withal, of a son of Esculapius, now desecrated to bacchanal revelry.

When I reached there I found everything in hubbub and smoke, for the meerschaum is not dearer to the German, than the regalia to the American student. The academic scions were lolling about in every imaginable posture; beds were chairs and chairs were beds; every body was talking and no body was listening. . . .

Mr. Peter Patrick, the host of the evening, was a genuine Paddy from the emerald isle. Though not overly gifted with the graces of person, being bandy-legged, still he was not ill-looking. He was, moreover a practical wit, the very impersonation of quizzicalness. Of course he was very busy and had not much time "to blarney," as he called it. What with the bustling about, now cracking an egg, now stirring the yolk and then beating the white, his face got very red and all that he could tell us was "make yourselves *agraable.*" We of course answered that we were.

The conversation kept up pretty briskly for a while, but gradually flagged, through impatience, and the scattering fire showed that the talking battle was nearly over. Just about the time to commence work, one youngster, very long and gawky, rose up on his elbow from the far corner of the bed, stretched, yawned, and said, "fellows, it's getting dull, let's have a song; John, give us a song." Now John was the veritable original of the fat boy in Pickwick. Caesar would have been satisfied on first inspection that he "slept o' nights." He sang with loud and sonorous voice, several joining in the chorus, the following song, which whetted our appetites for the Christmas beverage.

(*Tune, Rosin the Bow*)

"Come join we all jolly young fellows
    In praise of this glorious grog;
Let's on the shelf lay our studies
    And drain off a glass of egg-nog.
                                Chorus.

"Professor may talk of the fountain
    That drips from Pieria's brink,
But when you've climbed up the mountain
    You'll find there is nothing to drink.
                                Chorus.

"The dandy may sip up his champagne,
    And whiskey may do for the prog,
But the surest of cures for true pain
    Is a bowl full of jolly egg-nog.
                                Chorus.

"Now may every true-hearted fellow
    As on through life's journey we jog,
At Christmas be never made mellow
    Except by glorious egg-nog."
                                Chorus.

The last note of this song had scarcely sunk into silence, when all our ears were pricked up to another sound far more pleasing. The soft, subdued note, which, like the matrimonial benediction, tells the unity of two elements, the "gugle, gurgle, gugella, gugella," knelled "the departing spirit" from the jug, and the thick, muffled sound told us that the communing had begun, in which, to use the language of transcendentalism, the spirit was being absorbed in the primordial elements of adolescent fowls—a glorious union of the vegetable and animal creation, where the one approximates nearest to vitality and the other to inanimateness. . . . I well remember my transcendental glow on approaching the brimming tureen, but alas! "there's many a slip twixt cup and lip."

The beverage is finished, the scramble for tumblers, gourds, cups, commences. "Fill up, gintlemen," said Patrick, "and before we drink I call for a *sintiment* from Tom Willoughby."

"A sentiment, a sentiment," was echoed round.

. . . "Gentlemen, may every *rock* that threatens the ship of State be a *Sham*-rock!"

Every fellow was about to shout out "good!" when "knock," "knock," "knock," at the door.

Consternation on every face was there, and "cheeks all pale and tremblings of distress."

"Knock, knock, knock," again at the door.

"The Proctor, by Jupiter," was the suppressed exclamation.

. . . One squad dropped their glasses and tumbled hurry scurry out of the back window, another huddled under the bed, and a third, "alas, the hour!" squeezed themselves into the closet.

But what was Patrick in the meantime doing? While the scuffle for place was going on, he deliberately emptied the tureen of egg-nog into the slop-tub and spread a dirty towel over it, pitched the tumblers, contents and all, out of the window on the heads of his retreating companions; then picking up "Abercrombie's intellectual powers," seating himself in a studying position, he halloed out, in a loud voice as though he was continuing an argument,

"How in the divil can ye say that sintiment has an organ distanct, whin it's only an amotion, and Sparzehim pratends so? I'll jist tell ye phraeknowledgy is a hombug."

This was uttered in the excited tone of one nettled in argument. His roommate stood with eyes and mouth wide open, completely dumbfounded at his audacity. Patrick commenced again, when "rap, rap, rap," at the door.

"Who's there?" said Patrick in an angry tone.

"Open the door," said a dry nasal voice from without.

"Go to the divil, I'm studying, I'll raeport you for botheration to me."

A silvery lisping voice here took up the burden; "Open the door, Mr. Patrick, we wish to speak with you."

"Arrah, you can't quiz me for old Pelasgi, *clair* out and don't bother *mae*."

"It's the Proctor and Professor," said the first voice again.

"Bless my sowl, gintlemen! I *crave* pardon; why really I had no idea 'twas you; walk in, walk in, be sated."

Sputtering out this, Patrick unlocked the door and ushered in his distinguished visitors.

"We were passing and thought we heard a noise in here," said the doctor.

"Noo *wander*, docthor, I always spake very loud against that Phrae-knowledgy as I concaive it militates against medicine."

"We are glad to see you studious and beg pardon for the interruption," said the Doctor, whose unsuspecting, innocent disposition might have been imposed upon.

A smile of triumph began to light up the visage of Patrick; but, alas, the minister of police, another Fouché, had taken the deception at a glance.

"Wait a moment, Doctor," said the Colonel; "Mr. Patrick, I'm almost certain I heard several voices in here."

"Yis, Ker-r-nal, you may have, I always was a sort of vintrilloquist." With this he made all sorts of unearthly noises, much to the amusement of his *visible* and *invisible* company, but the Colonel's laugh was loudest and most suspicious.

"What have you got in that tub, Mr. Patrick?" said the Colonel.

Unfortunately in throwing the towel over the bucket the handles raised a part of it and left the contents slightly exposed; of course it did not escape the quick eye of the officer. It was a poser and we all breathed thick, but his quick wit again triumphed.

"Oh, it's only the *soop suds* of my fit water."

At this answer the Colonel's eye twinkled and he choked down a laugh.

"Bless me, Mr. Patrick, you have a quantity of egg-shells."

"Arrah, Ker-r-nal, ould Ireland is great on poached eggs and potatoes, and that reminds me of a joke on two Irish boys, Pat and O'Brien; they lived in the same room and as I tould you were famous for eggs. Well, one day Pat walked in his room and saw O'Brien with the toongs houlding a paice of charcoal, sowsing it in a taa-kittle o' water. He saamed to be working so hard that Pat watched him a while, then tapping him on the showlder, says he, 'O'Brien, what is it ye are doing?' 'Why,' siys OBrien, 'I pit that aig in the pot and I want to pit in another, so I jist thought to mark the one in the pot to tell the one done first; but d—n the thing, it keeps a bobbing down as fast as I tooch it.' 'Bad luck to ye for a fool,' says Pat, 'why down't ye mark the one in yer hand.' With that both roared a laughing, and I niver sees aigs without reminding me of it."

Both gentlemen laughed loudly at the Irish joke, but the old dog was not to be thrown off the scent. When the laugh was over the Colonel snuffed up the air significantly and with comic gravity, "Mr. Patrick, I smell the fume of spirit very strong."

"Yis, Ker-r-nal, I wash my fit in whisky to kaipe from taking cowld."

At this answer there was a scarcely perceptible sniggle from under the bed and in the closet.

"Ahem! whose hat is that, Mr. Patrick?" pointing to one of extraordinary size.

"Mine, sir," said the undaunted Patrick.

"Suppose you try it on," said the Colonel.

Now it so happened that Patrick had a very small head and this was Tom Willoughby's hat.

"Certainly, sir." With that he carefully balanced it on his head and let it fall back on his straight collar behind. It was a sight for a Hogarth. I was crouched under the bed in a position to see the countenances; the Colonel's was swollen almost to bursting with laughter; the Doctor, who also began "to *smell* the rat," stood with his mouth wide open, and Patrick's look was indescribable; he felt that the game was up, but his lion heart determined to battle it out.

"Rather, (snort), rather, (snort), large," said the Colonel, gulping down laughter.

"Arrah, Ker-r-nal, you know I niver was much of a dandy."

Just as he finished the sentence, a suppressed tittering and a voice in a strangled whisper was heard in the closet. "Fellows, you squeethe me tho tight I'll thneeze."

"Put your finger under your nose, I'll kill you if you sneeze," in a loud whisper.

"Akish!" a half strangled cat sneeze was the only answer, and then the pent up flood poured out. The Colonel and the Doctor could hold in no longer. They staggered to the door, out of the room, and catching hold of the pillar for support roared with laughter. We *all* collapsed and such a burst of laughter never before rung in that room. Patrick fell down on the floor. I writhed and shouted and rolled under the bed. The poor little fellow, whose sneeze had betrayed us, and the other closet-boys, crawled out as limber as rags.

We were caught and shipped to the University Botany Bay, but as Marius in exile derived pleasure from the remembrance of the glory of Carthage, so our brief rustication was enlightened by recollection of that night's fun.

The day after the frolic, here and there an anxious visage and a *greasy coat*, tinged with an ochre yellow, were the only indicia to distinguish those who had escaped via the back window. The old hat is no doubt still kept as a relic in the Archives, as *escheated* property; it never has been claimed by any *heir*. Some anxiety was expressed about the appearance of a new hat, but Patrick was again too cute for the mirmidons of law. Said he to the owner of the fatal hat, "Do you go to town in a close hack, buy a cap, bring it home, souse it in lamp oil, sprinkle it with ashes, then do your best to rub it off and you will have the oldest *crown paice* in College."

The Colonel's eye twinkled when the *big head* next met him, but as he was an attentive student they winked at his first fault. Reader, I hope you will do the same at mine.

Jo of Mississippi.

THE FOOT RACE [15]

A night or two since the citizens of Natchez were somewhat excited by a foot race through some part of the city, the fugitive being a professor of the sublime art of *Heel Accomplishments* and the pursuer, staunch to his purpose as grim death to a negro, being one of our worthy constables. The pirouette and pigeon-wing maker labored under suspicions of want of honesty, and had been ordered to find bail for his appearance at court in the sum of $600. Anxious to keep the leader of the *haut ton* in Natchez from so indifferent and vulgar a place as the county jail, the generous-hearted constable spent most of the afternoon in going from place to place through the city with his prisoner striving to get bail; but, alas!—

> The more the bail they sought,
> The less the bail they got.

The shades of the night were fast approaching. The sun was going to bed; and so must the prisoner go to jail. As they had often called during the afternoon to get something to moisten their clay, the officer of law readily permitted the prisoner to go into a store to get a drink of water, when he rushed out of a back door, *chassaed* down an alley, *ballencez* to a dray, *ladies chain* with three dogs and a slut, *down the middle* of the next street, *crossed over* intending to *turn his partner* by a perfect *gallopade*, entirely neglecting the rules of the *cotillion*, or the languishing graces of the *waltz*. The pursuing constable being convinced that he stood no chance of *figuring* to advantage through the streets with one who had cultivated his heels so dexterously hoarsely called out "Stop G——r! or by Julius Cæsar I'll shoot you down." This threat, by the way, would certainly have been put in execution, as the pursuer had in his pocket a copy of the Free Trader, a large piece of junk tobacco, four segars and four of the protested *"rails."* This harsh roar of threatening brought the dancing master "all up standing." The suddenness of his stop enabled him, as he lifted one leg to a horizontal level with his eyes

[15] *Mississippi Free Trader and Natchez Weekly Gazette*, Thursday, July 2, 1840, p. [1].

à la Celeste or Elssler, to make one of the most beautiful and brilliant *pirouettes* ever seen in the South. He whirled like a top, and fell, with all the languishment of an over-wearied and dizzy *danseuse* in the hurricane waltz into the safe and confiding arms of constable D——.

How warm and affectionable was the grip of the law upon one who had made such a public display of his accomplishments! He was housed safely that night—sure!

GRACEFUL GESTURE AND MODERN DANCING

By H. St. Maur Stuart [16]

H. St. Maur Stuart presents his compliments to the Ladies and Gentlemen of Natchez and announces [that] his classes for instruction in Graceful Gesture and all that is essential in Modern Dancing will commence on Thursday the fourth of February at 3 o'clock P. M. The course will consist of 20 lessons for $12.

HIGH FINANCE FOR A PROFESSOR

By R. C. Beckett [17]

My FORMER school teacher, James Wightman, was a great practical joker. One day, when he had just returned home from the war, while he was riding along the highway he met another ex-Confederate. They got to talking over war incidents and finally Mr. Wightman, who was of Irish extraction, suggested that they get down and take a drink. The stranger assented, but asked, "Where is anything to drink?" Mr. Wightman said, "I can supply it." So they got down, sat on a log, and Mr. Wightman pulled from an inside overcoat pocket a bottle of whiskey, and together they took a good "horn." They then got fluent, and after a while Mr. Wightman suggested to the stranger, "It's your time to treat." The stranger willingly assented, "But," said he, "I've got plenty of money but no whiskey." "Well," said Mr. Wightman, "I'm just opposite; I've got plenty of whiskey but no money; so I'll furnish the whiskey and you put up the cash." Accordingly the stranger paid for a drink apiece. Then, after more talk, Mr. Wightman treated again and then the stranger, and so on. As a consequence, Mr. Wightman had all he wanted to drink, treated his companion constantly, and had more money than he started with. This was certainly high finance.

---

[16] Natchez *Daily Free Trader*, February 18, 1858. This advertisement was given to me by Dr. Charles S. Sydnor, Professor of History in the University of Mississippi, who has in preparation a volume on the old Natchez region.

[17] "Antebellum Times in Monroe County," *Publications of the Mississippi Historical Society*, vol. XI, p. 94.

CHAPTER XIV

DUELISTS

The real thing in the Southern duello was something as grim as Steele in earnest or Swift in jest, as matter-of-fact as Fielding or Thackeray, as romantic as Dumas or Rostand. It was what ye will. Factually it was coffee at dawn, over the river to the Louisiana side (or down under the live-oaks by the Canal or out to the island in the Bay) by sunup, surgeons with sleeves rolled up and forceps and tourniquets handy, take your pick of pistols, flip for the sun, ten paces, to your marks, I'll shoot you if you jump the command, and fire at the word—with a very gory aftermath, the wailing of widows and the sigh of sweethearts and the cries of orphans. This is your Allen-Marsteller affair. Or, if you prefer "something in the meller-drammer line," take Moses Stevens and the golden-haired youth.

The Bob-Acres-and-Sir-Lucius-O'Trigger fiasco, however, is the duel for our money. That and its woods colt descendant. It is too bad that some of the most uproarious of the latter didn't get artistically recorded. Uncle Billy Hull, the old Methodist circuit rider, used to tell one on our gallery while the katydids were singing. It happened in Winston County "before the war," as I understood the story. It was "fought" on horseback. A stranger dandy attended a country frolic. The girls liked him too well. One of the hillbillies tied a red bandanna handkerchief to his coat-tails, and he swung them grandly unbeknownst. Guffaws and squeals having suggested something amiss, and an inspection of his costume having discovered the cause, the dandy challenged his insulter to a duel, on horseback with broadswords, in an old field, with a nicely curving rail fence for spectators. At the appointed time the dandy was on the spot, duly armed, mounted on a horse already skittish from unaccustomed caparisons. The hillbilly was late, but when he did appear he came with rings on his fingers, bells on his toes. His calico mustang pony was loaded from stem to stern with a cargo of skillets, tin pans, wash boilers, and shot gourds. The warrior's steed promptly *un-loaded* his rider as he leaped the rail fence and left for parts unknown. The difference was settled without further bloodshed. Some of the following accounts of duels are in similar vein, though they are not so comical as Uncle Billy's story *the way Uncle Billy told it*.

Imported to the lower South by French chevaliers, practised by the quondam military English and American colonial settlers around Mobile and Natchez and along the "Coast," and kept vigorously alive by hot-headed South Carolinians and touchy Virginians who poured into the lower river country with their belongings and their old colony manners, the duello lay like an incubus upon public conscience until after the sixties. In 1807 the Legislature of the Mississippi Territory memorialized its indignation and alarm, alleging that "this barbarous and savage conduct has of late attained a great degree of prevalence, to the destruction of the lives of some valuable members of society, and involving the feelings of others, who from principle and respect for the laws of their country, will not engage in this pernicious practice." The memorial heads up in a statute making dueling an offense against the laws of the Territory.[1] The Mississippi constitution of 1832 made ineligible for public office any man who should participate in a duel after 1833, and the state code contained strict prohibitory laws. But, like the prohibition laws of another sort a hundred years later, these were more honored in the breach than in the observance. Practically every county or small-city newspaper of the twenties to sixties is witness to the illegal persistence of "this barbarous and savage conduct": "unfortunate affairs," "tragic occurrences," "unhappy transactions," "lamentable affrays," if the editor wished to observe a detached and decorous attitude; "horrid murders," "cowardly assaults," and "dastardly assassinations," if the victims happened to be his friends. Observance of "The American Code of Honor,"[2] by John Lyde Wilson, gave a cold and calculatingly murderous decorum to regular affairs; but it is doubtful that the majority were regular.

In a country of rugged individualism, an exaggerated sense of personal honor, and violent passions, it was felt to be cowardly and despicable to resort to the law for personal protection either of body or of honor. Thousands of men followed the precept of Andrew

[1] *Statutes of Mississippi Territory*, 1816, p. 219.
[2] For the text of the "Code," see Edward Chambers Betts' *Early History of Huntsville, Alabama, 1804 to 1870*, Montgomery (The Brown Printing Co.), 1916, pp. 41-44.

Jackson's "little, dumpy, red-headed Irish" mother: "Andy . . .
never . . . sue anybody for slander or assault and battery. *Always
settle them cases yourself.*" [3] There is some evidence that even
women occasionally resorted to arms, as two stories in another
chapter of this book, "The Ladies—God Bless 'Em," will show. Yet
there is abundant evidence that the pulpits and the newspapers
thundered anathemas against the custom, and that many men who
were unfortunate enough to be forced into duels fought against their
conscience as well as their pistoled antagonists. Though honor was
somehow involved, a stigma attached to this manner of vindicating
it. Places where duels were too frequent fell into disrepute. For instance, J. F. H. Claiborne, riding through the piney woods, remarks
that a fine watering place had been ruined because of several unfortunate affairs of honor there. Mississippians fought in Louisiana;
Louisianians, in Mississippi.

Even after the custom of regular, formal duels died out, the
tradition of settling personal difficulties by arms continued. If less
cold and calculated than the cartel affair, it was usually bloodier
and more often cowardly. How "The Mississippi Duello" impressed
a well-traveled Englishman in 1860 the selection of that title will
show. Of course it may be that the hotel loafer pulled the leg of the
foreigner in regard to some details, but that the case was easily as
bad as it appeared to him is proved by the fact that it was equally
bad in some Mississippi towns no longer ago than the turn of the
nineteenth century. There is hardly a courthouse in Mississippi
without the brown stain of some man's blood on its floors.

Against this sort of thing the pen or the tongue of the satirist was
less effective than against the regular arrangement. That ridicule
quite as much as the slow processes of civilization and the development of a more sensitive social conscience brought about the decline
of both forms of the practice is entirely probable. The history of
manners in England is clear on the point. Perhaps the following
stories were just as effective in their way for their age and place as
Sir Richard Steele's more urbane *Tatler* and *Spectator* papers were
for the men of England in the eighteenth century.

[3] W. H. Sparks, *The Memories of Fifty Years,* Philadelphia (Claxton, Remsen &
Haffelfinger), 1870, pp. 147-148. An "anecdote relative to [Jackson's] parting from his
mother in his outset in life," heard by the writer after J.'s "last term in the Presidential office had expired."

WHY ENSIGN MORIN WAS RETURNED TO FRANCE

(1740)

By the Chevalier de Louboey [4]

(To the Comte de Maurepas)

My Lord:—

....

The prompt departure of the *Profond* agitated me. In addition, an inflammation affecting my right arm caused me a very distressing fever. These conditions were aggravated by the last two actions of Morin, on account of the indignation which his cowardly and disgraceful conduct caused me.

Such were the causes which prevented me from giving in detail at the time to your Lordship the reasons that had led me to send him back to France. But, as I fear, my Lord, that you may think I have taken it upon myself too lightly to dismiss from the colony an officer commissioned by the King, I think that I am under obligation to inform you without concealment about the manner in which everything happened on this occasion, and to accomplish this with a little more order it is necessary to take up the matter at its beginning.

About three and a half years ago this little Provençal obtained a commission as a cadet in the Rochefort company and set out to go to his destination. Unfortunately for him he met on his way two or three young men who were going to the same port. Among these was one Detreans, a clerk in M. Salmon's office, with whom he had a very sharp quarrel which led that employé to slap his face. They grappled, they were separated, and the voyage was continued and reconciliation made on condition that no mention at all should be made of this occurrence.

Since that time the offended man, having been appointed to the position of ensign in the troops of Louisiana, embarked last year to come and take possession of his position at New Orleans. As he is haughty and turbulent, he did not stay there long without getting into a quarrel, from which he got out fairly well. This little advantage having increased his vanity, he became insolent on account of it and thought that he had the right to impose upon some of his comrades, several of whom were in no humor to endure his quarreling and his ill-placed arrogance. He found one who treated him so roughly that it revived

---

[4] *Mississippi Provincial Archives, 1729–1840: French Dominion,* Collected, Edited, and Translated by Dunbar Rowland and A. G. Sanders, Jackson, Mississippi, 1927, vol. I, pp. 415-418. Some liberties have been taken with the phrasing and the pronominal references of M. Louboey's letter, which is more soldierly than scholarly in style.

the old dispute. Some one spoke of it to M. De Bienville, who had permitted him to go to the war with him; but this discovery made M. De Bienville leave him at the Natchez and take Sieur Voisins in his place.

This obliged our man, as he said, to go down to New Orleans to clear himself of the original insult. Having found Detreans in the street the day after his arrival, he said, "I am coming to settle with you for the insult you have offered me." Detreans, who knew the hypocrite and who, besides, is not incapable of resistance, answered him readily and took his sword in his hand at once. Morin replied to him, "That's not the way I mean to fight; I want to see you with a pistol in your hand," inasmuch as Detreans had too great an advantage with the sword, since he had been a fencing-master's assistant at Paris. But Detreans, confident because of the weakness of this wretch, provoked him beyond endurance by insults and harsh treatment that a gentleman would be sorry to inflict upon the lowest of human beings. Striking Morin several times on the fingers with his sword, he forced him to walk backwards in order to march before a number of persons who had been witnesses of this base and infamous scene; all this without the offended man's having the courage to draw his sword.

Apparently his reflection during the night made Morin realize the full horror of his cowardice and made him form the resolution to go and find his adversary the next day a little before daybreak with two pistols loaded with two bullets each, and he offered Detreans his choice of them in order to settle the quarrel. Detreans, who I think does not like firearms, refused the proposal, rose to a sitting position, caught Morin by the arms, wrapped him in a curtain of his bed, and let him fall. His fall discharged a pistol, of which the shot struck two feet above the head of Detreans' bed. Detreans, thinking himself dead, fled in his shirt into the street, shouting "Murder! Murder!"

Morin followed him with the second pistol and kept saying to him, "Don't go away, come back. I have bullets and powder to load and finish our affair." But Detreans was so frightened that he thought only of finding a way to hide in some house. He reached the kitchen of Sieur Tixerant's negroes, slammed the door after him, and waited until his adversary had retired, to go and dress and lay a complaint before the clerk in order to have an investigation made and to bring a criminal prosecution against him.

A cloud of witnesses prejudiced by the action of the day before rose against him so that he would have been convicted and sentenced, although this affair is not so disgraceful as the public represents it. In addition, Morin had left one of his pistols and his hat in the house of Detreans, and they were material and convincing evidence against him.

These, my Lord, without evasion and without partiality, are the dismal and unhappy details of an occurrence that is as contemptible as it is unusual. I have thought that in view of the character with which Morin was invested, it was not proper to permit that a report should be made in which these exploits might have been diminished, augmented, and amended unreservedly.

My Lord,
of your lordship,
The very humble and very obedient servant,
LOUBOEY.

At New Orleans,
January 4th, 1740.

DUEL BETWEEN CAPT. ALLEN AND
DR. MARSTELLER

(Vicksburg, July, 1843)

By H. S. Fulkerson [5]

WHEN the fighting ground was reached—a grove of cottonwood and cypress, immediately on the bank of the river [Louisiana side, opposite Vicksburg]—Allen was greatly excited. He stripped himself to the skin as low as the waist; was very vociferous, and confident of killing his antagonist, and his countenance bore a marked expression of ferocity. Marsteller said nothing, and was perfectly calm as he awaited the settlement of the preliminaries. He had only taken off his coat and loosened his shirt collar.

A few of us spectators busied ourselves at an attempt at reconciliation, but our efforts availed nothing towards a settlement. Marsteller, as the challenged party, had the choice of weapons and the naming of distance. He had procured a pair of heavy pistols—not duelling—which he chose, to be filled with buckshot, and named the distance at ten *feet*—not paces. Under the apprehension that he meant paces when he said feet, he was inquired about it, but he repeated *ten feet*. Allen won the position and the word. It was about midday. The pistols were loaded, the distance was measured, and they took position north and south—Allen north. Knowing the nature of the loads of the pistols, there was a general movement on the part of everybody present to get out of range by moving off at right angles to the fighters, leaving the second who gave the word, alone in his danger. As the writer was not

[5] *Random Recollections of Early Days in Mississippi*, Vicksburg, Miss. (Vicksburg Printing and Publishing Company), 1885, pp. 46-48. For note on the author, see p. 307.

the special friend of either party he very appropriately got up on the top of a *fence* near by!

As they stood in position Allen held his pistol perpendicularly *down,* while Marsteller held his almost perpendicularly *up.* After the second had called out "gentlemen, are you ready," intending to follow immediately with the words fire—one—two—three, Allen cried out "stop," and told the second to state again *how* the word was to be given— thought to have been a ruse on the part of the Captain to disconcert the Doctor, but the Doctor gently lowered his pistol when Allen called "stop," and when Allen said "go ahead" the Doctor again elevated his pistol and quietly waited for the word.

As they stood at this moment, in the deep shadow of the tall cottonwoods, in ten feet of each other, Allen with his ferocious look, his high cheek bones, smooth face, closely cut hair, slender, but tall, half nude form, with pistol down, and Marsteller in his shirt sleeves, with collar of the period, open, with his reddish whiskers and slightly bald head, rotund and rather heavy figure, with pistol up, calm and self-possessed, they made a picture not likely to be seen oftener than once in a lifetime.

The second called out distinctly but with trembling voice: "Gentlemen, are you ready? fire! one, two, three." They fired, both of them so nearly together at the word "one" that it seemed to the bystanders to be but a single loud report. A great volume of smoke completely enveloped them, and we all looked on in profound silence till it rose and disclosed the two figures standing and looking savagely at each other, and each with apparent astonishment that his adversary was not prone upon the earth, and we, the spectators, equally surprised. Immediately, Marsteller began to sink slowly to the ground, and Allen turned away bloody and limping in the direction of my perch. I reached him as he sat down upon a log near by, and shall not soon forget the mingled anguish and anger of his face as he replied to my question about his wound. A single ball had passed through both thighs high up. A single ball had struck Marsteller in the hip and he lay upon the ground where he had stood.

Allen's friends conveyed him to his skiff as soon as possible, and thence to his home, he himself being the bearer of the first intelligence of the fight to his wife. Marsteller as soon as he had recovered somewhat from his first prostration, demanded another fire, and upon being told that Allen had been carried off badly wounded, insisted that he should be called back, saying, "I am not satisfied." He crossed the river to his room, probed the wound with his own instrument, and himself, unaided, extracted the ball and *never went to bed for the wound.*

A peace was patched up by their friends, but came near being broken on several occasions by Marsteller's lingering desire for another "shot." Allen did not shrink from another encounter, but friends would interpose and calm them down.[6]

DUEL SUBMARINE

By Minnie Walter Myers [7]

THE affair was between Monsieur Marigny, who belonged to one of the oldest families of Louisiana, and Mr. Humble. Marigny was sent to the legislature in 1817, at which time there was a very strong political opposition between the Creoles and the Americans. . . . Catahoula Parish was represented by a Georgia giant, an ex-blacksmith named Humble, a man of plain ways but possessed of many sterling qualities. He was remarkable as much for his immense stature as for his political diplomacy. It happened that an impassioned speech of M. Marigny was replied to by the Georgian, and the latter was so extremely pointed in his allusions that his opponent felt aggrieved and sent a challenge to mortal combat. The Georgian was nonplused.

"I know nothing about this dueling business," said he. "I will not fight him."

"You must," said his friend. "No gentleman can refuse."

"I'm not a gentleman," replied the honest son of Georgia; "I am only a blacksmith."

"But you'll be ruined if you don't fight," urged his friends. "You will have the choice of weapons, and you can choose in such a way as to give yourself an equal chance with your adversary."

The giant asked time in which to consider the question, and ended by accepting. He sent the following reply to M. Marigny:

"I accept, and in the exercise of my privilege, I stipulate that the duel shall take place in Lake Pontchartrain, in six feet of water, sledge hammers to be used as weapons."

M. Marigny was about five feet eight inches in height, and his adversary was seven feet. The conceit of the Georgian so pleased M. Marigny, who could appreciate a joke as well as perpetrate one, that he declared himself satisfied, and the duel did not take place.

---

[6] According to Fulkerson, Allen was afterwards elected governor of Louisiana.
[7] *Romance and Realism of the Southern Gulf Coast*, pp. 71-72.

ALFRED W. ARRINGTON [8]

Alfred W. Arrington (1810–1867) was a native of Iredell County, North Carolina. In 1819 he moved with his father to Arkansas. A preacher at eighteen, he made a reputation for his pulpit eloquence, but on account of the development of a skeptical attitude toward religion, he abandoned the ministry for the law. After acquiring a flourishing practice in Arkansas and serving for a term as member of the state legislature, he moved to Texas. On a visit to the East in 1847, under the pseudonym of "Charles Summerfield" he published serially in newspapers some sketches which were later gathered into *Desperadoes of the South-West* and *Sketches of the South and South-West*. After a career as a judge in Texas, he removed to New York in 1856 and published *The Rangers and Regulators of the Tanaha*. He spent his last years in the Northwest, dying in Chicago in 1867. His posthumously published *Poems by Alfred W. Arrington* (1869) contains a memoir by his wife which is said to be the chief source of information about him.

The following story, "Moses Stevens," is a fair sample of the lurid contents of *Desperadoes of the South-West*. It is so melodramatic that the impression it produces upon a modern reader is likely to be one of naïve grim humor.

MOSES STEVENS

By Alfred W. Arrington
(Charles W. Summerfield, Pseud.) [9]

SOME years ago, there lived not far from Vicksburg, a well known duelist, of the above name. He was commonly called "the Yankee Peddler," being a native of New-England. The fact may surprise some persons— that a man educated in the land of steady habits should ever turn desperadoe. But such is often the case with those who emigrate to the South and West; and, indeed, it may be that it is a touch of the savage in their nature which determines such persons to seek a more congenial climate, where the lion's blood in their veins may bound freer under

---

[8] Biographical facts from the *Dictionary of American Biography*, ed. by Allen Johnson and Dumas Malone.

[9] *The Lives and Adventures of the Desperadoes of the South-West: Containing an Account of the Duelists and Dueling; Together with the Lives of Several of the Most Notorious Regulators and Moderators of That Region.* By Charles W. Summerfield of Texas. New York: William H. Graham. Brick Church. 1849. The story is Chapter V, p. 67 ff.

the noons of a more fiery sun. But however it may be accounted for, the fact of the great change that comes over the spirit of their dreams is undeniable.

This change is never instantaneous, but is wrought out into a sound conversion by degrees, under the influence of the new manners and customs and passional attractions, which gradually permeate their old prejudices and leaven their entire nature.

When a Yankee first settles in the South he is a most amiably timid and modest being; eschews the grocery and gaming-table, and is perfectly horrified to see a young female whipped until her bare back is cut into ribbons of gory flesh, and the woods all resound to the cry of her howlings for mercy!

At this stage of his moral progress the Yankee is considered as decidedly green; he is not yet acclimated. You can tell him there as he walks along the streets by his deprecatory air—which looks like a mute apology for presuming to be in the world, and seems to say to every body, "don't shoot me, good people, I can't fight a duel!" He is called a coward and subjected to various annoying insults which, as yet, he bears with the meek patience of a martyr.

By and by, his thrift and cunning economy make him wealthy; he buys him a few negroes, and begins to be weary of being termed a coward, assumes a fiercer look, and learns to spout thunderous oaths of daring menace; nay perhaps, if you will observe him closely, when he stoops forward, you will see the white handle of a genuine bowie peeping out from beneath his satin vest. This is the Yankee's second stage of moral progress, his transition state, as the geologist would say. At length some desperadoe, presuming on the New-Englander's reputation for cowardice, undertakes to cowhide him. The Yankee cuts his enemy wide open with his bowie knife.

He has passed through his transition state; he has written his diploma as a doctor of desperadoeism with his own hand and in blood! and the hand that has once been stained by that tint of gory crimson, wanders ever after to the hilt of the dagger at the least sign of insult and opposition, as if moved by an invincible instinct.

Ye need not ask now who is the most pitiless of all desperadoes, the harshest to his friends, the cruellest to his foes, the fellest of all tyrants to the poor negro slave? All will recognize him at once in the transmuted son of New England. Such is the fact, however it may be explained; not universal, indeed, but alas! too frequent.

Such a desperadoe was Moses Stevens. He came to Mississippi when but a youth of eighteen. He then possessed the mildest manners, and strictest puritanic morality; and was particularly noted for that hard-working practicability of purpose and pursuit so characteristic of his countrymen in general. Rapidly, by his industry and rigid economy, he amassed wealth in land and negroes, and arose to respect and influence, till at length he was run on the Whig ticket for a seat in the lower house of the Mississippi Legislature. And now the shameless stipendiaries of slander set to work to blacken the hitherto unimpeachable reputation of the new politician. He was accused of every crime that stands recorded in the criminal calendar, and sins, never before heard of, were moulded by plastic fancy for the occasion. His name filled the newspapers with detestable scandal, and supplied the foaming stumporators with a theme for the most bitter philippics.

The temper of Stevens became roused by the unmerited denunciations heaped upon him; excited to a like fury with his foes, he repaid them in kind for all their unmitigated tirades of abuse. It was supposed that the Yankee would not fight, and one Allen Simons, a noted duelist, was selected by the opposite party as a proper person to send him a challenge, and if he refused to accept it, as a matter of course, he was degraded and the political contest would be thereby determined. They were miserably deceived in their man. Stevens accepted the challenge. His hand was as firm as his aim was sure, and he shot his adversary through the heart the first fire!

Other personal rencontres followed in rapid succession, and in all of which Stevens displayed the same cool courage, and always came off victorious. He soon became insolent, overbearing, and excessively quarrelsome. Up to the year 1834 he had killed his half-a-dozen men.

In the autumn of that year he was one day in a country grocery, about ten miles from Vicksburgh. A mixed company was present, to whom the desperadoe was boasting of the number of victims he had slain, recounting with a savage delight the several circumstances of honor attending the separate death of each, and spicing the whole with the usual exaggerations supplied by the vanity of boasters. As he went on thus reciting the bloody narration, and dwelling with a peculiar gusto on the parts presenting the most enormous cruelties, his quick eye wandering around the circle of his eager auditors for sympathy and the customary approbation that was wont to greet his stories, caught the gaze of a man fixed upon his face, that instantly arrested attention and made him start almost from his seat, as if thrilled with a momentary dread.

The man, or rather youth, for to judge from the extreme juvenility of his appearance he could not have seen more than nineteen summers, was a stranger; one whom no person present knew, nor recollected to have ever seen before. He was tall, but slender in shape almost to a defect, with that exquisite symmetry of proportion and graceful round-ing of the trunk and limbs that never fail, when possessed by a beauti-ful woman, to win for her the epithet of *sylph-like*. His hand was very small, white as snow, and regular as if cut with a chisel. His hair as fine as silk, and of a bright golden yellow, fell in natural ringlets around his fine spherical head, veiling from the view of the beholder the well developed brow, which, however, appeared not to be very broad or high. By a singular contrast to his other features his eye was large, and seemed to be nearly all iris—and such an iris! It was blue as the tints of a Southern sky, one hour after the rising of the sun of early spring, when not a single wreath of cloud dimples the pure serene, and in its centre the small pupil glistened like the first star of evening, seen in the crepuscular light of heaven as a diminutive jet of flame. The whole expression of its orb was abstract and dreamy, the ideal look of the mournful poetic soul which, once seen, haunts the depths of memory forever. The face was pale, almost colorless, and sweetly sad, and tinged, so to speak, all over with a melancholy smile—like that we sometimes behold on the features of the recent dead!

There was nothing in the appearance of the stranger youth to excite alarm, unless it were, perhaps, that stedfast, piercing gaze of his strange, wild blue eyes, immoveably fixed on the face of Stevens, as that ferocious wretch painted, as with words steeped in blood, his re-volting story of conflict and death. That mysterious gaze seemed to possess the power of penetrating the lowest depths of the human mon-ster's soul, and to be reading all the recorded sins of that "Conscience which makes cowards of us all" alike!

Disconcerted, surprised, if not alarmed, Stevens shrank from that glance, and cast his eyes on the floor, but still made an effort to pro-ceed with his narrative. But he felt that the gaze of the stranger was upon him, and he began to burn with shame and indignation at the reflection that he had encountered one look of a mortal man which had mastered his own spirit as with a mysterious spell. He felt in his heart that he was become a coward!

Again he raised his eye to the face of the stranger, and met the same mysterious gaze, the same calm expression, as of a feeling unknown to earth, a look that seemed to be a question from Eternity saying— "Murderer, where are thy victims?" He observed now, also, that the hands of the youthful intruder no longer hung motionless by his side, but the left was in his coat-pocket, and the right, thrust into his bosom, grasped something which gleamed through the clasp of his fingers like silver.

The desperadoe comprehended, at a glance, the peril. He was in the power of an enemy. Mastering, however, by a great effort of self-control, his fears, he took his resolution quick as thought: to gain time, and if possible, obtain the chance of an equal combat. This, or instant death, was the only alternative. For he was a profound judge of character, and knew that he had now to deal with no common foe, and that a single violent gesture, or movement to grasp a weapon, would be the signal for a stab at his heart.

He therefore assumed a look of careless good-humor, and addressing the stranger in a friendly tone of well-feigned familiarity, inquired—"You have listened to my idle stories with some appearance of curiosity, young man; what do you think of my powers as a story-teller?"

The stranger replied—and his voice was so low, soft, and musical, that it sounded like a silver-whispered flute in a moonlight serenade, breathing melodious love— "I was not thinking of your power as a story-teller; I was wondering at your prowess as an assassin!"

Stevens made answer, "I was but joking, I assure you."

"You lie!" was the calm response.

The desperadoe turned pale as death; but again, instantly gulping down his emotions, he proceeded, "How do you know I lie? You are to me a total stranger. I am positively certain that I never saw you before in my life."

"That matters not, Mr. Stevens, I have known you as an assassin since I was ten years old; and I now know you for a dastardly coward."

"Who are you?" exclaimed the desperadoe, in real surprise as well as consternation.

"I am the son of a man you murdered."

"You must be mistaken in me, young man; what was your father's name?"

"That you shall never know, infamous liar and poltroon, till I whisper it in your dying ear, as the sound of a signal to bid your soul down to eternal torture. Man of blood, your last hour is come!"

The last sentence was repeated in a shrill trumpet tone that made every hearer start. It deprived Stevens of the faculty of speech. He sat dumb and trembling, like a sinner at the bar of the final judgment.

The stranger youth contemplated him in much scorn, and with a look of infinite contempt, for a few seconds, and then said, in caustic, cutting accents—"I had thought to slay you where you sit, base wretch as you are; but I disdain to kill even a murderous coward without giving him a chance for his life. Poltroon, will you meet me in a fair combat?"

A gleam of savage joy shot across the face of Stevens as he answered —"I will. Name your time, place, and seconds."

"That is soon done," replied the stranger. "Meet me to-night precisely at twelve o'clock, at the old waste house, in the pine woods, five miles east from this place. Bring with you a single friend; I will contrive to have one also present. We two only will enter the house, armed each with a bowie knife, or dagger, at our option. Our friends will lock the door from the outside, swearing first, on the Holy Gospels, to leave us alone for the space of twenty-five minutes. Are you agreed?"

"But the house to which you refer," suggested Smith, "has not been inhabited for eight years. The windows and doors are exceedingly strong, almost half covered with bars of iron; and are, moreover, securely fastened; so that we cannot possibly gain admission. Therefore it would be best to name some other place."

"I have the key," retorted the youth, drawing a large one from his pocket, covered with red rust. "Are you satisfied?"

"I am." At this answer of the desperadoe, the young man, without uttering another word, turned upon his heel and left the room; mounted his horse, which had been hitched near the grocery door, and rode slowly off in an easterly direction, not by the main road, but through the pine woods, which were there thickly set with an almost impenetrable undergrowth of young bushes and tangled vines.

The rumor of this strange challenge and prospective duel, flew around the neighbouring country like the wind; and two hours before the time appointed, a large crowd of spectators were assembled, eager to witness the expected scene.

It was a night without moon or stars, of a thick, pitchy darkness, with a drizzle of light sifted rain from the ebon clouds, low-lying overhead. The spectators carried in their hands long torches made of rich pine knots, whose red, flaring lustre reflected among the green boughs of the dense surrounding grove; and the clustering vines that were intertwined with their luxuriant foliage all over the lonely walls and mouldering roof of that old building, presented a scene at once picturesque and savage.

Ten minutes before twelve o'clock, Stevens, accompanied by a chosen second, arrived. His countenance was flushed, his nerves were tremulous, and his whole air and demeanor gave evidence of the high excitement under which he was manifestly laboring. He appeared to be intoxicated.

The stranger had not yet made his appearance. Minute after minute rolled away, and still he did not come. The spectators looked disappointed. They thought themselves in danger of losing their promised sport.

It was three minutes till twelve. Stevens stood with his fine gold repeater in his hand, gazing on the slow-moving index that glittered beneath the polished crystal, with the most intense anxiety. At last both hands were perpendicular, one above the other, and directly over the figures XII. A sneering smile played around his coarse features, and he said aloud, "I am here at the time; but where is he?" Hardly had the last word died on his lip, when a loud voice from the old house shouted in a clear, reverberating tone—"Here!"

A key grated in the rusty lock, the bolt was drawn back, the door opened, with a harsh, creaking noise, on its old hinges, and the stranger stepped from the sill.

We pause a moment, to survey his friend, who was by his side. He was a stranger also: a man of Herculean size, and exceedingly wild aspect. His hair was long, coal-black, and straight as an Indian's. His skin was swart, sun-burnt, almost copper-colored. His face and forehead, a huge mass of bones, with outlines sharply projecting, were repulsively ugly; and his dark eye flashed rays that seemed sparks of fire to scorch the beholder, with that strange, fascinating glance, deep and dreamy, so peculiar to the aboriginal Americans, and which so strongly reminds one of the look of certain wild animals. Both were literally loaded down with arms.

The arrangements were immediately made for the duel.

The stranger stripped off his coat, vest, and shirt, and tied a red silk handkerchief around his waist. His weapon was a single long dagger, not very broad, but keen as a razor, and double-edged. His other arms he handed to his friend.

The weapon of Stevens was an enormous bowie knife, heavy as the war-club of a savage.

The stranger exacted a solemn oath from the seconds, that after the two foes entered the house they would neither open the door themselves, nor suffer any one else to open it. It was also agreed that all the spectators who bore torches should retire some twenty paces from the house, so that no ray of light might penetrate through the crevices in the wall to illuminate, however feebly, the deadly gloom within.

All the preliminaries being thus adjusted, the combatants were placed by their seconds in opposite corners of the room, when the latter withdrew, locked the door, and left the foes alone with death!

At first they both stooped down, and stealthily untied and laid off their shoes, so as to make no noise in walking across the floor. The same thought had struck them at the same time—to manoeuvre for the advantage!

The young stranger moved in a circle, and softly as a cat, around the room, till he got within four feet of the corner, where his enemy had been first placed. He then paused to listen. For a few seconds he heard nothing in the grave-like silence but the quick beats of his own heart. But presently there crept into his ear a scarcely audible sound, as of suppressed breathing, in the opposite corner of the room, which he himself had just before left. His foe was trying the same stratagem. The manoeuvre was repeated several times by both, and with a like result. At length the youth concluded to stand still, and await the approach of his adversary. Motionless now himself, and all ear, a soft noise like the dropping of flakes of wool became distinctly audible, and slowly approached him. When the sound appeared about three feet from where he stood, he suddenly made a bounding plunge with his dagger aimed in the air where he supposed the bosom of his foe to be. Stevens, at the time, was stooped forward, thus seeking for the advantage; and the point of the dagger-blade, by a singular fatality, perforated his right eye, and pierced deep into the brain. He fell with a dull, heavy sound on the floor. He had "fought his last battle!"

The seconds waited with breathless anxiety until the expiration of the twenty-five minutes. They then unlocked the door, and the crowd rushed in with their flickering torches. A most hideous spectacle presented itself. There lay the gory trunk of Stevens, the head severed from the body, and placed as if in savage mockery on the breast of the dead—and there was still sticking in the bloody right eye the fatal two-edged dagger, almost up to the silver hilt in the now soulless brain. The stranger was standing in the middle of the room, with a large hawk-billed pocket knife in his hand, and red-stained with reeking gore with which he had evidently performed the work of decapitation. On his face was still the same calm look and the same melancholy smile. He seemed, in fact, to be conscious of nothing, save his own dreamy thoughts, that wandered through wide eternity!

The spectators crowded with mute countenances of horror around the mutilated corpse, and for a moment lost sight of the living foe; till, maddened at the lamentable sight, some one cried out, "arrest the murderer;" and all the crowd cried, "seize him, seize him!" They turned to seize him; but both he and his second had disappeared, and were nowhere to be seen. Neither was ever afterwards heard of in that region of the world.

Eighteen months ago I met them both at St. Antonio in Texas. The acquaintance was accidental, and formed under peculiar circumstances, that gave me their full confidence, and accordingly I received from them a clear and complete narration of the facts herein before related, most of which I had previously learned from witnesses of the transaction. Their history since that dreadful combat has been deeply tinged with the romantic; but its occurrences must be left for some future work or other pen than mine. I am not permitted now to give their names; but will only state, that one of them has gathered imperishable laurels in the present Mexican war, and is altogether one of the most remarkable men of the age.

The story of this murderous affray created an immense sensation at the time, and went the rounds of the public papers. We have thought it as worthy of preservation as many other combats of a like kind, which are so carefully engraven on the tablets of veritable history. And we cannot forbear remarking now that we have brought the dreadful narration to a close, what a noble heroism was here displayed only for the purpose of destruction. Search the annals of all time, and you cannot find a more lofty daring. Never did the leaders of the mightiest armies —the most reckless heads of forlorn hopes, exhibit a truer courage; no, not "Murat, with his white plume, charging" through the hail of a hundred pieces of artillery; nor "the man without a fear," when he stood, the foremost foot, on the dreadful bridge of Lodi; nor the dauntless Ney, he who was called "the bravest of the brave," when he led the Old Guard to the last charge, on the field of Waterloo; nor any world-butcher of them all, as they marched to meet death, with music to cheer them on, and gaudy banners tossing in the breeze above them, and the eyes of Europe and of all the world, to witness their brilliant achievements!

Not so is it with the desperadoe. His fame shall not flourish in the eulogy of sonorous dispatches. The trumpet-tongue of history shall not discourse of his deeds to the drowsy ear of distant time. No column shall point its tall spire above his lonely grave. But still he is nevertheless a hero, as mad as the maddest of them all; covered with everlasting infamy, I admit, but a real death-defying hero notwithstanding.

True, he sacks no cities, lays waste no fair fields, burns no costly monuments, and hears not behind him, on his desolate track, the mournful wailing of widowed nations, the howls of despair from an orphaned world. But still I maintain that he is a genuine hero in any acknowledged historical sense of the word.

His motto is ever the death-song of the Indian brave—

> "The prospect of death, with the brave I have borne,
> I fear not to bear it alone;
> I have often faced death when the hope was forlorn,
> I shrink not to face it with none!"

With the meet opportunity of correct education, and favorable circumstances—how fit were such a man to defend the glorious cause of liberty against the banded despotisms of all the world! What a martyr to chaunt love-hymns amidst blazing fagots. As it is, we behold him but a mere fire-brand of ruin, whose glaring flame goes out at last in blood!

Thus do circumstances create for us all our destiny; even if that destiny be of our own choosing; for what, and how, and when we shall choose, is fixed in the inevitable circumstance that precedes and super-lies all choice and even being. The flight of a bird, or the fall of a feather, may determine whether the child shall be born on this or on the other side of a given range of mountains; and that accident alone decides whether he is to be a saint or an assassin, a blessing or a blight to mankind.

Such are ever my reflections when I behold the loftiest natural en-dowments in a state of passional subversion, and the noble fires of genius that were given to man to warm and irradiate the world, per-verted to incendiary purposes—torches, not to enlighten, but to con-sume. Ah, me! The holiest flame on the altar of the social institute, if misplaced, becomes the means of an inextinguishable conflagration.

Not such will be the reflections of many who will glance over these flying sketches. They will doubtless condemn the spirit of the whole, as pandering to the natural appetite for destruction common to man, with the wolf and the raven. I am conscious that I lay myself liable to the severest critical animadversions; for the minute description of murders is the surest method of making murderers, just as experience proves, that one public execution generally harbingers many a succeed-ing series.

We say "guilty," then, oh most consistent critic; but we plead, in arrest of thy judgment, benefit of clergy, according to the universal common law of custom, as exemplified by all drivers of the quill. The historian paints his page with blood; the poet sings it; the tragedian acts it; the newspaper teems with carnage. It is sanctioned by our laws. The uproar of a universal war resounds throughout the world; and from the hut of the poorest peasant to the summit of imperial thrones. Education is a drill; life a truceless campaign; and death the only last-ing peace. Ceaseless conflict is the order of nature. We must, whether we will it or not, do battle with all sorts of foes—with the wear and tear of the physical elements—with disease, danger and toil. From rank to rank, in the ascending scale of society, a fierce competition, that never knows relaxation, prevails among all. And how can it be other-wise without the abolition of individual property, which would be the death-warrant of our race, the signal of a world-wasting famine? For-ever, then, few and far between will be the bugle-notes of the peace party, sounding to uncertain parley, not heard or heeded in the general din of a conflict, that rolls around the globe.

Let us not then blame with merciless severity the unfortunate des-peradoe, victim to the natural propensity of imitation, who but follows too faithfully in the footsteps of all society. Let us forbear to crucify the duelist until we cease to adore the fortunate usurper. And when we no longer gloat over the butchery of millions, then may we weep logical tears on the lone grave of one. But while the gorgeous funeral of Napoleon attracts the eyes of all mankind, we may well wink hard, and let pass the story of the bloody achievements of Bowie, and the petty dealers who traffic in single deaths!

WALKING INTO A LION'S DEN

By Reuben Davis [10]

. . . I was in Jackson late in the winter [of 1841], and one day while walking with Governor Alcorn and Governor Clark, invited them to go with me to a certain restaurant, well known as serving fine oysters, to take lunch. This house, although on the main street, was approached by a side entrance, a long outside stairway, with a sort of platform at the top, from which the door opened into a small entry. When we got to the place, the colored waiters were gathered upon the pavement, but that passed unnoticed, as we all knew their habits of idle curiosity as to what happened on the street. Neither did we attach any importance to the fact that one of them kept repeating, "Walk up, gentlemen, walk up," but all the while waited for us to go on, instead of preceding and ushering us into the room, as was his duty.

Whether it was fright, or a desire to get up some excitement, I do not know, but none of the servants warned us that Colonel McClung was in the eating-room, and that he had driven every one out of the house. He had been drinking heavily for some days, and had reached a state of actual insanity. The room was a very long one, and had two narrow tables extending the length of it. We were fairly within the room before we saw McClung seated at the head of one of the tables, and then it would have been instant death to attempt a retreat. He had a large dueling-pistol on either side of a wine bottle that stood be-fore him, and a bowie-knife was disposed between them. His face was deeply flushed, and his bloodshot eyes gleamed angrily from beneath a mass of tawny hair. It was like walking into a lion's den, but we had

[10] *Recollections of Mississippi and Mississippians*, pp. 215-218.

no choice. Neither Alcorn nor Clark had any weapon, and I had only a small pocket-pistol.

Now McClung did not like Clark, and he hated Alcorn with a singular intensity of hatred. We went up to the end of the unoccupied table, and after saluting McClung with elaborate courtesy, I took the seat at the head with my friends on either hand. Our eccentric neighbor spoke to me cordially, but treated the others with marked coldness. The waiter, whose black face was ashy with terror, served us hastily with wine and oysters, and disappeared without ceremony.

I whispered to Alcorn not to exasperate McClung by seeming to ignore his presence, but to ask him to take a glass of wine. He did so, and McClung, after glaring at him for a moment, replied with a fierce emphasis, "Not with *you*, sir; I drink my own wine," pouring out a tumbler full, as he spoke.

I don't suppose three men ever despatched food with more celerity than we did those unlucky oysters, or with less appreciation of its flavor. McClung had now begun to tell a story of how he had that day been attacked by three assassins in that very room, and got up to show just how he drove them off. Brandishing his bowie-knife, he rushed down between the two tables, just grazing Clark's back as he passed him with a furious lunge. When he sat down again, he began to flourish his pistols, regardless of the fact that they were hair-trigger, liable to go off at a touch. As soon as it seemed prudent, our party rose to leave, not forgetting to go through the most careful parting salutations. Just as we reached the door, McClung jumped up with a pistol in each hand, and ordered us to stop.

Coming closer, McClung addressed me first. He said, "Now, Davis, you don't believe one word I have said. You *can't* believe anything you don't see, but I don't care—you are made so, and can't help it. I like you, and won't try to make you say you believe anything. You can go, but these gentlemen are different, and they have got to say they believe every word I have told them, or I will shoot them on the spot." Wheeling round, he pointed both pistols at Alcorn, and said, "Do you believe I told the truth?" Alcorn immediately replied, as blandly as possible, "Why, colonel, do you suppose any gentleman ever questions what you assert?"

McClung scowled at him, and turned upon Clark, who made the same reply. We were then permitted to depart, which we did with more haste than ceremony. We did not even stop to chastise the rascally waiter who had served us such a trick.

SIR WILLIAM HOWARD RUSSELL

William Howard Russell (1820–1907) was a crack war correspondent of the London *Times*.[11] Born and educated in Ireland, he began reporting for the *Times* in 1841. During these troubled times in Ireland, he scoured the countryside and visited the hospitals to get information from both sides. After an interval in which he read for the bar and taught mathematics, he became regularly attached to the *Times* as a reporter. In 1860 he founded the *Army and Navy Gazette*, which he owned and operated until his death. In March, 1861, he sailed for the United States to report the progress of the controversy between the North and the South. At this stage the *Times* supported the cause of the South. Russell, however, soon found that his sympathies were on the other side. His articles on the South secured for him the intense dislike of that section. Reporting the disorderly retreat of the Federals after Bull Run, he brought down a storm of Northern disapproval upon his head. His *Diary North and South* (3 vols., 1863–65), from which the selections for this book were taken, is a fine piece of reporting. He was a matchless *raconteur*. William Makepeace Thackeray is said to have remarked that he would pay a guinea a day to have Russell dine at the Garrick Club and talk. Before his death in 1907, Russell published books on the Crimean War, on India, on Canada, on the Atlantic telegraph, and on later wars and travels.

THE MISSISSIPPI DUELLO

By William Howard Russell [12]

June 16th, [*1861*].— ....

When my work was over I walked out and sat in the shade with a gentleman whose talk turned upon the practices of the Mississippi duello. Without the smallest animus, and in the most natural way in the world, he told us tale after tale of blood, and recounted terrible tragedies enacted outside bars of hotels and in the public streets close beside us. The very air seemed to become purple as he spoke, the land around a veritable "Aceldama." There may, indeed, be security for property, but there is none for the life of its owner in difficulties, who may be shot by a stray bullet from a pistol as he walks up the street.

I learned many valuable facts. I was warned, for example, against

[11] Biographical data from the *Dictionary of National Biography, Twentieth Century* (1901–1911).
[12] *My Diary North and South,* Boston (T. O. H. P. Burnham), 1863, pp. 300-301.

the impolicy of trusting to small-bored pistols or to pocket six-shooters in case of a close fight, because suppose you hit your man mortally he may still run in upon you and rip you up with a bowie-knife before he falls dead; whereas if you drive a good heavy bullet into him, or make a hole in him with a "Derringer" ball, he gets faintish and drops at once.

Many illustrations, too, were given of the value of practical lessons of this sort. One particularly struck me. If a gentleman with whom you are engaged in altercation moves his hand towards his breeches pocket, or behind his back, you must smash him or shoot him at once, for he is either going to draw his six-shooter, to pull out a bowie-knife, or to shoot you through the lining of his pocket. The latter practice is considered rather ungentlemanly, but it has somewhat been more honored lately in the observance than in the breach. In fact, the savage practice of walking about with pistols, knives, and poniards, in bar-rooms and gambling-saloons, with passions ungoverned, because there is no law to punish the deeds to which they lead, affords facilities for crime which an uncivilized condition of society leaves too often without punishment, but which must be put down or the country in which it is tolerated will become as barbarous as a jungle inhabited by wild beasts.

Our host gave me an early dinner, at which I met some of the citizens of Jackson, and at six o'clock I proceeded by the train for Memphis. The carriages were, of course, full of soldiers or volunteers, bound for a large camp at a place called Corinth, who made the night hideous by their songs and cries, stimulated by enormous draughts of whiskey and a proportionate consumption of tobacco, by teeth and by fire. The heat in the carriages added to the discomforts arising from these causes, and from great quantities of biting insects in the sleeping places. The people have all the air and manners of settlers. Altogether the impression produced on my mind was by no means agreeable, and I felt as if I was indeed in the land of Lynch-law and bowie-knives, where the passions of men have not yet been subordinated to the influence of the tribunals of justice. Much of this feeling has no doubt been produced by the tales to which I have been listening around me —most of which have a smack of manslaughter about them.

VICKSBURG DUELLING GROUND [13]

THE duelling ground opposite Vicksburg was shown me. Years past it was a frequented battle-field! but of late years the *duello* is scarcely

[13] From "Arrows from a Tourist's Quiver," by "the pen of one of the most distinguished and popular writers of the South, whose well established literary reputation, second, perhaps to none, is acknowledged throughout the United States," in *Southern Field and Fireside*, vol. I, No. 39 (Augusta, Georgia, February 18, 1860), p. [305].

known in Mississippi. Here occurred, twenty years ago, the political duels between Prentiss and General Foote. The former was lame, and always wore a cane. On the ground he leaned upon it, placed, as usual, in front of his left knee, which was supported by the pressure. General Foote's second objected to the cane, saying "it would turn a ball." Prentiss flung it away with a smile of scorn on his fine face, saying, "Tell General Foote he may stand behind that sapling," and, standing on one leg, with his cigar in his mouth, he reserved his fire and wounded his opponent.

Here, also, Colonel Claiborne fought, I believe, with Foote. He was taken suddenly ill the evening previous to the day set for the fight, and the second of the opposite party called to inquire if he would be well enough to be on the ground. "If he is not there," said his spirited young wife, "*I* will take his place!" The Colonel, however, was on the ground, and came off victor.

The most desperate contest which ever took place on the shores of this river was in 1829, between Col. Bowie and a gentleman of Natchez. Twenty gentlemen were ranged on a side to see fair play, but at the second fire the whole forty went into the melee with dirks and pistols, and a battle of the most desperate character was fought, during which three men were killed, and seven or eight combatants, including the surgeon of Col. B., wounded! But all that wild spirit of ill-directed courage and false chivalry is departed; and it is not many years since General Duffield, of Natchez, received a piece of plate from the citizens for refusing to accept a challenge under aggravating circumstances. The duel is now given up pretty much to members of Congress. Without question, the brave man who can refuse to fight shows more real courage than he who dares not refuse! A duel is no evidence of courage, nor proof of right! It accomplishes nothing! It is as resultless as it is sinful and absurd. Brave men seldom go armed! Brave men never draw a weapon, unless they intend to use it in defense of, or taking of, life. As a general thing, a man who goes armed is a timid man, or a quarrelsome man! Secret weapons are unworthy a brave and peaceable gentleman. As society advances in refinement and intelligence, secret arms are laid aside, and men trust to the laws, rather than to their own red hand, for protection and security of person and property. But *au revoir*.

CHAPTER XV

HA'NTS

A FRIEND of mine who is a folklore authority has complained that in the South the orally current folk-tales have a tendency to run to ghost stories, this type outnumbering all others. Such is the one, well known in the South, called "Big 'Fraid and Little 'Fraid." There was once a man who had a pet monkey and a trifling little boy. When the boy was sent to drive the cows home, instead of doing his errand promptly he would play along the road. The father decided to cure the youngster by frightening him as he came by a graveyard at dusk. One evening when the boy was overdue, the father snatched a sheet off the bed and slipped down to the grave-yard and hid behind a tombstone. Unbeknownst to him, the monkey had copied him, bringing a sheet off the baby's cradle. While the father was waiting, the little boy cut through the graveyard behind, and seeing a little shrouded figure behind a little tombstone watch-ing a big shrouded figure behind a big tombstone, cried out, "Look out, Big 'Fraid!" The father turned and seeing a small ha'nt behind him, ran. The monkey followed after him. "Run, Big 'Fraid!" said the boy; "run, or Little 'Fraid 'll ketch you!"

Most of the humorous stories about ghosts turn on some such trick as this. Either the plot succeeds and someone is badly frightened, or something goes wrong and the frightener, if not hoist by his own petard, is made to skedaddle by a real ghost or the intended victim.

Until quite recently little effort has been made to collect and print such folk-tales or folk-tales of any kind floating about the country-side in the South. Scholars who have interested themselves in the subject find, however, that the folklore of the region is rich in them, many of them being of Old World origin, with modifications to suit the American scene.[1]

[1] See Professor Ralph Steele Boggs' "North Carolina Folk-Tales Current in the 1820's" and "North Carolina White Folk-Tales and Riddles," *Journal of American Folk-Lore*, vol. XLVII (Oct.-Dec. 1934), pp. 269-329, which give a large number of examples and an excellent bibliography.

One of the most elaborate stories of the supernatural is the "Bell Witch Legend," still known in Mississippi and Tennessee. Its origin in the ante-bellum period and the unusual quality of its humor are sufficient justification for including it here. Its length, however, makes impracticable the inclusion of more than one other tale of the sort. The other one is from Alabama and has most of the plot features common to the practical joke motivated by fear of the supernatural.

THE BELL WITCH OF TENNESSEE AND MISSISSIPPI:
A FOLK LEGEND

By Arthur Palmer Hudson and Pete Kyle McCarter [2]

THE legend of the Bell Witch recounts the misfortunes of a family named Bell who moved from North Carolina to the midlands of Tennessee in the early 1800's and then, in one branch, to northern Mississippi, about forty years later. It is well known to oral tradition in the designated sections of the two latter states. The Tennessee versions of it have been made the subject of at least two obscurely published books. In 1894, at Clarksville, Tennessee, appeared M. V. Ingram's *An Authenticated History of the Famous Bell Witch. The Wonder of the 19th Century, and Unexplained Phenomenon of the Christian Era. The Mysterious Talking Goblin that Terrorized the West End of Robertson County, Tennessee, Tormenting John Bell to His Death. The Story of Betsy Bell, Her Lover and the Haunting Sphinx.* This book professes "to record events of historical fact, sustained by a powerful array of incontrovertible evidence. . . . The author only assumes to compile data, formally presenting the history of this greatest of all mysteries, just as the matter is furnished to hand, written by Williams Bell, a member of the family, some fifty-six years ago, together with corroborative testimony by men and women of irreproachable character and unquestioned veracity." Ingram's book is now rare and hard to get. Drawing on much the same sources and telling much the same story is Harriett Parks Miller's *The Bell Witch of Middle Tennessee* (Clarksville, 1930). This pamphlet and letters from residents of Middle Tennessee attest the independent oral survival of the legend in that region. As late as 1910 it was still told, "under the most appropriate surroundings—country parties, hayrides, and fireside gatherings."

In northern Mississippi, where descendants of the original family concerned still live, the legend survives in somewhat fragmentary but

[2] Reprinted from *The Journal of American Folk-Lore,* vol. XLVII (January-March, 1934), pp. 45-63.

independent, orally traditional form. Of the considerable number of people who told it, or parts of it, to us, a few said that they had seen "the book" (Ingram's) a long time ago, and most of the others had heard of a book; but we were unable to find a copy in Mississippi.

Our following version of the legend has been recovered exclusively from oral tradition in Mississippi, and was put together before we ever saw a printed version. Most of our sources know the main outlines but remember especially some particular episodes or motives. A few tell the whole substantially as we reproduce it. But there is great diversity in the details and motives. We have taken the main outline on which all agree and have sketched in, as consistently as possible, the minutiae from numerous Mississippi sources. The dialect used, the few simple figures of speech, and the folk locutions are genuine and are true to the speech of our informants.

Back in the days before the War there lived somewhere in old North Carolina a man by the name of John Bell. Bell was a planter and was well-fixed. He had a good-sized plantation and a dozen niggers of field-hand age, and mules and cows and hogs a-plenty. His family was made up of his wife, a daughter thirteen or fourteen years old they say was mighty pretty, and two or three young-uns that don't figure much in this story. Until he hired him an overseer, Bell got along fine.

The overseer was a Simon Legree sort of fellow, always at sixes and sevens with other folks, and especially with the niggers. He didn't even mind jawing with his boss. They say Mr. Bell was half a mind to fire the scoundrel and hire another one. But he tended to his business. He had a way with the women-folks. Some say he had an eye open for Mary, the daughter. And Mrs. Bell stood up for him. So he stayed on for a good while, and the longer he stayed the uppiter he got. Whenever he and Bell had a row—and their rows got bigger and bitterer—the overseer went out and blacksnaked three or four niggers, for they were the only critters in the shape of man that he could abuse without a come-back. He was the worst kind of a bully, and a man of high temper, in fact, a regular overseer of the kind you hear about in Yankee stories.

Mr. Bell had a tall temper too, and the men did not spend a lot of time patting each other on the back and bragging about each other's good points. A stand-up fight was bound to come off.

It did. Some say it was about the way the overseer had beat up one of the niggers. Some say it was about something Mr. Bell heard and saw from behind a cotton-house one day when Mary rode through the field where the overseer was working a gang of niggers. Bell went away blowing smoke from his pistol barrel, and mumbling something about white trash. The overseer didn't go away at all.

Of course Bell was brought into court, but he plead self-defense, and the jury let him off. He went home, hired him another overseer, and allowed that everything was settled. But the truth was that everything was now plumb unsettled.

That year and the next and the next the crops on the Bell place were an out-and-out failure: bumblebee cotton and scraggly tobacco and nubbin corn. His mules died of colic or some strange disease like it. His cows and hogs got sick of something the horse-doctor couldn't cure. He had to sell his niggers one by one, all except an old woman. Finally he went broke. He got what he could for his land—lock, stock, and barrel—and moved with his family to Tennessee. They say that where he settled down the town of Bell, Tennessee, was named for him. Anyway, he bought him a house and a patch of land near the home of old Andy Jackson, who had knocked off from being President and was living in a big house called the Hermitage.

Not long after the move to Tennessee, strange things began to happen in the Bell home. The children got into the habit of tumbling, or being tumbled, out of bed at least once a week, and of waking up every morning with every stich of the bed-clothes snatched off and their hair all tangled and mussed up. Now for young-uns to tumble out of bed and to wake up in the morning with their heads uncombed is a mighty strange thing, and the Bells realized it. The children couldn't explain this carrying-on, for they were always asleep till they hit the floor; and it was a peculiar fact that they were never tumbled out while awake.

The old nigger woman told them it was the ha'nt of the overseer Mr. Bell had killed that was pestering the children. She was as superstitious as any other nigger, and she said she had always felt jubous about what the ha'nt of a man like the overseer would do. But she had spunk, and one day she allowed she would find out whether she was right by spending the night under the young-uns' bed. In the middle of the night Mr. and Mrs. Bell were fetched out of their bed by a squall like a pant'er's. When they lit a lamp and ran into the room, they found the old nigger woman sprawled in the middle of the floor, dripping cold sweat like an ash-hopper, her face gray-blue as sugar-cane peeling, and her eyes like saucers in a dish-pan. She was stiff-jointed and tongue-tied. When they got her sitting up and her tongue loosened, she screeched: "Hit's him! Hit's him! Fo' Gawd, hit's him! Hit peenched me all over, stuck pins in me, snatched de keenks outen ma haiuh, an' whup me, Lawd Gawd, how hit whup me, whup me limber an' whup me stiff, whup me jes' lack *him*. Ain't gwine back dauh no mo', ain't gwine back dauh no mo'."

The Bells were so scared they told some of the neighbors. Old Andy Jackson heard about it and decided to ride over. He didn't take any stock in ha'nts, and as he rode through the gate he spoke his mind out loud about tarnation fools that believed nigger tales about them. He hadn't got the words out of his mouth before something whaled him over the head and skipped his hat twenty or thirty yards back down the road. Old Andy didn't say any more. He motioned his nigger boy to hand him his hat, and he went away from there.

It seems like the Witch could get hungry like folks, and was satisfied with folks' grub. But it had to be the best. One day the old nigger woman came tearing into the front room where Mrs. Bell was quilting and said the Witch was back in the kitchen drinking up all the sweet milk.

Mrs. Bell was scared and said the old woman was lying.

"Come see fo' yo'se'f, missus. Come see fo' yo'se'f. Ah was back dauh a-mixin' up de biscuit, an' Ah retched ovah to git a cup o' miu'k, an' fo' Gawd, de cup was in de middle o' de auh, an' de miu'k was a-runnin' rat outen hit—an' hit wa'n't gwine nowheah, missus—hit wa'n't gwine nowheah. Jes' run outen de cup, an' den Ah couldn' see hit no mo'."

"You're just seeing things," said Mrs. Bell.

"Jes, whut Ah ain' doin'—ain' seein' de miu'k. Go on back in de kitchen efen you don' believe hit. Go on back dauh an' look fo' yo'se'f. . . . No, ma'am, Ah hain' gwine back in dat place. No, ma'am, dat ha'nt kin guzzle an' bile up all de miu'k de cows evah give 'fo' Ah raise mah finger to stop hit."

Mrs. Bell went back into the kitchen and looked. There was a cup there that had had milk in it, and the milk was gone, sure as shootin'. She was now as scared as the old nigger woman, and sent right away for her husband to come out of the field.

They couldn't figure out how a ghost could drink milk, or what becomes of the milk if he does. Does the milk dry up into the ghost of itself? If not, where does it go when the ghost swallows it? Ghosts can't be seen. At least, this one couldn't. They could see through where it was. If they could see through it, why couldn't they see the milk as plain when it was inside the ghost as when it was outside? The old nigger woman said the milk was running out of the cup, but it "wa'n't gwine nowheah." An old Holy Roller preacher from down in Talla-hatchie bottom who rode over to talk about it argued that if the old woman's tale was so milk must be of a higher class than folks. When it turns into the soul of itself, it leaves nothing behind; but folks leave behind a corpse that must be covered up with dirt right away. Folks argued about it on front galleries in the summer time and around the fire in winter—but they didn't argue about it on the Bells' front gallery or by the Bells' fire. And the preachers preached about it at camp meetings.

But the Witch didn't let up on the Bells' grub. No one ever saw it; but lots of times some member of the family would see something to eat dive out of the cupboard or pop out of the safe. The Witch's favorite was cream, and he got to skimming it from every pan in the spring-house. The Bells were never able to get any butter from the churning.

Mr. Bell might have stood for having his young-uns' rest disturbed and his old nigger woman all tore up this way, but he couldn't stand for letting the ghost eat him out of house and home. So he called the family together and allowed he would move again—this time to Mississippi, where land was rich and cheap. Mrs. Bell raised up.

"Pa," said she, "it seems like to me we have been gettin' along tolerable well here. I don't see any use moving away. What would be to keep the Witch from following us down there?"

"Nothing in the world," spoke up a hide-bottomed chair from a corner of the room. "I'll follow you wherever you go," the Chair went on. "And I'll tell you what: if you stay on here, I won't bother you much; but if you go traipsing off to Mississippi—well, you'll wish you hadn't."

Mr. Bell was scared and bothered, but he studied a while and screwed up his courage enough to ask the Witch why he couldn't live where he pleased. But there was no answer. He asked some more questions. But the Chair had lapsed into the habit of silence that chairs have.

Mary, Mr. Bell's daughter, was now old enough to argue with the old folks about things. She was pretty as a spotted puppy, they say, and had lots of spunk and took after her pa. She sided with him. Girls always like to be moving. So when the family got over its scare about the Chair they argued back and forth. But finally Mrs. Bell and what they remembered about the Witch got the upper hand. Mr. Bell and Mary gave up the idea of moving to Mississippi—for a while anyway.

And for a while the Witch eased up on them. It even did some good turns. One day Mr. Bell was talking of visiting a family across the creek where he had heard everybody was sick. "I have just come from there," said a Voice from the eight-day clock, and went on to tell how well everybody was and what everybody was doing. Later Mr. Bell met up with a member of the family and learned that everything the Witch said was so.

Maybe because she had taken side with him in the argument about going to Mississippi, the Witch was partial to Mrs. Bell. The old nigger woman said the ha'nt sided with her because she had stood up for the overseer when Mr. Bell wanted to fire him in North Carolina.

One Christmas time the family was invited to a taffy-pulling. Mrs. Bell was sick and couldn't go. They talked about whether they ought to go off and leave their mammy feeling poorly. Mr. Bell was invited too, and they needed him to do the driving; so Mary and the children begged him to take them. Mrs. Bell told them to go ahead, she didn't need them and could make out all right. So they all piled into the wagon and started.

But before they got far one of the wagon wheels flew off and let the axle down into the road with a bump. It looked like a common accident, and the old man climbed down and put the wheel back on the axle and stuck the linchpin in. He looked at all the other linchpins and saw they were on all right. Before long another wheel flew off. They looked on the ground for the linchpin but couldn't find it there. Mr. Bell whittled a new one, and when he went to put the wheel back on he found the old one in place. He fixed the wheel and drove off again, telling all of the children to watch all of the wheels. Soon they saw something like a streak of moonshine dart around the wagon, and all four wheels flew off, and the wagon dropped kersplash into a mud-hole. They put them back on, turned round, and drove back home, going quiet and easy, like sitting on eggs.

When they got there, they found their mammy sitting up by the Christmas tree eating a plate of fresh strawberries, and feeling lots better.

Other pranks were laid to the Witch. Often when the old man and the boys would go to the stable to catch the horses and mules for the day's plowing or a trip to town, the critters would back their ears and rare and kick and stomp like hornets or yellow-jackets were after them. Some morning they would be puny as chickens with the pip, and caked with sweat and mud, and their manes and tails tangled in witch-locks. The neighbors said that off and on they met an unbridled and bare-backed horse, and the horse would stop, and something on his back that they couldn't see would talk to them—but not long—they had business the other way.

Maybe because Mary had sided with her pa against her mammy and the Witch, the Witch was harder on her after the argument than on anybody else. She would wake up in the middle of the night, screaming and crying that something cold and heavy had been sitting on her breast, sucking her breath and pressing the life out of her.

One time she was getting ready to go to a play-party. Some of the young sprouts were waiting for her in the front room. While she was combing her long, black hair, it suddenly was full of cuckleburs. She tugged and pulled and broke the comb to untangle it, and when she couldn't, she leaned on the bureau and cried.

"I put them in your hair," said the Witch from the looking-glass. "You've got no business going to the party. Stay here with me. I can say sweet things to you."

She screamed, and the young fellows rushed in the room, and when she told them about the Voice they shot at the glass with their pistols. But the glass didn't break. And the Witch caught every bullet and pitched it into their vest pockets and laughed. So they called it a draw and went out of there. And Mary stayed at home.

Mary was now mighty near grown. She had turned out to be a beautiful woman. She had lots of beaux. But whenever one of them screwed himself up to the point of popping the question he always found that the words stuck in his throat and his face and ears burned. For young fellows these were strange signs. But it was always that way. And none of them seemed to be able to ask Mary the question. They laid it on the Witch, and finally quit hitching their horses to the Bell fence.

All but one. His name was Gardner. He was a catch for any girl, smart as a briar, good-looking, easy-going and open-hearted, and the owner of rich bottom land, a passel of niggers, and a home as big as the courthouse, with columns as tall and white. He got all wrapped up in Mary, and they say Mary was leaning to him.

The way of the Witch with him was different, more businesslike. Maybe it was because the Witch realized this was the man Mary was setting her heart on. One night when Gardner was walking up the row of cedars in the Bell yard to see Mary, something he couldn't see reached out from a big cedar and touched him on the shoulder, and a voice said, "Wait a minute." Gardner was afraid to wait, but he was more afraid to run. So he waited.

"You might as well understand, here and now, that you are not going to have Mary Bell."

"Why not?" Gardner asked.

"You might have guessed from all that's happened round here. I'm in love with her myself. It's going to be hard to get her consent, and it may be harder to get the old man's. But she's not going to marry you. I'll see to that. If you open your mouth about it to-night, you'll be dead as a door-nail before morning."

Gardner studied a while and said, "If you'd only come out like a man."

The cedar tree stepped out and snatched his hat off and stomped it.

"Well, I reckon I'll have to lay off for a while," says Gardner. "But I do love her, and I'd go to the end of the world for. . . ."

"Well, you don't have to go that far, and it wouldn't do you any good if you did, and if you love her the only way you can keep her out of hell is to get out yourself. If you keep on hanging round here, I'll make it hell for you. Now this is how far you go. Pack up your traps and get out of the country, hide and hair. Go any place you think the Bells won't hear tell of you—and go before breakfast. If you slip out quiet without raising any rookus I'll never pester you again. What's more, on the day you get married I'll give you a pair of new boots you'll be proud of all your life."

Gardner couldn't see why the Witch's promise of a pair of wedding boots was in the same class as the threat of death before breakfast, but he didn't split hairs, and he didn't argue any more. He picked up his hat, sneaked back to his horse, and rode off.

He never said or wrote a thing to the Bells about what had happened, part because he was scared, but more because he was ashamed of being scared. He left the neighborhood before sunup and moved to the western part of the state. He got somebody else to sell out for him. They saw the town of Gardner, where he settled, was named after him when he got old and respected.

After he had been there a while he fell in love with a girl and got engaged to her. And they say that when he was dressing for the wedding he couldn't find his boots. He looked high and low, every place a pair of boots was liable to be and lots of places where they couldn't possibly be, but no boots could he find. He was about to give up and go to his wedding in his sock feet, when a Voice told him to crawl out from under the bed and look in the bed. And there between the sheets he found a pair of shiny new boots. He put them on and went his way rejoicing and thinking of how well a ghost kept his word, and wondering if the boots would ever wear out and if they were like the Seven-League boots he had read about in old McGuffey.

But they looked like natural boots. He told some of his friends how he had got them. They thought he was a liar. But they had to own up they were wrong. One day Gardner's house-boy made a mistake and carried them instead of another pair to a cobbler. The cobbler said they were in perfect shape, that they were not made by mortal hands, and that the soles were sewed on in a way that no man or man-made machine could have stitched them. And there is a lady in this neighborhood who has seen the boots.

While Gardner's mind was getting mossed over about Mary, Mr. Bell decided again to move to Mississippi. It looked like his move from

North Carolina was jumping from the frying pan into the fire, but he figured maybe the skillet wouldn't be any hotter. Gardner's break-up with Mary and Mary not marrying hung heavy on his mind. Mrs. Bell raised up again, telling him about rolling stones. And the Witch horned in. By this time the family got used to the Witch and would talk free with him, but respectful. Every time the question came up there was a row between Mr. Bell and Mary on one side and Mrs. Bell and the Witch on the other. The old nigger woman told Mr. Bell the ha'nt didn't want him to move because he was afraid of witch hunters in Mississippi. She said there were powerful ones down there.

And so one winter after the crops had petered out on him again, he sold his place dirt cheap. But the old nigger woman told him to wait till spring to start. She said Easter was early that year and there would be plenty of time to pitch a crop. Good Friday would be a good day to leave, she said, for the ha'nt would have to go back to his grave and stay three days under the ground and would be puny-like several days more. While he was in good working order he could be in two or three places at once and be in any of them in the bat of an eye, but then he would have to lie low, and that would give them plenty of start. So Mr. Bell early on Good Friday stacked his furniture and duds in a couple of wagons, climbed into the front one with Mary, put the old nigger woman and his biggest boy into the hind one, and told Mrs. Bell, "Git in with old Patsy if you're a-comin', and don't forgit the young-uns."

And that was the way the Bell family came to Mississippi. Mr. Bell bought him a little place in Panola County, ten miles east of Batesville on the Oxford road. He was all ready to begin life over again without supernatural interference.

But the Witch made a quick come-back, not before the family got there, but before they moved into their new home.

When Mr. Bell first got to Batesville, or Panola as they called it then, he left the family there and went out to look at the land he aimed to buy. When he got a place that suited him, he went back to town for his family and stuff. There was some sort of hitch, and the wagons did not get started till late in the evening. As the wagons moved slowly out of town, dark clouds began to roll up in the south and west, and before they had gone three miles the storm broke. Dark came on earlier than usual, for the clouds hid the sun. The rain beat down on the wagon covers. Every now and then the lightning flashes lit up the swaying trees on each side of the road, the draggle-tailed horses, and the road itself,—a long, muddy creek,—and then it was dark as a stack of black cats. The folks all stopped talking. There was nothing to listen to but the beating rain and the thunder and the suck of the horses' feet and the wheels in the mud.

All at once the hind wagon, with the family in it, slid to the side of the road and sunk into the mud up to the bed. Mr. Bell saw it in a lightning flash and came back. It couldn't be moved; the horses had no purchase and the wheels were in too deep. The fix they were in wasn't dangerous, but it was mighty uncomfortable.

And then the Witch took a hand.

"If you'll go back to your wagon and stop your cussin'," said the empty dark beside the wagon, "I'll get you out. Hump it back to your wagon now—light a shuck!"

Mr. Bell waded back and crawled in.

And then the horses and the wagon and the furniture and the family and the dog under the wagon and the calf tied behind and everything else but the mud on the wheels riz up about eight feet high and floated down the road till they were just behind the front wagon, and then they settled down easy and went on home without any trouble.

The family got settled down in their two-story double-loghouse amongst the cedars on the Oxford road.

A few nights later, the Witch spoke up from one of the andirons and told Mr. and Mrs. Bell he was in love with Mary. He said he wanted to marry her. Mr. Bell was shocked and surprised. He explained, respectful but emphatic like, that he could never dream of letting a daughter of his marry a ghost, not even so noble a ghost like the one he was talking with.

"I got a claim on you, John Bell," said the Witch. "I got a claim on you and on yours. I got a claim." And his voice was deep and hollow-like.

This was a point Mr. Bell maybe didn't want to hear any more about. So he said, "Have you spoken to Mary?"

"No, not spoken."

"Well, how do you know she would have you?"

"I don't. But I haven't got any reason to believe she wouldn't love me. She's never seen me. She doesn't know whether she would or not. Maybe she would consider it an honor to be married to a ghost. Not many girls are, you know. Why, it would make her famous."

"I don't want any daughter of mine getting famous that way. And besides, what if you were to have children? What in the world do you reckon they'd be like? Like you or her? Maybe half good human meat and bone, and the other half sight unseen. Or maybe they'd be the vanishin' kind and goin' round here and raisin' hell invisible. Do you think I want a passel of soap-suds young-uns floatin' round here and poppin' up into puffs of wind every time I p'inted to the stovewood pile or sprouts on a ditch bank? Not on your life. I reckon plain flesh and blood's good enough for Mary."

"But, John Bell, I love Mary. And remember. Remember."

"So do I, and that's why I'm not a-goin' to let you marry her. Why, when she got old and hard-favored I reckon you'd quit her for some young hussy. You could do it easy enough. Mary'd have a hard time keepin' up with a stack of wind and a voice, and I'd have a hard time trackin' down and shootin' a low-down, no-count dust devil. When Mary marries, she marries a man that's solid and alive in body."

"I gather, John Bell, that you're opposed to me courting your daughter. But she's the one to say, and I'm going to talk to her about it. You'll be my father-in-law yet, or you'll be a-mourning, a-mourning."

"But what kind of wedding would it be like?" Mrs. Bell put in. "Think of it. Mary standing in front of the preacher and the preacher saying, 'Do you take this woman?' to a vase of flowers. And the ring floating down to Mary from the hanging-lamp maybe, or rising up from under a bench. I won't stand for it. I've stood for a lot things, and you can't say I haven't been a friend to you. But I won't stand for Mary being a laughing-stock and disgrace to the family."

"If we're a-goin' to add to this family," Mr. Bell took up, "we're a-goin' to be able to see what we're addin'. I don't even know what shape you've got, if any."

"Oh, I can give you some idea what shape I have. I'll let you shake hands with me. But you must promise not to squeeze. We're very delicate, especially when we touch folks. Here, hold out your hand, and I'll put mine in it."

Mr. Bell held out his hand, felt something, and grabbed it. It was, he said later, the hand of a new-born baby—soft and crinkly and warm and just about the size of a new-born baby's hand.

"How big are you all over?" he asked.

"I can't tell you that."

"Well, there's one other thing I want to know. How do you get into this house any time you want to when every window and door is locked and barred? Do you ooze through the walls?"

"No. It's a lot easier than that. If you'll watch the corner of the ceiling up there, you'll see."

And all the rest of his life Mr. Bell swore to trustworthy witnesses that he saw the corner of the ceiling raised a good three feet and then let down again—all without the slightest racket.

"Do you mean to tell me that anything with a hand like that can h'ist the top off of the house that a-way?"

"Sure," came the answer. "But—about Mary. I'm going to talk to her right off."

"Don't," said Mr. Bell. "Do you want to drive her crazy?"

But the meeting was over, for there was no answer. And the fire had died down, and the andiron looked glum.

The story is kind of skimpy here. Nobody seems to know what the Witch said to Mary or what Mary said to the Witch.

But the family noticed next day that she was drooping and wasn't minding what was going on around her. For days she wandered about the house and up and down the yard under the gloomy old cedars, like somebody sleep-walking. And the color left her face, and deep in her wide-open black eyes was a far-away look, like she was trying to see something that ought to be but wasn't there. Every day she got up later and went to bed earlier.

And finally there came a day when she didn't get up at all. In the evening a screech-owl hollered in a cedar right by the gallery.

That night her fever was high, and by midnight she was raving. "We've put off seein' a doctor too long," said Mrs. Bell.

"The roads like they are, it'll take me two hours goin' and him and me two hours comin'," said Mr. Bell. "It'll be might' nigh daylight before we get back. But I reckon you're right, and I'll go as quick as I can saddle a horse."

"No use," said a Voice. "All the doctors and medicines in the world won't cure her. But if you want one, I'll get him, and get him a lot quicker than you can."

The doctor got there just as the old eight-day clock struck one. "I heard somebody hollering at my window about midnight, telling me to come out here right away. When I got to the door, nobody was there; but I thought I'd better come anyway." He was a young doctor just starting out. "Say, what kind of road overseer and gang do you fellows have out this way? Last time I came over this road, about Christmas, it was the worst I ever saw. Why, I picked up a Stetson hat in the middle of a mud-hole near the four-mile board, and by George there was a man under it. 'You're in the middle of a bad fix, old man,' I said. 'Hell,' he said, 'that ain't nothin' to the fix this mule's in under me.' I had to lift up my feet half the way to keep them from dragging in the mud by the horse's belly. But to-night my horse skimmed over it in an hour. Well, who's sick out here?"

"It's her mind and nerves," he told them after he had questioned them and examined Mary. "I won't conceal from you, she's in pretty bad shape. And medicine won't do her any good. You've just got to be gentle and careful with her. Humor her and be patient with her. I'll give her something to put her to sleep when she gets like this. Watch her close and don't let her get lonesome. She's young and strong and ought to come round in time."

But she never did. For a month she lay there on the bed, looking at nothing and yet straining to see something. Something too far off. At night her pa and ma took turns sitting up. They didn't want the neighbors in. They called the doctor back a few times, but he shook his head and said he couldn't do any more. So they would watch and wait, wanting to do something, but helpless.

One night her ma was sitting there, holding Mary's hand and stroking the dark hair back from her forehead. Suddenly Mary pushed her mother away and sat up and looked across the foot of the bed, as if somebody was standing there.

"Mamma," she whispered, "Mamma. . . . I see him. . . . at last. . . . And I think. . . . I think. . . . I'm going. . . . to love him."

And she died with the only expression of happiness they had seen on her face in months.

Some folks have tried to explain Mary's strange death. A few say the Witch tortured her continually and kept her in such constant terror that her mind was affected. Others have heard that a school teacher ventriloquist that was jealous of Gardner played tricks on her and the family, and then when she wouldn't have him tormented and frightened her to death. Some believe she was in love with the overseer from the first, and then when he was killed she was in love with the Witch and didn't want to live because she knew she would never be happy with him until she too became a ghost.

But she died, just the same. And they say that on the day of the funeral, when the coffin was carried from the house to a wagon a great black bird flew down from the sky and hung in the air just above the wagon. And around its neck was a bell that tolled in the mournfullest tone ever heard by the ear of man. And when the funeral procession began to move, the great bird floated just in front of it all the way to the graveyard and circled round and round the grave during the burial, the bell tolling all the while. And when the mound was rounded up, the bird swung high up in the air and flew away to the west and finally became just a little speck above the treetops and disappeared. But long after it was gone the mourning notes of the bell floated back to those who stood and watched.[3]

Such is the Mississippi version of the Bell Witch legend.

A GHOST STORY "AS IS" A GHOST STORY

By an Old Alabama Correspondent [4]

"Won't you take somethin' Murd?"

"Thank you," was the decided response, and into the only grocery of V. we walked.

"What will you have, gentlemen?" was the kind query which saluted us from behind the counter as we entered.

"Brandy-toddy," answered my friend.

"Give me same." Our liquors mixed and tumblers raised, I sat mine down without putting it to my lips, and looking the bar-keeper full in the face, pronounced slowly and very distinctly, the letters "s-n-o-t."

"Sir!" answered he, in a tone of voice which showed that, although he had never travelled, he was yet sensible of the dignity "that doth hedge" a bar-keeper.

"I merely asked, in short metre, for *'some nutmeg on top!'*" innocently responded I. Murd laughed, our liquor went the way, if not "of all flesh," of at least a good deal of it, and I threw down two dimes to pay for it.

"You owe me nothing, sir," said the bar-keeper, in whose mind an idea had evidently formed, "that last wrinkle makes us square."

Mounting my horse, I was at home in just the one-twelfth of the twenty-fourth, of the three hundredth and sixty-fifth portion, of the one-hundredth part of a century.

'Tis strange "to what base uses we come at last." Now it has been so long since I tasted a drop of anything, but what was really villainous, that I conscientiously believe, and I speak it with all due respect to the feelings of the distillers of corn juice, that the base *smell* of some of "Dicky Jones's" gourd, would knock the breath out of me, and a *taste* of "Dr. Otard's" best, would throw me into fits. Speaking of guns, why the devil didn't Byron, when he took it on himself for the good of gentlemanly drinkers to prescribe for the "after claps"—why, I

---

[3] The remainder of the article from which this is reprinted is devoted to a comparative study of the Bell Witch legend, showing the oral independence of the Mississippi version, indicating that its line of development is in the direction of the vampire type of folk-tale, and pointing out motives in other folk-tales (chiefly European) analogous to those in the Mississippi tale.

[4] *Spirit of the Times*, vol. 18 (December 16, 1848), pp. 506-507.

ask, didn't he give a prescription that was effectual. Hock and Soda! forsooth, why didn't he recommend a thimble wine glass of "the nectar that Jupiter sips," taken immediately after rising. The one would have been about as sensible (and as obtainable in this section) as the other. Now, although the "peerless poet and the poet Peer" was drunk often enough to require a remedy that was infallible, yet a hundred to one, he never tried his boasted remedy twice during his life—for if he had ever used it once, and I doubt it, he would have been forced, with the same disgust which Lord Chesterfield once made a noted inquiry, to ask "do men drink Hock and Soda twice?" It won't do. I know a kink worth two of it, but let us change the subject to

THE MAN WHO HAD NEVER SEEN A GHOST.

Around the mind of every one, be he learned or simple, rich or poor, old or young, there lingers a superstition most unaccountable and abiding. Whether this feeling is innate, or is impressed upon the mind in its tender state with such force by extraneous causes as indelibly to tinge it for all after life, is a point it is here needless to argue. Enough that the fact is incontestable. Who, when riding a lonesome road on a lonely night, has not, from inadvertently thinking upon "the tales old gossips tell," worked himself into such a state of nervousness, that the hooting of the night owl would send the blood rushing to the heart; or the sudden cry of the whip-poor-will, make his hair stand on end. Who, I care not how callous or indifferent he may be, has ever passed a lonely grave yard at the dead hour of night, without an undefinable feeling of awe stealing over him. Anything bordering upon the supernatural, however much our common sense may reject it, *will* at once arouse all the latent superstition of our nature, and leave for the time an impression on the mind, despite all the efforts of reason to prevent it.

The great "meteoric shower" of '35, that splendid phenomenon prepared by dame nature for the gratification of those learned in her mysteries, was productive in this part of the world of considerable alarm. Many there were who confidently predicted a speedy termination of all mundane matters, others believed it was a sign sent from on high, to warn mankind of the impending danger of continued sin, while not a few, having no fixed opinion regarding the matter, and perfectly indifferent on the subject since there had resulted no harm, looked upon the occurrence only as a d—n fuss generally in the regions above.

Among those of the latter class, was Major RHODES. A man noted more for strong prejudices, dogmatical opinions, a pompous diction, and a long purse, than for refinement of education or a possession of any of the gentler virtues, the Major bore a very respectable but by no means popular position in the estimation of his neighborhood.

Shortly after the "falling of the stars," Maj. Rhodes happened in town, and there being quite a crowd at the grocery, the conversation naturally turned upon the recent wonderful event, and the effect it had produced upon each one present; all having expressed their different views, DAVE LAWSON asked the Major what *he* thought of the matter.

"Why, Sir," answered the Major, "I didn't see them, but if I had I shouldn't have cared a continental d—n; it takes something worse than falling of stars to scare Maj. Rhodes."

"Well, I know one thing," rejoined Dave, "if it didn't scare you, it did me. I never was as bad scared but once before, and that was when I saw the ghost at Bently's grave yard."

"D—n the ghost at Bently's grave yard," quickly answered Maj. Rhodes. "If you've told that tale once, Dave Lawson, you have a hundred times, and if you'll agree never to tell it again, I'll treat the whole crowd."

"Why, Major, maybe you have seen one there yourself," added Dave, "you appear to be so touchy 'bout it."

"No, Sir, I never have," was the reply, "but if I had, 'twould take a dozen ghosts to scare Maj. Rhodes," saying which, that worthy untied his horse "Pomp" and left for home.

To a full understanding of the above conversation, it is necessary to state that it had ever been the boast of Maj. Rhodes that he was perfectly inaccessible to fear from anything supernatural—averring that, although he had never seen a ghost, he had just as leave see one as to see a dead cow, and would have about as much fear of the one as the other. Dave Lawson having always had his own opinion of the Major's courage on this point, had long had it in contemplation to put it to the test—and for this purpose, had made the story about seeing the ghost at Bently's grave yard, for the purpose of getting the Major ripe for his project. The grave yard above spoken of, was as lonely a spot as ever the eye of man rested upon—lying immediately contiguous to the road with a small knot of woods intervening, with its old dilapidated palings tinged with black, and the few white slabs of marble, it was well calculated at all times to impress the passer-by with thoughts of sadness.

Being directly upon the road leading from Major Rhodes' house to town, and the Major frequently being detained in town waiting for the mail, thereby being compelled to pass the spot at night, there were not wanting opportunities for Dave Lawson to put his purposes into execution.

Some time having elapsed, and Maj. Rhodes happening in town, it struck Dave that, as it was a drizzling, rainy evening, with every appearance of a bad night, the time had arrived when to put his long cherished plan in effect, provided he could ascertain that Rhodes was going home.

"Bad evening, Major," says Dave.

"Yes," answered Rhodes, "I shouldn't be surprised if we had a bad night."

"Not going out of town to-night," continued Lawson.

"Yes, responded the Major, "I *am* going home. *I* don't mind the rain when I'm on Pomp."

Being satisfied on this head, Dave Lawson sought out his tried crony Rube Davis, and imparting his plan, to which Rube joyfully acceded, they soon procured the paraphernalia necessary to the success of their enterprise, and by hard riding reached the grave yard by dark. Tying their horses out of reach of discovery, and dressing themselves, each in a whole sheet with a long, conical paper cap on their heads, Dave stationed himself in the skirt of woods before spoken of as intervening between the grave yard and the road, while Rube Davis took a position some one hundred yards lower down the road, for the purpose of cutting off retreat in the event a retreat was attempted. Being thus stationed, they in silence awaited the coming of their victim.

By this time night had set in black as pitch, the rain was falling in a constant steady stream, while the rumbling of distant thunder, the fitful gusts of wind, and the quickening flashes of lightning gave unmistakable indication of a coming storm.

Some hours elapsed, and our ghosts were beginning to think "they were in for it," when the sound of a horse's feet coming full gallop gave assurance that "the game was up." Nearer and with quickened speed as he approached the lonely spot, came the horseman, when, having arrived opposite the grave yard, out stepped Dave Lawson, dressed in the habiliments of the grave, and exclaiming as he stepped into the road, with a voice of sepulchral awfulness—

"Rhodes, I want you!"

"Wo, Pomp," exclaimed the terrified major, "wo, Pomp! oh Lord have mercy!—wo, Pomp, I say!"

When Dave made a step toward him, he wheeled Pomp and just got him straightened for all he had in him; then out stepped Rube, and in a voice of deep solemnity exclaimed—

"Rhodes, I must have you!"

"Wo, Pomp!—Now I lay me—Our Father who art—Wo, Pomp!—My heavenly father!" screamed the agonized victim. Then seeing Rube advance toward him, he reined Pomp full in the woods, sunk both rowels up to their heads in his flanks, swam a creek, intersected another road leading by his house, and was at home "before a minnow could swim a branch."

Arrived at home hatless, coatless, and nearly senseless, he changed his clothes, and ordered a pallet before the fire, on which he threw himself, and there on that pallet, with the startling events of the last hour before his mind, he made a vow, "If ever I pass Bently's grave yard again at night, may I land in h—ll!"

Alabama, November 22, 1848.   *The Very Young 'Un.*

CHAPTER XVI

GREENHORNS

BOTH the word *greenhorn* and the character which it names appear to be old. The Farmer-Henley *Slang and Its Analogues Past and Present*[1] defines the word as "A simpleton; a fool; a gull; also a new hand." The third synonym harks back to the sixteenth century in England, to Shakespeare, Ben Jonson, and Dekker, and to such titles as *The Gull's Horn Book*. In the *Adventurer*, No. 100 (1752), occurs a description that might apply to any number of bumpkins who wandered about the streets of small Southern towns and cities a hundred years later: "A slouch in gait, a long, lank head of hair and an unfashionable suit of drab-coloured cloth would have denominated me a GREENHORN." Scott used the word in *Guy Mannering*, Thackeray in *Pendennis*, and Washington Irving in *Tour of the Prairies*, all published in the first half of the nineteenth century.

It would be difficult, and perhaps useless, to find in artistic American or Southern regional humor of the first half of the nineteenth century many specialized analogues of the following anecdotes about greenhorns. The greenhorn is certainly not prominently present in *Georgia Scenes*.[2] There are, however, shoals of him among the Virginia emigrants who got trimmed by the sharpers in *Flush Times*. Mr. Thomas Jefferson Knowly, candidate for admission to the bar, is one variety of him. Perhaps the classic example in the fiction of the period, however, is Sut Lovingood.

Despite his apparent scarcity in conscious literature,[3] the greenhorn is a common *dramatis persona* of real pioneer life, and the

---

[1] Curiously enough, it does not appear in J. R. Bartlett's *Dictionary of Americanisms*, Fourth Edition, Boston, 1877.

[2] Ned Brace pretends to be one, but only as a "plant" for his practical jokes.

[3] Perhaps he is implicit in the larger type whose evolution is sketched by Jennette Tandy's *Crackerbox Philosophers in American Humor and Satire*, New York (Columb. Univ. Press), 1925, chapters I and II.

oral stories told about him are legion. He is a common subject for the ridicule of the political speaker of the Davy Crockett type. A Mississippi politician of the 1830's illustrated the divagations of a shifty opponent who was trying to track him on his most popular courses, with the following story. A green hand was conducted to a field by his employer and told to plow a straight furrow. "How 'm I goin' to plow straight?" he asked. "See that red cow, yonder?" asked the farmer. "Well, you make a bee-line for her, turn round when you get to her, and when you get back make another bee-line for her." Returning to his field some hours later, the farmer was horrified to find it criss-crossed like a crazy-quilt, and asked profanely why it was so. "Well," said the new hired hand, "you told me to plow for that red cow, an' I did, an' 'tain't my fault if the old hussy poked 'roun' over the whole dam' field."

The immigrant Irishman, however, is the favorite stock greenhorn in the South. In one rural Mississippi story, Moike was given his first stalk of Louisiana sugar cane and told how to peel and eat it. Moike's expression of keen relish darkened somewhat toward the end of the first chew. "Good, Moike?" "Tastes foine, but bejasus it's dom hard to swallow." Another story turns on the Irishman's first acquaintance with mosquitoes and lightning-bugs. Pat and Casey were tramping 'cross country in search of a ditch-digging job. Benighted, they were tortured by mosquitoes. They built a little brush arbor over them and found a brief surcease. After a time Casey awoke his companion with the horrified exclamation, "Begorry, Pat, the spalpeens be afther us wid their lanthorns!"

The Yankee, particularly the city Yankee, is perhaps next. A man whom we should to-day call a city bum applied at a Mississippi farm for a job. The first job (not chore; the word isn't used down there) was feeding the mules. "Give 'em a bundle of fodder apiece and ten years o' corn in the year." At his supper table some minutes later the farmer heard a hullabaloo in the "lot." At the gate he met his new man, limping and bleeding. "What's the matter?" "Matter, mister!" snarled the hand. "They took the fodder all right, but when I tried to pour the corn in the ear of the first one, he r'ared up an' bit an' stomped an' kicked hell out of me."

HOW TO CATCH AN OWL[4]

A WESTERN paper mentions the following as an easy method of taking owls: When you discover one on a tree, and find that it is looking at you, all you have to do is to move quickly round the tree several times, when the owl in the mean time, whose attention will be so firmly fixed, that forgetting the necessity of turning its body with its head, it will follow your motions with its eyes till it wrings its head off.

The same paper proposes a method of taking rabbits, equally easy and effectual. "Place (says the writer) apples in the parts where they frequent after sprinkling them with snuff, and when they come to smell, the sudden effort to sneeze which they make never fails to break their necks, and even in some cases has been known to throw their heads a foot beyond their tails."

A militia captain in one of the northern states, during the late war, being told that a regiment was to be *organized* for some special service, exclaimed, "The darned fools, they'd better stick to the drum and fife than go to the expense of buying *organs*."

An Irishman who had never fired a gun in his life took it into his head to go a shooting. It was not long before he saw a little wood pecker busily engaged in perforating a tall cherry tree. Pat crept slyly as far as he durst without alarming the bird, and after making two or three circumbendibuses around the tree, as the little feathered mechanic performed a similar revolution round its trunk, he thought he had at last got a good chance for a shot; so shutting both eyes fast, he blazed away. The bird more scared than hurt by the attack, took to its wings, while Pat, sure as he could be, that he had brought down his game, commenced searching for it amongst the weeds at the foot of the tree. As he was thus engaged, a frog started before him and began hopping round the tree. Pat in an ecstacy of his joy at having found as he supposed, the object of his search, soon seized poor croaker, and while he eyed his lantern jaws and freckled skin with somewhat of amazement, exclaimed, "Arrah, now, but sure you were a pretty bird before I shot all the feathers off you."

---

[4] *The/Alabama/Almanack/For the Year of Our Lord 1824:/Being Bissextile, or Leap Year, and the 48th-49th of American Independence./Containing the rising and setting of the Sun—the rising and setting of the Moon—the Moon's place in the Signs of/the Zodiac at Noon—Moon's Phases—/Eclipses, Festivals, &c. &c.,/caculated for the Meridian of Huntsville./By* John Beasley, Astronomer,/Morgan County, Alabama./Huntsville:/Printed and Sold by Boardeau & Adams,/At the Office of the Alabama Republican.

THE FRENCHMAN AND THE TURKEYS

By Satchel, of Alabama [5]

IN A recent visit to one of the Southern counties of this State, I met with a clever old "French gentleman"—one of the few yet living in Alabama, to whom Congress donated a valuable tract of canebrake, which the vivid imaginations of the French emigrants transferred into an El Dorado, in which perpetual spring would reign, and the olive and the vine grow without the labor of cultivation. The history of this French settlement in Alabama, if ever written, will contain more of seeming romance than reality. After the exile of Napoleon, a few of his devoted followers—disgusted with the scenes that presented the French, one day as the idolators of "Republicanism" under Napoleon's rule, and the next day crying "Viva la Bourbon!" with the earnestness of maddened zealots—determined to seek in the Western World a home for themselves, and perchance a home, at some future day, for their Emperor. Among them were the scar-worn veterans of a hundred fights, as well as the *élite* of French society, during the glorious days of the Republic. They landed at Philadelphia, and without delay proceeded to Mobile, in order to possess themselves of the land which Congress had granted them. They were, for the most part, men who had devoted their lives to the art of war, and women who had graced the drawing rooms of Paris and Versailles. Of course they knew nothing of Western life, and in after days, when some of them became planters and in some degree reconciled to their adopted country, they used to laugh over the many incidents which, in their early history, disgusted them with the country and the people—who, however kind in their deportment, were not exactly of the character to please men and women who had lived in the shadow of Royalty all their lives. The story related to me by my friend "the French gentleman" above alluded to, was well calculated to disgust them with the country, and particularly with its *game*.

When the emigrants were preparing to leave Philadelphia, they were advised, as they were moving to a new country, to possess themselves of fire-arms, ammunition, &c., which they were very careful to remember. On the voyage to Mobile they had no use for them; but so soon as they reached land, and were ready to commence their journey up the Warrior River, they prepared their arms expecting to meet an enemy "in every bush." In those days there were no steamboats; and all the trips from Mobile to the up country were made in "pole-boats"

[5] *Spirit of the Times,* vol. 18 (March 11, 1848), p. 14.

—which caused the journey to be exceedingly tedious. The French emigrants numbered several hundred, and as they progressed very leisurely, they soon found their provisions growing short. But they were told game was plenty, particularly *turkeys,* and when their chickens and pigs were gone, they could live on turkey meat.

"Dis vat da say," remarked our French friend, "but, ma Foi! such turke!"

"Was it not good?" we remarked.

"Goot? I vill tell you, Sar. I been look all day for game; I keep my gun mit me, an ven I say 'no game dis day,' I see a dree all cover mit somethin. I say, vat dat? and den enebodee say *Turke,* TURKE, TURKE! I call enebodee, come here,—and den I say—ven I say von, doo, *dree,* den enebodee shoot! Ven I say *'dree,'* den comes de Turke. Vel, we have plente fresh meat. Ve dake him to de cook, vat cook in de cete ov Paris—and say vat ve vant. De cook say he no like him smell, —he *stink;* but ve say cook goot as you can—an he smell shweet den. Vell, he cook him—and he *stink vorse:* but dis var de Turke, de Turke Americ, *and he mus be goot!* Von shentleman sa—vat you call him— ah! dis it—*paur boil him* an de stink go way. Vell ve do dat—ve have him cook paur boil, but he stink vorse, *dam vorse!* De diable! vat *sal* ve do! De cook say, somebodee tel him he no Turke; he—vat you call him. Ah! I got him—he dam *Turke Bussart!* Vot you tink. Ve cook, ve bake, ve boil, ve *paur boil,* de dam Turke Bussart—vot stink so bad as a skunk, and ve tink him a good Turke!"

Our French friend here evinced symptoms of having a stray emetic in his stomach; but he says he is always affected in this way when he recollects having masticated, some 20 years ago, *the leg of a Turkey Buzzard!*

ALABAMA, 26 Feb., 1848.

A THEATRICAL DENTIST

By Sol Smith [6]

THE new theatre in Natchez was situated at the extreme end of main street, and in a graveyard. Two hundred yards of the street leading to it had been cut through this "last receptacle of humanity," and every day, in going to rehearsal, our sights were regaled with the view of leg-bones sticking horizontally out of the earth ten or twelve feet

[6] *Anecdotal Recollections of Sol Smith,* Philadelphia, A. Hart, late Carey & Hart, [Dedication dated St. Louis, July 4, 1845], p. 128 ff. In the original, the three paragraphs descriptive of the theatre at Natchez are printed as a footnote to the sentence beginning "Most of the company of Mr. Caldwell had assembled at Natchez." For note on Smith, see p. 252, *supra.*

above us, the clay having gradually washed away and left them thus exposed.

The dressing-rooms for the gentlemen were under the stage, the earth having been excavated to make room for them. Human bones were strewn about in every direction. The first night, the lamplighter being a little "pushed" for time to get all ready, seized upon a scull, and sticking two tallow candles in the eye-sockets, I found my dressing-room thus lighted.

In digging the grave of Hamlet, I experienced no difficulty in finding bones and sculls to "play at loggats with."

Most of the company of Mr. Caldwell had assembled at Natchez [fall of 1828], nearly a week before the theatre opened. Time hanging rather heavily on their hands, they set to amusing themselves as well as they could. There was a Mr. Tooley in the town, a justice of the peace, a member of the church, and a violent opposer of the theatre. On the previous season he had connived at the escape of a negro thief, merely because he committed the felony in the theatre—telling the sufferer (who was no other man than myself) that he was served rightly, and it was a pity he had not lost everything he possessed, so that he would thus be prevented following his criminal profession! Among the new engagements this season was a Mr. Carr, a kind of "rough-shod" vocalist—a cockney Jew, who could bellow out "Oft in the stilly night" like a clap of thunder, and warble "Wha'll be king but Charlie?" like a bull. We learned that this vocalist had been a dentist, and he had communicated his intention of singing and drawing teeth in the western metropolis on his arrival there—in short, he expected to charm the lovers of harmony with his *wocal* powers, and line his pockets by the exercise of his dental acquirements. These two persons were the ones chosen by the lovers of mirth as the *Dram. Personae,* for the joke which was to make the time pass lightly for at least a day.

In due time, Dr. Carr received the following note:

"Natchez, Nov. 28, 1828.

"Sir:—For some years our town has been visited by quacks, who have passed themselves off for dentists, imposing on the people and pocketing their money without rendering them any essential service.

"My wife has for a very long time been in need of having a very difficult operation performed on her teeth and jaws, which I have been unwilling to employ any of the numerous pretenders who have visited this place to do, hoping that some gentleman would arrive with whom she might be intrusted with safety. I have been told by a friend from Philadelphia that you stood very high in that city as a professor of dentistry, and the object of this note is to request that you will favor me with your company to dinner at half-past one o'clock, bringing your instruments; and I assure you I will make it worth your while to perform the operation required, as money is no object to me in comparison with Mrs. Tooley's comfort.

"Your having adopted the theatrical profession is an additional inducement with me to employ you, as I am always glad to have it in my power to benefit those engaged in it, considering it as I do, the noblest profession on earth. Your complying with this request may be beneficial to you in more ways than one. Be punctual at half-past one.

"Yours respectfully,
"J. Tooley."

When this letter was handed to Carr by a negro boy, he was enraptured. Several of us *happened* to be present; he immediately excused himself to us, and saying he had an appointment, he began to prepare for his visit. He had swallowed the bait, hook and all. A few minutes before the time appointed, the performers (by mere accident) again happened to be strolling along the street which led to the justice's house. Punctual to his time, Dr. Carr was seen bustling along, with a miniature chest of drawers under his arm, and dressed up in the finest manner. Every one asked him to stop, on some pretence or other. All we could get out of him was, that he " 'ad a werry himportant haffair hon 'is 'ands, and 'e vas hafraid of being too late."

Precisely at the time appointed, he knocked at the justice's door. A servant inquired his business. "Tell the squire that Dr. Carr vishes to see him." "The squire is just sitting down to dinner." "Yes, I know it—please to deliver my message." In a few minutes the servant returned, and asked him to walk in.

The doctor accordingly stepped into the dining-room, bowing and scraping. After the usual salutations, the justice inquired his business. "I'm Doctor Carr." "Ah! Dr. Carr, how do you do? Well, Dr. Carr, how can I serve you?" "I am Dr. Carr, from Philadelphia, you know." "Well, Doctor, to what am I indebted for this visit?" "Vy, you know I 'ave come to see you, I've brought my hinstruments." "Brought your instruments?" "Yes—I belongs to the theatre, you know—I've brought my hinstruments—I'm going to dine with you, and then I'm going to hoperate on your vife."

At these words the justice seized a chair, and, raising it over the poor doctor's head, exclaimed—"You infernal playactor! if you don't instantly leave my house, I'll perform an operation on your head!" As he was about to suit the action to word, the doctor, in utter surprise, made a precipitate retreat, roaring murder! At the street-door his foot slipped, and he fell headlong down the steps, his hinstruments flying in every direction.

On being questioned in the evening about his "appointment," poor Carr, with an exceedingly chop-fallen countenance, replied, "That 'ere hinvitation, and the 'ole concern vas a wile 'oax!" [7]

A FOX CHASE IN MISSISSIPPI

BY WHICH CAPT. BEEROM AND BARON BLUCHER LOST THEIR "FORTUNES IN PROSPECTIVE" [8]

Mr. Editor.—You are a treasure to a man waiting for a steamboat. What a crowd of subscribers you could get on the banks of the Styx? weary souls that know no pastime—how like them is the still incarnate mortal who is tied to a steamboat landing, waiting for the next boat.

Were you ever here in Natchez? It is the prettiest and best shaded village this far South. It is buried in China trees—the foliage of which is nearly black, and so dense that the sun cannot penetrate it. I have learned something of this quiet vicinity during my delay here. There is but one hotel, and of an evening a knot of gentry sit at the corner, and the stranger may sit near enough to hear what is public.

You have faithfully recorded the feats and the toils of those who pursue the feathered and the finny tribes—but there is higher game, more ardently hunted, and this place has been, and still is, a hunting ground to be noted. Here is about the centre of cotton growing—out of which, in the days when the staple was of more value than at present, enormous private fortunes have been accumulated. "Is that a *swan* I see"—to be sure; was ever an heiress that was not a beauty? or if not a beauty, her wit is sparkling, or her step majestic, or she

---

[7] There are two possible identifications of the Squire Tooley of Sol Smith's anecdote. Both give pictures of an individual quite different from the villain of Sol's piece. One of these is described in John G. Jones's *Complete History of Methodism. . . . Mississippi Conference* (I, p. 248). His christian name was Adam. He was "an Englishman by birth, but previous to 1760 we find him living in New Berne, North Carolina. . . . He came to Natchez as a Methodist . . . previous to 1803, as that year he is mentioned as one of the trustees of Jefferson College. His house became a resting-place for itinerant preachers . . . he subscribed and paid fifty dollars toward the building of the first Methodist church in Natchez in 1807. . . . We feel assured that he died in the Lord." The other, the more likely candidate, was Adam's son, Dr. Henry Tooley, born at New Berne, N. C., 1773, doctor and preacher, who settled in Natchez not later than 1811, for in 1812, like his father, he was a trustee of Jefferson. He was "prominent and useful as a citizen, often filling responsible positions in . . . the city" (*ibid.*, pp. 249-250).

[8] *Spirit of the Times*, vol. 18 (August 26, 1848), p. 313.

has the intellectual brow of her father. At all events, the gilded frame attracts. Consequently, at the proper season, and when all the pretty birds are wintering at home, it is not astonishing that many nice young men have business at Natchez.

I have amused myself with looking over the register at "the Mansion House," and to some of the names there is a story. For instance, here are Capt. Beerom and Baron Blucher—they were distinguished travellers, who stopped to see the country, with some thoughts of making investments in cotton planting. And gallant looking men they were— such as seem sent into the world expressly to storm a battery or the fortifications of a woman's heart. The Captain was tall, muscular, erect, with a soldier-like bearing, and was said to hold a commission in some European mounted regiment. But the Baron—with his pink cheeks and raven moustache, he was perfection to look upon. The way he broke his English was distinguished.

They bought no plantations, notwithstanding they passed a winter here, but very soon after their arrival it was apparent they had made a selection of the properties they desired to own. How the acquaintance was made, I have not heard, which is the more to be regretted, as it is the only part of my story which might be of use to future "followers of the sport"—but so it is, that not much time elapsed before they became the constant cavaliers of two of the wealthiest, if not the loveliest, of the natives. To and from their morning calls they charged up and down the decorous streets of the town with a desperate horsemanship —which the Mayor had to put a stop to. And if, of an afternoon, you should lose your way upon a cross road or shady lane, it was not improbable that you would meet one or the other couples, they and their horses, all their company.

The nerves of a small town are easily jarred, and the antics of these strangers, jumping their horses over drains, wheelbarrows, and such small obstacles, looked like an attempt to astonish. This, in a country where one of the first things a boy learns is how to ride, was, you must admit, a little unsafe. I need not tell *you* what a Southern boy and his horse will dare attempt, and they will do it, too, if neither gets his neck broke, which sometimes happens.

Alas! for the Captain and the Baron—puffed up with the fame they had secured by frightening the citizens and bewitching the ladies, they were one day heard to lament that there was no fox hunting to be had. In Germany it was their favorite sport, and deprived as they were of the old familiar sound of hound and horn, there was danger of their manhood becoming musty.

"No fox hunting!" said an accidental hearer amongst the ladies.

"Why, gentlemen, we have plenty of young men who do nothing else, at this season. My cousin runs a pack every other morning, and I'm sure he would be delighted that you should join him."

And accordingly the cousin waited upon the gentlemen, and arrangements were made for a start the ensuing morning, as soon as possible after daybreak.

"I say, Sam," said one of the regular huntsmen, "I will make you two bets—one, that neither of those chaps will attend—the other, that one out of the two gets his neck broke, or thereabouts."

And although between daybreak and sunrise the next morning the valley of the Saint Catherine echoed with the cry of the pack, and hot and fast spurred the riders, whose healthful whoop disturbed the slumbers of many a fair pair of eyelids, and after the due time the "varmint's" brush was taken, yet the expected guests had not appeared.

As they returned to the place of meeting, with occasional comments not much to the advantage of the absent strangers, the Captain, to his credit be it said, with a party of city friends, loomed up in the distance. With many graceful apologies for mistaking the hour of meeting, and regrets that the Baron was suffering with a headache, he hoped it would not be impossible to get up another start.

This was at length assented to, after a short time allowed for the horses and dogs to blow. The ground was changed, and after a brief delay a well known veteran fox, an ancient customer, who many a time before had led the pack, was up and away. With many a joyous whoop, giving new life to the thoroughbreds who had already done a morning's work, with hasty adieus to the city spectators, off they went, the old fox, as was expected, taking the most villainous course which the face of the country presented.

"I say, Sam, I want to see those toes go through the grape vines. Do you think Lucy can clear the Bayou this time?"

"Bayous" are ravines or rain gullies of any width and depth, and in a field grown up in sedge grass, they cannot be seen by a rider until he is upon them.

On dashed the crowd, the Captain, with his fresh horse, riding on his stirrups, toes out (is that German fashion?), going for speed, and leading the way. Mile after mile was passed, over fallen timber and fence gaps, and through treacherous bottoms abounding in dangerous sink-holes, and still horses and riders were right side up. And now the course lies through an old cotton field thrown out and grown up in sedge grass, sloping on the far side towards the creek.

"Better let me lead, Captain. Look out for the Bayous."

But alas for the unbeliever! While the shout of warning was still ringing upon the air, the martingaled head of the Captain's mare mounted towards the sky—a yawning chasm was before her checked speed—a leap alone can save her—one moment of doubt, and in that moment the treacherous bank crumbles beneath her, and horse and rider seem to melt into the earth. "The rude sons of the hamlet" took it flying, showing to the fallen *a shower of horse shoes,* but generously forbearing to fall in on top, and when the old fox, as usual, had placed an impassable cane brake as a stopper, "the guest" was carefully dug out of the soft bottom, and returned to his admiring friends.

The Baron was never in health for a fox chase, and the Captain probably wondered, with Lord Chesterfield, if ever people "hunted twice." Their fair acquaintances looked lightnings at "those coarse young men,'" but "the accident" had somehow sullied the bloom of their chivalry, and one fair spring morning the illustrious visitors disappeared, unwedded and alone.

Yours,   JERSEY.

NATCHEZ, Aug. 1, 1848.

A VERY FAMILIER EPISTLE FROM 'AMITO'[9]

'COLLAMAR has come,' and two jets have issued from the Sahara of a Southern tour in summer time. The one, full of life and vigor, sending a noble, steady stream 'sky high,' and diffusing its fraught waters over the meadow and the highland of its own adamantine boundaries. Boundaries, said I? I am loth to use the word—so versatile and ever-varying are the conceptions and correspondings of thy numerous friends, dear 'Spirit' and essence of 'Times past, present,' and, I may safely add, the 'future.' Hast not recognized thy own 'fair form' in the fountain simile?

The sister jet comes from the brain-dottings of 'Old Knick,' whose 'gossip familiar' with kind readers comes like the sunshine and clouds of an April day—laughter-provoking and saddening in the same breath.

Indeed, I love you!—for there is a something familiar in thy very look, for erst in boyhood I wandered by the clear rivulet of thy wit and humor—and half fearing, yet not undaunted, buffeted the welling tide of deeper thought that, like our own noble river, came ever onward. 'Twas in boyhood I did 'all this,' but the season and the climes of many sister States in riper years have found me still at my boyish avocation.

Surely 'love begetteth love,' and why should I not 'yearn toward thee,' for in times back (and not so long neither,) I have communed with thee under varied cognomens, and at sundry times and places. On

[9] *Spirit of the Times,* vol. 19 (August 25, 1849), p. 313.

the clear waters of 'La Belle River' (*not* whilst yet a brook), from the land of 'Tar, Pitch, Turpentine *and* Lumber,' as we school-boys used to have it—from the snow-clad hills of the North, (though you *didn't* publish one of my *poetical* effusions, but recommended a longer communion with the muses—ah! that *was* a 'cut direct!')—from the groves of the sunny South, ('where the race horse gently runs his course, and the cock crows *precisely* at 12 o'clock, my friends')—from all these have I communed with you and your readers—'*kind* readers' indeed you were—and you have borne with me with an ever-enduring patience—Caudle-like.

And now I find myself in this 'fair city of an hundred hills,' dozing away the long summer months. And wonder not, therefore, that I should turn eulogist after so long a season, and tell you so frankly that I like you, and how like big drops in summer rain your correspondings come—each drop separate and distinct, yet a miniature deluge in itself.

This ever-blossoming South of ours is not so bad a land, with its broad savannas—its noble rivers—and its majestic evergreen, unending forests, stretching as far as human vision goes, and then commingling as it were its waves of green—of Hope—with arching Heaven's ether-blue of truth and purity.

But I would be poetical and 'contrawise,' and *might* turn uninteresting. But the land is 'not so bad,' poetry or prose. So, leaving these trite themes 'for those whose heads have not commenced turning gray, and whose hearts are not turned grayer,' let us discourse of other matters.

By the bye, there was a stray thought (all my thoughts are stray, and I am the 'Ranger,') flitted across my mind just then that reminded me of a story of my old friend Mr. M——, of Yazoo County. Shall I tell it to you for what it is worth? It made me laugh 'consumedly' when related to me—and then beyond the mere story, there is a some-thing so decidedly American—so especially South Western in it, that, as a mere evidence of our independence of character, it is worthy of record.

Mr. M—— had occasion to visit New Orleans during the winter of 1845, and obtained from his factor in this city various letters of introduction to merchants in New Orleans, and among the rest, one to a French house of eminence. The day after his arrival he made it his special business to call upon the houses to whom he carried introductory letters. About mid-day he found it convenient to call upon his friend the Frenchman. Being ushered into the handsome counting-room, he was invited by the principal to 'take a seat,' which without farther words he did, 'crossing his legs à la American,' and at the same time taking a bird's eye view of the 'arrangements.' Without any farther notice upon the part of his French acquaintance, who commenced talking his interminable jargon to some fellow countrymen who were having a chat with him, Mr. M—— continued his mental observations, noting incidentally that not much of the conversation was addressed to him, or if it was, not in a comprehensible tongue. His 'sovereignty,' offended with this cavalier treatment, he waited 'till a pause in the conversation, and then relieved himself thus to his astonished auditory:

'E Pluribus Unum! *Magnum* Bonum! Mahola tosh! *Good morning, gentlemen, and be d—d to you!' He* interprets thus—'I am one among you! As good as *any* body! May-be so! Good morning, gentlemen, and be d—d to you!'

He left—*he* did, and it is upon record that our French friend has been especially polite to his Yazoo County sovereigns since that occurrence.

VICKSBURG, July 20, 1849.

EXPEDISHUN TO THE LOWER REJIN OF LOOZEANA

By Mike Shouter [10]

To the Editor of the "Coon Run Banner."

TICKEER TAVERN, YAZOO CO., MISS., NOV. 18, 1856.

The last time you was down in our range, I happened to let it leak out that I was 'bout gwine on a expedishun to the lower rejin of Loozeana, to that sitty of unhearn-of wikkedness, frogs, katfish and Frenchmen, called Orleans, of which so much has been hearn, spoke, and writ, and the half not told; an' soon as you hearn me say I was gwine thar, up you jumps, an' sez you to me, sez you—Uncle Mike, sez you, do write to us all about what you sees, an' I'll print it in the Banner.

Well, sez I, I will, on one condishin.

What's that, sez you?

It's this here, sez I—that you won't make any mistakes in the spellin', nor put in none of yure commense in 2 the tex'.

Very well, sez you, I won't, by hokey.

Good as tater, then sez I, I'll write—an' if you've a stray quarter 'bout you, we'll take a drink on the stren'th of it. So we adjourned over to the nearest dead-fall, tuck a whoppin' horn of Ball Face, an' you paid for it like a white head. However, this ain't the pint—so we'll jest proceed in the nateral way.

[10] The New Orleans *Weekly Delta*, vol. I, No. 51 (November 23, 1856), p. 1.

Well, when everything was fixed up, off I started.

When I got down to Satartia, waitin' for the steamboat to come along, sez I to myself, sez I, I ixpect that are tarnation boat will be 'bout a year 'fore she gits here, but I hadn't more'n got the words outen my mouth, when here she come, a snortin' an' a blowin' like a bar an' a whole team of dogs atter him, tearin' threw a cane-brake. Well, toreckly she hauled up to the side of the bank, to take on some cotton, an' put off a few bar'ls of whisky, an' I went aboard as sassy as a meat-axe, an' struttin' 'bout dex as large as life. Several fellers from my neck of woods was gwine along with me, an' soon as I got on, they jumps on too, an' thar we was, a whole team of us. In about a minit the boat she put off, an' jest as we was gittin out of site of the town, I don't b'leeve I ever felt so bad in all my born days: For, thar was the tops of the houses—7 or 8 of them in a bunch—fast reseding from the site, an' the pickteresk view of the gable end of Bill Piers's grocery dwindlin' down to a pint—of which, alas! I was about to look on it, prehaps, for the last time! The site was more than I could stand, an' my pheelinx (too deep for expreshun) was about to bust out at my eyes, when a sentiment lower down, in the way of a drought in the stomach, absorbed the moisture in my eyelids,—an' I was dry as a powder-horn! Boys, sez I, look here! We've been on this dug-out 'bout a coon's age, an' I ain't hearn one of you say "treat" yet! With that, Jo Cole sed he had a few bushels of corn left at home yet, and as long as that lasted, he'd be dad burned if Uncle Mike should suffer for a drink. So we walked down to the bar, an' tuk a horn all round. Then we walked out on deck, whar the Cap'n of the boat was standin' (he was one of the nicest fellers you ever see) chawin' backer an' cussin' the deck hands in the most bewtiful style you ever hearn, an' sez I, Cap'n, s'pose we take a drink? An' we tuck it.

Then we went out on the guards, front of the wheel-house, to take a look at the alleygaters an' the cypress trees, an' the long moss, an' the bull-frogs sportin' from bank to bank; an' then we went in agin, an' we all tuck a drink.

In about a minit or 2, a gentlemun with store clothes on, an' a whoppin' site of har under his nose, cum up to our crowd, an' sez he, "gentlemen, 'spose you jine me in a drink?" So we tuck another small horn all round.

Then the gentlemun with the har under his nose an' the store clothes on, sez he to me—as I was the oldest man of the party, an' the cutest lookin' of all of em—sez he to me, "thar's a sight of trees about here, an' cane-breaks, an' a great scarcity of houses; an' sez he, it strikes me this must be a great country for *game?*"

"Yes," sez I, "one of the greatest you ever see; you can have any kind of game you like, from Sunday mornin' to Saturday night."

"You *bag* a great deal then?" sez he.

"Yes," sez I, "all that comes in reach; an' I, for my part, never pretends to quit till my bag is chock full, an' my briches pockets, too, fit to bust," sez I.

"What kind of arms is most in use?" sez he. "Pistols and bowie-knives," sez I!

"The deuce you say," sez he; "whar I cum from they uses mostly rifles and double-barrel fowling pieces!"

"Yes," sez I, "that's the fashion in some places whar they like to take it at long taw, so as to keep out ov danger; but I, for myself, when it comes to close quarters, likes pistols and bowie knives."

"When I was in India," sez he, "whar we amused ourselves in the jungles, an' had sometimes to fight the tiger, pistols was in great demand."

"Yes," sez I, "nothin' like pistols for fightin' the tiger, an' a bowie knife in case of a accident; for then, if he happens to claw you a little too strong, you can jest show him the weapons till he 'turns' to suit you, an' you are bound to win!"

"So you have the tiger, too," sez he, "an' pray what other kind of game have you?"

"Well," sez I, "the 'tiger' * is in genully considered the best, an' then we have poker an' eucre, an' a occasional game of 'seven up' or 'old sledge!' " Moar nex time, an'

Yourn till deth,   MIKE SHOUTER.

*—By the term "Tiger," Mike means "the game of Farro."

ENOUGH, ENOUGH! [11]

A FRENCHMAN who knew very little of our language, unfortunately got into a difficulty with a back countryman, and fight he must, and that, too, rough and tumble. But before he went at it, he was anxious to know what he should cry if he found himself whipped. After being informed that when satisfied, all he would have to do would be to cry out enough, at it they went; but, poor Monsieur in his difficulties, forgot the word, and finding his eyes likely to be removed from their sockets, he began to cry out, but instead of saying what was told him, he commenced bawling lustily, "hurrah! hurrah!"

To his astonishment the countryman kept pounding harder, when Monsieur, finding there was no use in hallowing, turned and went to

[11] The *Tuskaloosa* [Alabama] *Independent Monitor*, Wednesday, April 29, 1846.

work in such good earnest, that it was not long before the countryman sang out in a stentorian voice—"Enough!"

"Say that again," said the Frenchman.

"Enough! Enough!" cried he again.

When the Frenchman in his turn exclaimed—"Begar, dat is the vere word I vas try to say long time ago."

DUMPLINS [12]

A YANKEE pedlar dining at a house where they happened to have apple-dumplins for dinner, wanted to ask for the sauce which was prepared for the dumplins, but forgetting the name of it, said "I'll thank you for some of that truck that you wallow your dumplins in!"

THREE TO ONE [13]

A YANKEE and a Southerner were playing poker on a steamboat. After a while the Southerner remarked that he had not seen an ace for some time.

"I guess you haven't," replied the Yankee, "but I can tell you where they all are. One of them is up your shirt sleeve there, and the other three are in the top of one of my butes."

[12] Hotchkiss & Co's. *Louisiana and Mississippi Almanac, 1833.* . . . New Orleans (Hotchkiss & Company).

[13] *Southern Journal,* vol. XI, No. 6 (Monticello, Mississippi, August 17, 1850), p. 1.

CHAPTER XVII

THE LADIES—GOD BLESS 'EM!

OLD-FASHIONED novels and Southern silver-tongues to the point, and also mainly to the contrary, the woman of the lower South was all your fancy painted her, and a good deal that is unimaginable unless you have chatted with nice, white-haired old ladies in hickory chairs on tall-columned verandahs, or visited with great-framed, iron-gray, pipe-smoking chatelaines in the breezy dog-trots of two-story double-log houses, or gossiped with bonneted crones in the cabins.

She was "The Natchez Beauty" of the 1840's, who drank George Joseph Vinnigerholtz's juleps at the Mansion House, or those at the Shakespeare, crowned with a moss rose. She was Christian Schultz's "virgin queen before the Gordian knot is tied . . . yet the Cyprian goddess for ever after." She was W. H. Sparks's "mother when her nap was up," rubbing her hand over the rifle barrel to get the sight clear; or she was the sister of that lady, Marion Beck Forrest, riding through Coldwater swamp, determined to take her chickens home, pa'nter or no pa'nter, and, later, h'isting her cowed soldier son on top of a sack of grist corn. In a tight place, she was writing Jeff Davis to let her man come home and marry her, all bein' willin' 'cep'n Jeems's cap'n. She's lovely Miss Clemmie, whom the Feds and Confeds won't leave a man living to make her his wife. She's a lady of character, ready to settle the hash of the negro equality tribe "at Masons and dixon line," with a pair of Colt's repeaters. In truth, she's the infinite variety that woman has always been since the world began, but more so. For she was a pioneer, a lady of the Big House, doctor and nurse to the negro slaves, dispenser of household and plantation justice, a queen and huntress chaste and fair, a trull at Natchez-under-the-Hill, an Indian fighter, a mother of sons terrible in battle. She was all these things and plenty more. Oratory cannot spoil her nor fiction stale her infinite variety.

THE ABUSED RUSSIAN GRAND DUCHESS

By Alexander Beaufort Meek [1]

AMONG a company of German colonists, who arrived at Mobile, in 1721, there came a female adventurer, of great personal beauty and high accomplishments, and evidently possessed of much wealth. It was generally believed, as she herself represented, that she was the daughter of the Duke of Wolfenbüttel, and the wife of the Czarowitz Alexius Peter, the only son of Peter the Great, and that, being cruelly treated by her husband, she had fled from him, for refuge in these far colonies, while he represented that she was dead. This belief was confirmed by the Chevalier d'Aubant, who, having seen the princess at St. Petersburgh, recognized her features in the newcomer; and upon the strength of this opinion, formed a matrimonial alliance with the repudiated wife.

After many years' residence in the colony with all the style of a court—the Chevalier went to Paris with his princess. Here for some time, her story obtained general credit, and it was not until after the death of her husband, that she was discovered to be an impostor.

It was now proved that the pretended arch-duchess was only a humble female, who, having been attached to the wardrobe of the Princess of Russia, had robbed her of large quantities of jewelry and gold, and had fled to America. By a similarity of appearance with her mistress, she imposed upon the credulity of the young officer, who lived in splendor upon her ill-gotten wealth, and died in blissful ignorance of the truth of her history.

"TEN OR A DOZEN OF THE FINEST LADIES"

By Thomas Rodney (to Caesar Rodney) [2]

Natchez Augt. 9th 1804.

My dear Son

. . . .

Apropos, last Evening I walked up to Major F. L. Claiborn to see M^{rs}. Poindexter a young Lady I had lately married to the Att^y. Genl. but the Ladies were out at M^r. Wallaces in the next Square, and on

---

[1] *The Southwest: Its History, Character, and Prospects, A Discourse for the Eighth Anniversary of the Erosophic Society of the University of Alabama, December 7, 1839*, Tuscaloosa (C. B. Baldwin, Printer), 1840, pp. 15-16. For the same story, see A. J. Pickett's *History of Alabama* (pp. 225-226; giving, also, a footnote reference to Martin's *History of Louisiana*) and P. J. Hamilton's *Colonial Mobile*, pp. 89, 164.

[2] "Thomas Rodney," by Simon Gratz, Esq., in *The Pennsylvania Magazine of History and Biography*, vol. XLIV (1920), pp. 55-56. For biographical note, see p. 55, *supra*.

hearing I was there M^rs. Claiborn was sent by the Ladies to Invite me over there, and when I went, found an Assembly there of Ten or a dozen of the finest Ladies of the City and Territory—where they had met to spend the Evening, Shields & other gentlemen were there & Shields's beloved Miss P. Dunbar, &c &c. They were mostly young Ladies and young married Ladies, and spent much of the Evening in selling Pawns &c and would not Excuse me from Entering into the Amusement with them—the pleasantry Ended with Music; and then a flock of the Ladies, & some of the Gentlemen, Conducted me nearly to my Lodging with a Lamp carried by one of the Ladies who walked with me—I mention this merely as a Trait of the Chearful and pleasant Manners of the place and tho I sit here on the hills of the Mississippi distant, far distant, from my friends, my sweet friends of Delaware, yet that my Situation is not altogether solitary—the young people as well as the old seem pleased with my Company and I am often told that I am the only person that Ever was in the Territory that no one has ever said a word against—Yet I have done nothing more than Endeavor to Conduct myself up rightly with placid and good manners to all—

"LIKE A CHOIR OF SERAPHS"

By Thomas Rodney (to Mrs. Anna D. Postlewait, Natchez) [3]

Town of Washington March 13th 1805.

Dear Madam,

Inclosed you will receive a Certificate of your Marriage—It has always been my Custom to place this in the hands of the Lady for Safe Keeping.

And please to permit me to say your Marriage pre-sented a pleasant scene. The Ladies appeared, I will not say, like a band of Sirens, but like a Choir of Seraphs just descended from above. Their Music and Charms were Enchanting and spread blissful pleasure around—and permit me to tell Miss Dunbar your Successoress that there was nothing lacking to have turned the Forrest into a perfect Paradise but her neglecting to dress & ornament the House throughout with flowers, to have made it a representation of the bower of the primeval pair of the human race—She ought to have done this on such an occasion, as the God of nature himself had dictated its propriety, by previously dressing the woods and fields with flowers—therefore when such an occasion happens again she ought not to omit this beautiful and delightful part

[3] *Ibid.*, pp. 186-187.

of the Paradisal Scene—and permit me to say to the Young ladies further that tho they appeared like a Choir of Cherubims and perhaps hereafter may be such, yet that at present they are Mortals and are only sent here a while to beautify adorn and replenish the Earth—Therefore I wish them all happy Matches and as soon as they please—
God bless you with health and prosperity—Adieu.

Thomas Rodney.

Please to present my congratulations and Respectful Compliments to M^r. Postlewait.

LADIES AND GENTLEMEN OF NATCHEZ

(1808)

By Christian Schultz, Jr., Esq.[4]

MY STAY at Natchez was but two days and two nights: of course you will not expect me to say any thing respecting the manners of its inhabitants, as the result of my own observations. Yet as this was always one of the principal items in my catalogue of inquiries, you may be sure I did not neglect it on this occasion.

"The ladies in general are extremely delicate, which never fails to please, and excite the warmest sensations of the beholder. They are fond of dancing and all the other gay amusements, and though chaste as the virgin queen before the Gordian knot is tied, yet indulgent as the Cyprian goddess for ever after." Although this character, (given me by a married gentleman of the town,) may be applicable to a few, yet I entertain too exalted an opinion of the sex to make it general.

The gentlemen pass their time in the pursuit of three things: all make love; most of them play; and a few make money. With Religion they have nothing to do; having formed a treaty with her, the principal article of which is, "Trouble not us, nor will we trouble you."

I had the curiosity the next morning to count the number of boats then lying along the Levee, and found they amounted to eighty-three, all loaded with the produce of the upper country as far as the 42d degree of north latitude. When I went on board of my own boat, (which was very early, and before the sun had risen,) I discovered

[4] *Travels on an Inland Voyage through the States of New-York, Pennsylvania, Virginia, Ohio, Kentucky and Tennessee, and through the Territories of Indiana, Louisiana, Mississippi and New-Orleans; Performed in the Years 1807 and 1808; Including a Tour of Nearly Six Thousand Miles. With Maps and Plates.* In Two Volumes. New-York: Printed by Isaac Riley. 1810. Vol. 2, pp. 133-136. For biographical note on Schultz, see p. 89, *supra.*

that my visit was as unwelcome as it was unexpected. I was so unfortunate as to disturb the morning slumbers of exactly one quarter of
a dozen of the copper-coloured votaries of the Cyprian queen, who it
seems had undertaken to enliven the idle hours of our Canadian crew.
The *ladies* really seemed ashamed; but whether from a conviction of
their being the intruders, or considering me as such, I am unable to
say. Suffice it, I took my leave until they had time to decamp.

"MOTHER'S NAP WAS UP"

By W. H. Sparks [5]

NOT ten years since, I spent some time in Eastern Mississippi. I met
at his home a gentleman I had made the acquaintance of in New
Orleans. He is a man of great worth and fine intelligence: his grandfather had emigrated to the country in 1785 from Emanuel County,
Georgia. His grandson says: "He carried with him a small one-horse
cart pulled by an old gray mare, one feather bed, an oven, a frying-
pan, two pewter dishes, six pewter plates, as many spoons, a rifle gun,
and three deer-hounds. He worried through the Creek Nation, extending from the Oconee River to the Tombigbee.

"After four months of arduous travel he found his way to Leaf
River, and there built his cabin; and with my grandmother, and my
father, who was born on the trip in the heart of the Creek Nation,
commenced to make a fortune. He found on a small creek of beautiful
water a little bay land, and made his little field for corn and pumpkins
upon that spot: all around was poor, barren pine woods, but he said it
was a good range for stock; but he had not an ox or cow on the face
of the earth. The truth is, it looked like Emanuel County. The turpentine smell, the moan of the winds through the pine-trees, and nobody
within fifty miles of him, was too captivating a concatenation to be
resisted, and he rested here.

"About five years after he came, a man from Pearl River was driving
some cattle by to Mobile, and gave my grandfather two cows to help
him drive his cattle. It was over one hundred miles, and you would
have supposed it a dear bargain; but it turned out well, for the old
man in about six weeks got back with six other head of cattle. How or
where, or from whom he got them is not one of the traditions of the
family. From these he commenced to rear a stock which in time became
large.

[5] *The Memories of Fifty Years: Containing Brief Biographical Notices of Distinguished Americans, and Anecdotes of Remarkable Men; Interspersed with Scenes
and Incidents Occurring During a Long Life of Observation Chiefly Spent in the
Southwest*, Philadelphia (Claxton, Remsen & Haffelfinger), Macon, Ga. (J. W. Burke
& Co.), 1870. For biographical note on Sparks, see p. 75, *supra*.

"My father and his brothers and sisters were getting large enough to help a little; but my grandfather has told me that my father was nine years old before he ever tasted a piece of bacon or pork. When my father was eighteen years of age he went with a drove of beef cattle to New Orleans. He first went to Baton Rouge, thence down the river. He soon sold out advantageously; for he came home with a young negro man and his wife, some money, and my mother, whom he had met and married on the route. Well, from those negroes, and eight head of cattle, all the family have come to have something.

"I was born nine months after that trip, and grew up, as father had done before me, on the banks of that little creek. I doubt if there ever was a book in my grandfather's house. I certainly never remember to have seen one there, and I was sixteen years old when he died. I think I was very nearly that old before I ever saw any woman but those of the family, and I know I was older than that before I ever wore shoes or pants. Nearly every year father went to Mobile, or Natchez, or New Orleans.

"The first time I ever knew my mother had a brother, I was driving up the cows, and a tall, good-looking man overtook me in the road and asked where my father lived. I remember I told him, 'At home.' He thought it was impudence, but it was ignorance. However, he was quite communicative and friendly.

"That night, after the family had gone to bed, I heard him tell my mother her father was dead, and that he had disinherited her for running off and marrying father. I did not know what this meant; but the next day father came and told mother that her brother wanted to be kind to her, and had proposed to give him a thousand dollars of the estate of her father, if he and she would take it and sign off. That was the word. I shall not forget, so long as I live, my mother's looks as she walked up to father and said: 'Don't you do it, John. John, I say, don't you do it.' Uncle had gone down to grandfather's, and when he came back, mother had his horse saddled at the fence. She met him at the door, and said: 'You don't come in here. There's your beast; mount him, and go. I am not such a fool as my John. I was raised in Louisiana, and I remember hearing my father say that all he hated in the laws was that a man could not do with his property, when he died, what he pleased. I haven't forgot that. I have not seen nor heard from any of you for fifteen years, and never should, if you hadn't come here to try to cheat me.'

"I was scared, and my father was scared; for we knew there was danger when mother's nap was up. Uncle did not reply to mother, but said: 'John, you can sign off.'

" 'No, John can't; and I tell you John shan't! so now do you just mount that horse and leave.'

"As she said this she lifted the old rifle out of the rack over the door and rubbed her hand over the barrel to get the sight clear. 'I am not going to tell you to go any more.'

"It was not necessary—uncle went; but he kept looking back until he was at least a quarter of a mile from the house. Mother turned to father and said: 'Now, John, you go after my share of father's truck, and go quick.' He did as she bid him: everybody about the house did that. Well, he was gone three weeks, and came home with six thousand dollars, which he had taken from mother's share; but she said she knew he had been cheated.

". . . I got two thousand of it, one negro, and two hundred head of cattle. . . . I was twenty-one years old when I learned my letters. I have been lucky. . . . Come, Sue, can't you give the gentleman some music? Give me my fiddle, and I will help you."

"ALWAYS SETTLE THEM CASES YOURSELF"

By W. H. Sparks [6]

JACKSON was enterprising and eminently self-reliant; in all matters pertaining to himself, he was his own counselor; he advised with no man; cool and quick in thought, he seemed to leap to conclusions, and never went back from them. An anecdote relative to his parting from his mother in his outset in life, illustrates this as prominent in the attributes of his nature at that time. The writer heard him narrate this after his return from Washington, when his last term in the Presidential office had expired.

When about to emigrate to Tennessee, the family were residing in the neighborhood of Greensboro', North Carolina.

"I had," said he, "contemplated this step for some months, and had made my arrangements to do so, and at length had obtained my mother's consent to it. All my worldly goods were a few dollars in my purse, some clothes in my saddle-bags, a pretty good horse, saddle, and bridle. The country to which I was going was comparatively a wilderness, and the trip a long one, beset by many difficulties, especially from the Indians. I felt, and so did my mother, that we were parting forever. I knew she would not recall her promise; there was too much spunk in her for that, and this caused me to linger a day or two longer than I had intended.

"But the time came for the painful parting. My mother was a little,

[6] *Ibid.*, pp. 147-8.

dumpy, red-headed Irish woman. 'Well, mother, I am ready to leave, and I must say farewell.' She took my hand, and pressing it, said, 'Farewell,' and her emotion choked her.

"Kissing at meetings and partings in that day was not so common as now. I turned from her and walked rapidly to my horse.

"As I was mounting him, she came out of the cabin wiping her eyes with her apron, and came to the getting-over place at the fence. 'Andy,' said she, (she always called me Andy,) 'you are going to a new country, and among a rough people; you will have to depend on yourself and cut your own way through the world. I have nothing to give you but a mother's advice. Never tell a lie, nor take what is not your own, nor sue anybody for slander or assault and battery. *Always settle them cases yourself!*' I promised, and I have tried to keep that promise. I rode off some two hundred yards, to a turn in the path, and looked back—she was still standing at the fence and wiping her eyes. I never saw her after that." Those who knew him best will testify to his fidelity to this last promise made his mother.

LIKE MOTHER, LIKE SON

By John Allen Wyeth [7]

MACBETH's surpassing apostrophe to his fearless wife might well apply to this Southern mother, who consecrated eight sons to the god of war:

"Bring forth men-children only."

One or two incidents in the life of General Forrest's mother will serve to emphasize what has been said in regard to her physical prowess, as well as her strong and determined will. They are not the less interesting in the fact that the same characteristics belonged to her illustrious son, who at the period mentioned was but a boy fifteen years of age.

When the Forrests first settled in Mississippi, so sparsely peopled was this part of the country, from which the Indians had but recently been removed, that it was some ten miles to their nearest neighbor. Roads were practically unknown, and those that existed were little better than bridle-paths through the woods and canebrakes, and had to be traveled on foot or on horseback.

On one occasion Mrs. Forrest and her sister, Fannie Beck, who lived with her, started out on horseback to pay a visit to this neighbor. When they were leaving for home late in the afternoon, her hostess presented her with a basket containing several young chickens.

---

[7] *Life of General Nathan Bedford Forrest*, New York and London (Harper Brothers), 1899, pp. 8-10. For biographical note on the author, see p. 331, *supra*.

Their return trip was without incident until they had arrived within a mile of their cabin. The sun had gone down and it was beginning to grow quite dark. At this moment they heard the yelp or scream of a panther in the dense woods, and only a few yards distant. They realized at once that the hungry beast had scented the chickens and was bounding through the cane and undergrowth to secure its prey. At the first yelp of the animal the horses became frightened and broke into a run. Their riders, or at least one of them, were alarmed, and both urged their horses towards home as fast as they could go with safety over the narrow and rough trail. Mrs. Forrest's sister shouted to her from her position in front as they were galloping along to drop the basket and let the panther have the chickens, which would stop it, but Marion Beck was not that sort of woman. There was too much determination and Scotch grit in her, and she declined to do as she was bid. She was "not goin' to let any varmint have her chickens," and on they sped, the horses holding the panther safely in their wake, until they approached the creek which ran near by their cabin. On account of the high banks of the stream and the depth of the water, they were compelled, as they reached it, to slacken their speed almost to a standstill to prevent their falling as they slid down the declivity and struck the water. This slowing-up enabled their swift pursuer to gain on them rapidly, and, mad with hunger to such a desperate degree that it had lost the natural fear of human beings, the beast leapt from the top of the bank, striking Mrs. Forrest upon the shoulder and side of the neck with his front paws, while the claws of the hind feet sank deeply into the back of the animal she was riding. Smarting under the pain and wild with fright, the horse plunged forward so quickly that the hold of the panther was torn loose, and at the same time the rider's clothes were ripped from her back, and several deep, lacerated wounds were inflicted in the flesh of the shoulder as the beast fell into the water. The screams of the women brought the whole household out from the cabin, which was situated on the opposite bluff, and Bedford Forrest came running with his dogs to the rescue. The mother, still holding on to her basket of chickens, was lifted from her saddle and tenderly cared for by her eldest son and his aunt. As soon as she was made as comfortable as possible, young Forrest took his flintlock rifle from the rack above the fireplace and started toward the door to call his dogs. His mother asked him what he was going to do. He said, "Mother, I am going to kill that beast if it stays on the earth." She tried to dissuade him from going into the woods at that hour, asking him to wait until daylight, when he could see what he was doing. The boy replied that by that time the trail would be so cold the dogs would not be able to follow it;

that he was going now while the scent was fresh; the hounds would soon run it into a tree; and away he went into the darkness.

The hounds soon picked up the trail, and followed it for miles through swamps and briers and canebrakes, until nearly midnight. After an hour or so of the chase, the boy perceived it would tax his strength sorely to keep up with the dogs, and fearing that they would get out of hearing and reach of him he cut a small grapevine, tied it around the neck of one of the oldest hounds and held fast to the other end of the tether. At times the other dogs would get out of hearing, but the captive hound followed unerringly upon the trail, and after a while, far in the distance, he heard the baying of the pack, which told him they had at last treed the panther. It was too dark when he arrived to see the beast, so he waited patiently until the day began to break, and then he saw it lying stretched at full length on a huge limb, lashing its cat-like tail from side to side and snarling with its white teeth at the dogs, which had never taken their eyes from it or given it a minute's peace. Putting a fresh primer in the pan of his flintlock, and taking steady aim, the young huntsman sent a bullet through its heart, and it fell limp and dead to the earth. Cutting off the scalp and ears, he started for home, where about nine o'clock the same morning he arrived to show his mother the trophy he had won.

THE NATCHEZ BEAUTY

(1 8 4 0) [8]

SHE has a form delicately moulded, slight, graceful, faultless. Her hair is the raven, shaded, lightened, brightened with a sun-burst. Her forehead is the ivory throne of a calm, proud intellectuality; her eyes dark, thrilling, relenting from the rapid and searching glance into a dreamy tenderness; her movement carries soul with it, and the indication of her irresistible influence.

Her voice is the murmur of spring doves, low and deep with holier passions than man can know, pulsating upon the heart of the listener, and teaching him with the majesty of female virtue. This is not fancy's sketch.

THE NATCHEZ BEAUTY [9]

THE editor of the New Orleans Sun is in the utmost distress respecting the "Natchez Beauty." After quoting our brief description of her peerless form, the Sun says:—

[8] *Mississippi Free Trader and Natchez Gazette*, vol. V (Thursday, March 12, 1840), p. 2.
[9] *Mississippi Free Trader and Natchez Gazette*, Natchez, March 26, 1840, p. [2].

Who is she? What's her name? Is she rich? Her temper? Where from? How old is she?—Did she spring from the sea, like *Va*-nus? or burst from the brain of Jove, like Miner-*vy?* Is she Whig or Loco Foco? Does she write poetry?—Her nose—what of her nose? Gods! that you should have said nothing of her nose! Is it a Grecian nose? Roman nose? or pug nose? Don't keep us in suspense—what's the order of her nose? "Let us not burst in ignorance, but answer us." Oh! that we were she, and her were us!—for she moves in matchless and queen-like beauty, and we move in a pair of three-dollar breeches.

Let us write a piece of poetry for her album.—Here it is:

TO THE NATCHEZ BEAUTY

A sunlight beauty, through and through
   Each limb, and every feature, gleams,
And on her lips nectarean dew
   Seems fresh, as on the morning streams:
And never yet shone half so bright
The Latmian shepherdess of night,
Or Sol, upon his throne of light,
   Amidst his native beams.

I look on Leda when I soar
   Upon my fancy's subtle wing,
And deem it honor to adore
   So proud, and fair a thing;
But thou more potent art than she,
More exquisite in harmony
And light—and almost forcing me
   To stammer as I sing.

I throw aside my song, and break
   The pen that traced—or struggled to—
Your picture, for I would not make
   A mockery of you:—
If eye-sight ever fell upon
So faultless and so fair a one,
From day-dawn to the setting sun
   I'd like such maid to woo.

We confess that we consider the poetry too indifferent to inscribe either in the Album of the "Natchez Beauty" or in pencillings of light to make the least impression on the tablet of her splendid intellect: but if any one *knows* any thing about the *nose* of the "Natchez Beauty," for mercy's sake let him *disclose* what he *knows* about that *nose,* as it *shows* that the Sun's *repose,* his joys or *woes,* from his ears to his *toes,* depend upon what any one may *disclose* in regard to that *nose!*

BATHING.—THE LADIES [10]

CLEANLINESS of body is in closer connexion with purity of mind than is generally imagined, and both ought to be associated with our ideas of personal beauty and loveliness. The Grecian fiction, of Venus being of "ocean born," is typical of the aid which beauty is expected to derive from frequent ablutions and bathing.

Females are not, we fear, adequately impressed with the full importance of the practice here recommended. They often spend much time at the toilet—great pains and expense are incurred to obtain, select, and arrange the finest materials for dress, and to display colors in the most tasteful contrast—but is that which ought to precede all these arrangements, the tepid or warm bath regularly used? If had recourse to on the morning after the fatigues and exertions in a ball-room, or an excursion of pleasure in a carriage or on horseback?— Some ladies will say, aye; but I greatly fear they are in so small a number as to be considered exclusives of the first water, even though they may not show off in silks and brocades.

"ALL WILLIN' 'CEP'N JEEMS' CAP'N"

By Varina Howell (Mrs. Jefferson) Davis [11]

THERE were some quaint appeals made to Mr. Davis, and his sympathy and sense of humor brought him into correspondence with the writers, or induced him to make as quaint endorsements on their letters.

One girl, whose sweetheart was a gallant soldier in the Fifth South Carolina Regiment and who had fought bravely all through the Seven Days Battle, made the following earnest request:

Dear Mr. President:—

I want you to let Jeems C. of Company Oneth, South Carolina Regiment, cum home and git married. Jeems is willin', I is willin', his mammy says she is willin', but Jeems Capn he ain't willin'. Now when we are all willin' 'cep'n Jeems Capn, I think you might

[10] *Arkansas Times and Advocate,* Little Rock, Monday, July 24, 1837.
[11] *Jefferson Davis, Ex-President of the Confederate States of America: A Memoir by His Wife,* 2 vols., New York (Belford Company, Publishers), c. 1890, II, pp. 325-326.

let up and let Jeems come home. I'll make him go straight back when hes done got married and fight just as hard as ever.

Your aff. friend, &c

Mr. Davis wrote on the letter, "Let Jeems go," and Jeems went home, married the affectionate correspondent of Mr. Davis, returned to his regiment, and fought as well as ever.

MISS CLEMMIE'S ALBUM

By Frazar Kirkland [12]

DURING the last visit of the Federal forces under Major-General A. J. Smith, to Holly Springs, Mississippi, in August 1864, the following lines were penned by Colonel A—— on the last page of a young lady's album, all others having been appropriated by real or pretended admirers in 1861. The black crape at the top of five loving epistles, and the broad, dark borders of five cards in the album, proved that ten of Miss Clemmie's admirers had fallen victims to Federal bullets, and that Yankee lead and steel were even more potent than Cupid's arrows. The females of the family being at the time residents of the elegant mansion, the book was returned to the centre-table with these lines—

TO MISS CLEMMIE

'Tis certain, Miss Clemmie, whether Fed or Confed,
In the plain course of nature you're destined to wed.
Some "Lord of Creation" will lovingly kneel,
And pour forth his tender and fervent appeal,
If the Feds and Confeds will cease this vain strife,
And leave a man living to make you his wife.

FED.

EPITAPH ON A FAITHFUL WIFE

By Augustus Barnard Longstreet [13]

HE SLEEPS by the side of his wife, of whom he never thought himself worthy, and who never thought herself worthy of her husband. In every innocent amusement of his life she went hand in hand and heart in

---

[12] *The Pictorial Book of Anecdotes and Incidents of the War of the Rebellion.* . . . Hartford, Connecticut (Hartford Publishing Company), 1866, p. 630.

[13] Carved on the tomb of Longstreet and his wife in St. Peter's Cemetery, Oxford, Mississippi; quoted in Wade's *Longstreet,* pp. 356-357. For biographical note, see p. 316, *supra.*

heart with him for over fifty-one years. Death was a kind visitor to them both.

CHANCE FOR A "LADY OF CHARACTER"

By Frazar Kirkland [14]

AMONG the documents left by the editors of the Memphis (Tennessee) *Appeal*, when they left that city, was the following gentle epistle from a secessionist woman, who had sent it to that paper for publication:

A CHALLENGE

where as the wicked policy of the president—Making war upon the South for refusing to submit to wrong too palpable for Southerners to do. And where as it has become necessary for the Young Men of our country, My Brother in the number to enlist to do the dirty work of Driving the Mercenary from our sunny South, whose soil is too holy for such wretches to tramp And whose atmosphere is too pure for them to breathe.

For such an indignity offord to Civilization I Merely Challenge any abolition or Black Republican lady of character if there can be such a one found among the negro equality tribe. To Meet me at Masons and dixon line: With a pair of Colt's repeaters or any other weapon they May Choose. That I may receive satisfaction for the insult.

Victoria E. Goodwin,
Springdale Miss April 27, 1861

THE ALMOST-TRAGEDY OF CARROLLTON [15]

A MOST extraordinary case came up yesterday before Justice Robinson of Carrollton. It grew out of one of the little gossiping by-plays of village life, and will furnish to our up-river neighbors "a laugh for a week, a joke for a month, and a good story forever."

It appears that a certain Madam *M.*, who is fair, young, and has a husband in California, considered herself vilely and villainously slandered by a Mr. *M.*, on the strength of a rumor put in circulation by a slave belonging to the masculine M., whose name, by the way, though commencing with the same letter, was far from being the same in sound or signification.

Goaded to madness by these calumnies, the lady undertook the defence of her own honor, and having no fear of "villainous saltpetre," she

[14] *Op. cit.*, p. 548.
[15] *The Southern Journal*, Monticello, Mississippi, August 17, 1850, p. [1].

appealed to that in her hour of anger. After the passage and re-passage of some hard messages and words, and moreover, after the masculine *M.* had heard the discharge of a gun, and the harmless rattle of some shot against a wood-heap, which gun, be it premised, was in the hands of the lady, and which wood-heap was near him, the masculine *M.*—he became alarmed, for he feared that the lady was practising with fire arms, for some deadly and dangerous intent. How prophetic were his fears, may be seen by the following belligerent missive:

CARROLLTON, August 4, 1850.

Mr. M——; SIR: Having been grossly and villainously slandered by you and your accomplice *M*aria, and furthermore molested by having spies set to watch my house at night, I demand satisfaction from you. I shall expect you to meet me with pistols as soon as possible.

——M——.

On the receipt of the e-pistol-ary document, *M.* the masculine, was overcome with great fear and trembling, and in haste he went to the distributor of justice for the town of *C*arrollton, and filed an affidavit against the fair calumniated.—In this affidavit, he charged that "on the fourth day of August, in the year of our Lord 1850, between the hours of 10 and 11 A.M., he received a challenge from Madam *M*——, in which he was invited to meet her in mortal strife, with pistols, against the peace of the State and the form of the statute in such case made and provided. Deponent therefore fearing that his life was in danger, prayed that she, the said Madam *M*—— be arrested, and dealt with according as the law directs."

Accordingly the lady was arrested and brought into court, to suffer disfranchisement and all the other penalties which the law affixes to the offence of which she stood charged.

The prosecution was conducted with much force and gravity, by lawyer Scott, and the defence was gallantly conducted by *M*essrs. Eliott of Lafayette and S. B. Reid of this city.

The facts stated in the narrative portion of our report, were brought out in evidence, and the case, after a lengthy hearing, was disposed of by binding over *M*adam *M*——to keep the peace for six months with the State of Louisiana, and more particularly with that very fractional portion of it whose fears were aroused by the fearful missive he received from the fair *M*adam *M*——.

In closing, we have to regret that, in consequence of a press of California matter, we have not space left for the speeches of counsel, and, more particularly, that of the youngest and most gallant of the three, which was, indeed, a forensic effort above all praise.

S. NEWTON BERRYHILL, THE "BACKWOODS POET"

"It is not through affectation," says the author of *Backwoods Poems*, "that I have given my book the title it bears. I chose this title in my boyhood, when I first conceived the design of publishing, some day, a book of poems. Nor is the title inappropriate. While I was yet an infant, my father, with his family, settled down in a wilderness, where I grew up with the population, rarely ever going out of the neighborhood for forty years. Save what I learned from books and newspapers, and from the conversation of those into whose society I was thrown—

> The little world in which I lived,
> Was all the world I knew.

"The old log school-house with a single window and a single door —described in one of my earlier pieces—was my *alma mater;* the green woods were my *campus;* and if I climbed Parnassus, 'twas not with Homer, 'by dint o' Greek,' but with trusty dogs, chasing the mottle-colored hare over the bush-covered hillock." [16]

Such a confession at once reminds one of Burns—

> That I for dear old Scotland's sake
> Some useful book or plan wad make,
> Or sing a sang, at least;

and this reminiscence is further strengthened by the author's simple admission of limited circumstances and opportunities, by his sturdy pride, and by his quiet trust in the power of native themes.

The hundred-odd closely printed double-column pages of *Backwoods Poems* bear out this modest Preface. The themes are homely and homefelt—local Indian legends, experiences of a pioneer boyhood, rural love, local politics and heroes, sectional patriotism, the Civil War, and the like. Without being slavishly imitative, almost every page is reminiscent of the good old poets of the Romantic Period—Ossian, Cowper, Burns, Wordsworth, Southey, Byron, Poe, Longfellow, Bryant, Whittier—notwithstanding the fact that he charges,

> Longfellow, Bryant, Whittier have sought
> To blacken us, *as British copyists ought*.[17]

[16] S. Newton Berryhill. *Backwoods Poems*. Columbus, Mississippi (Printed by Charles C. Martin, Excelsior Office), 1878.
[17] *Ibid.*, "The South's Response," p. 45.

In tone, most of the poems are sentimentally reminiscent, tender, or pathetic. A good number of patriotic pieces have a restrained ardor. Those humorous in spirit or treatment are the most attractive, and from these our selections have been made.

Two rustic courtship pieces—"Billy Boles, or the Shoemaker's Courtship," with its clever punning, and "In a Horn," with its high-spirited make-believe satire—are in the comic vein. "Betty Bell," with its huckleberry and persimmon dainties, and "Katy-Did," with love-making in the orchard, are a pair of pretty idyls. "Will You Come to the Bar" is a satire on the "doggery," or open saloon, of the Old South. "Tell Me Ye Winged Winds" turns out to be a descant on the inevitability of taxes. The social philosophy of "Uncle Sam Is Rich," and many of the economic ills and misadventures described therein, all symptomatic of the panic of 1857, might, with surprisingly few modifications, be applied to our own Year of Grace and the NRA. One of the chief comforts arising from the comparison, however, is our exemption from any regulation that

> petticoats to thirty yards
> Must lessen their dimensions.

I. IN A HORN [18]

Now, Tom, I wish you'd leave me;
I hate you in my sight;
I always thought you ugly—
Indeed a perfect fright.
You'd do in papa's cornfield
To scare away the crow—
But it is in a horn, Tom—
It's in a horn, you know.

What! kiss those horrid lips, sir,
That I can not see for hair!
I'd rather kiss a monkey,
Or hug a grizzly bear.
I wish you'd take your hat, Tom,
I wish that you would go—
But it is in a horn, Tom—
Just in a horn, you know.

[18] *Ibid.*, p. 44.

Pack up your gloves and vamose;
It is no use to woo;
For I will never marry
So plain a man as you.
I'm sure I wouldn't have kissed you,
But I thought 'twould make you go—
I'm talking in a horn, Tom—
Just in a horn, you know.

Don't put your arm around me—
I will not have it there;
And four and twenty kisses
Are more than I can bear.
O dear! the clock has struck eleven—
I wish that you would go—
But then it's in a horn, Tom—
All in a horn, you know.

II. KATY-DID [19]

O, Kate, you did, you know you did—
The fact you can't deny—
Let Harry squeeze your lily hand,
And kiss you on the sly—
Out where the red-cheeked peaches hung
And shed their fragrance round,
And mellow golden apples lay
Thick scattered on the ground.
O, Kate, you did, you know you did!
You needn't blush nor smile;
For 'mong the leafy branches hid,
I saw you all the while.

O, Kate, he did, you know he did,
While the purple sunset lay
Low in the west, and up the hill
Climbed the twilight shadows gray—
He pared a peach and threw the peel,
Which fell the letter K,
Then took your little hand in his,
And kissed your pout away.
O, Kate, he did, &c.

[19] *Ibid.*, p. 98.

O, Kate, you did, you know you did,
In the orchard linger long,
Till the round full moon rose in the east,
And I began my song—
Till Harry told the old, old tale
That maids have loved to hear,
Since the morning stars together sang .
In creation's natal year.
O, Kate, you did, &c.

WILLIAM WARD

A native of Litchfield, Connecticut (born August 23, 1823), William Ward moved at the age of sixteen to Columbus, Mississippi, to become a jeweler's and watchmaker's apprentice.[20] There he resided ten or twelve years, during which time he contributed poems and essays to the Philadelphia *Saturday Courier*. In 1850 he moved to Macon, Mississippi. In 1870 he became editor of the Macon *Beacon*. He died December 27, 1887. His poems, which have apparently not been collected, were published mostly in the Philadelphia *American Courier*, the Macon *Beacon*, and the New Orleans *Times-Picayune*.

The subject of "Katie Did" has intrigued several American poets, notably Philip Freneau ("To a Caty-Did," 1815) and Oliver Wendell Holmes ("To an Insect," 1831). In the latter's poem occurs the well-known epitome of the katy-did's song—

> Thou say'st an undisputed thing
> In such a solemn way.

In lightness of touch and delicate hints of domestic secrets Ward's poem is perhaps closest to Holmes's, though in its adumbration of a tender love idyl it also suggests the gentle pathos of Freneau's. Its closest neighbor for comparison is S. Newton Berryhill's, in this chapter.

[20] Biographical facts from Dabney Lipscomb's "William Ward, a Mississippi Poet Entitled to Distinction," *Publications of the Mississippi Historical Society*, vol. II (Oxford, 1899), pp. 22-42.

KATIE DID

By William Ward [21]

NAUGHTY Katie, saucy Katie,
  Is your secret aught to me
That you hide it, nor divide it,
  In a tree?
In the tree before the trellis,
  Where I have a secret hid,
And provokingly you tell us,
    Katie did,
    Katie didn't,
    Yes, she did,
    No, she didn't,
    Katie did.

Prithee, Katie, by what penance
  Are you nightly doomed to be
Trilling to the quiet tenants
  Of the tree,
Safely hidden from espial
  Of what Katie said or did,
That incessant, shrill denial,
    Katie did,
    Katie didn't,
    Yes, she did,
    No, she didn't,
    Katie did?

Little disputant, securely
  Ambushed, from intrusion free,
Don't I see you so demurely
  From the tree,
Peeping through the latticed branches,
  Where the moon its arrows slid,
Piping forth with cunning glances,
    Katie did,
    Katie didn't,
    Yes, she did,
    No, she didn't,
    Katie did?

[21] Quoted by Dabney Lipscomb, *op. cit.*, pp. 36-37.

Will you tell it, Katie, never?
  Must it still a secret be?
And forever and forever
  From the tree,
Will that answer shrill and lonely
  Mock us with the secret hid,
With these accents varied only—
    Katie did,
    Katie didn't,
    Yes, she did,
    No, she didn't,
      Katie did?

CHAPTER XVIII

DARKIES

THE Negro as a humorous character in fiction, poetry, and literary anecdote is of comparatively recent appearance.[1] Before *Uncle Remus,* various writers, among them William Gilmore Simms and Edgar Allan Poe from the South and Harriet Beecher Stowe and Stephen Collins from the North, tried their hand at portraying him. He was usually of the house or body servant class, and he spoke Gullah, or some dialect that passed for Gullah. In the Northern treatments of him he was sentimentalized; in the Southern, portrayed from the point of view of a slave-holding aristocracy that regarded him as a solemn appanage of the existing order. It was not until after the Civil War that a notable attempt was made to record his religious songs, F. S. Allen's *Slave Songs of the United States* (1867). This was so well done, however, that it has been reprinted recently without the necessity of editing.

The real "corn field" Negro, sentimentalized, certainly, and viewed, albeit intimately, from the white man's standpoint, but the authentic "corn field" Negro nevertheless, first makes his appearance in the poetry of a young Mississippian, but not before the 1870's. "The man who really discovered the literary material latent in negro character and in negro dialect," wrote the late C. Alphonso Smith, "was Irwin Russell (1853–79), of Mississippi. The two men best qualified to pass judgment, Joel Chandler Harris and Thomas Nelson Page, have both borne grateful testimony to Russell's genius and to their indebtedness to him. It is noteworthy also that the first

[1] "The great body of Southern antebellum humor centered about the poor white man. It may seem strange that the negro had so little place in the Literature of the Old South."

Thus remarks Dr. Jennette Tandy (*The Crackerbox Philosophers,* New York: Columbia Univ. Press, 1925, p. 66) and gives some of the probable causes.

marble bust that the State of Mississippi has placed in her Hall of Fame is that of Irwin Russell." [2]

Aside from their human interest as anecdotes, the following selections exemplify early attempts at giving humorous treatment of Negro character in Negro dialect between the thirties and the sixties. The first, from Hotchkiss & Company's *Louisiana and Mississippi Almanac* (1833), a street dialogue on the subject of diet, shows how far Negro dialect representation must go before it reaches the mellow richness of *Christmas Night in the Quarters* and *Uncle Remus*. Ingraham's illustration of Negro magniloquence, a fruitful subject of later humor, is quite as crude. The "Sambo and Cuffy" skit about "de armony," written in the fifties, is better, but the names of the interlocutors are still stereotyped. Thomas J. Shields' "A Negro Song," likewise of the fifties, is in the conventional language, and its subject matter, though it has piquancy, is really disguised social criticism of the white folks from the white folks' point of view.

The other selections, prose anecdotes for the most part, reveal various quirks and tricks of the Negro in his genial moods. One selection, from the "Diary of a Mississippi Planter," records the fecundity of one Amy and a few other matters relative to the life of a plantation. It is to be regretted that space does not permit representation of the simple annals of her husband Peyton, whose epitaph is given.

More to be regretted, however, is the fact that it seemingly did not occur to charming raconteurs of Negro yarns, the fathers and mothers of old men and women still living, to write down some of the family and plantation stories that one may yet hear. What they were like in Mississippi is beautifully illustrated by *The Tree Named John*,[3] which is composed of Negro stories (all of them in origin probably prior to and independent of *Uncle Remus*) heard by John Sale, of Columbus, Mississippi, on his family's plantation near Aberdeen.

STREET DIALOGUE—ON DIET [4]

Cuffee.—Wy, Cato, wat you goin to do wid dem are quash and dem are mutton chop wot you got in your basket?

---

[2] "Dialect Writers," in *The Cambridge History of American Literature*, vol. II, New York (The Macmillan Company), c. 1918, p. 353.
[3] Chapel Hill (University of North Carolina Press), 1931.
[4] *Louisiana and Mississippi Almanac, 1833*.

Cato.—Wy wot a fool question you ax, Cuff! I'm goin to eat 'em to be sure.

Cuff.—Eat 'em! My gosh! You die, Cato, sartin, you eat 'em.

Cato.—Wal pose I do, Cuff, wat den! I muss die when my time come, werrer no.

Cuff.—Yes, but you die fore you time come, sartin you take no better care you diup. De collar kill you sartin you eat dem are nassy quash and dem are ogis mutton chop.

Cato—[Looking black.] You tink so, Cuffee?

Cuff.—Tink so? Wy I no tink noffin bout it—I know so. I hab de proof all round me.—Twenty lebben my quaintance die sen de collar come, and dey all, widout deception eat one ting or anurrer. Ah, ha! wat you tink of dat Cato, ha?

Cato.—Dat is berry larmin, I muss say, Cuffee. But am you sure any on em eat de quash and de mutton chop?

Cuff.—Are I sure! Why how long you spute my word, Cato? I tell you dere was Sambo Cesar, he eat hearty meal o' pork an taters—nex day he was underneeve Potiphar's field.—Den dere was Pompey Ticklip, he eat a hearty dinner o' green peas and tinglingy bean, an in more dan tree hour he cotch a cramp, turn blue in de face, and foller arter Sambo Cesar. Den dere was Dinah Phillisy, a trong hearty wench as ebber walk on two leg, she pay no tention to her diup, but eat hot corn an succletash, got de diarry, and now she underneeve de sod too. Den moreober dere was Tom Traityshin, wot keep a wittlin house down suller, he eat seben hard bile eggs and a pown o' gammun for supper, dat dey needn't be loss, an fore mornin light he was wake up in tudder worl. Den moreover, besides, dere was—O loddy! dere was ebber so many ob 'em die wid eatin dis ting an dat ting an udder ting—I tell you, Cato, dat less you pay more tention to you diup, you sartin die sure as you lib.

Cato.—Wot mus I eat den, Cuffee?

Cuff.—Eat! Wy de safes way is to eat noffin at all, den you no spose youself.—

NEGROES—ARISTOCRATIC AND OTHERWISE

By J. H. Ingraham [5]

THERE are properly three distinct classes of slaves in the south. The first, and most intelligent class, is composed of the domestic slaves, or "servants," as they are properly termed, of the planters. Some of these

---

[5] *The Southwest*, Vol. II, New York (Harper and Brothers, Cliff St.), 1835, pp. 247-250. For note on Ingraham, see p. 73, *supra*.

both read and write, and possess a great degree of intelligence: and, as the negro, of all varieties of the human species, is the most imitative, they soon learn the language, and readily adopt the manners, of the family to which they are attached. It is true, they frequently burlesque the latter, and select the high-sounding words of the former for practice —for the negro has an ear for euphony—which they usually misapply, or mispronounce.

"Ben, how did you like the sermon today?" I once inquired of one, who, for pompous language and high-sounding epithets, was the Johnson of the negroes.—"Mighty obligated wid it, master, de 'clusive 'flections werry distructive to de ignorum."

In the more fashionable families, negroes feel it their duty—to show their aristocratic breeding—to ape manners, and to use language, to which the common herd cannot aspire. An aristocratic negro, full of his master's wealth and importance, which he feels to be reflected upon himself, is the most aristocratic personage in existence. He supports his own dignity, and that of his master, or "family," as he phrases it, which he deems inseparable, by a course of conduct befitting colored gentlemen. Always about the persons of their masters or mistresses, the domestic slaves obtain a better knowledge of the modes of civilized life than they could do in the field, where negroes can rise but little above their original African state. So identified are they with the families in which they have been "raised," and so accurate, but rough, are the copies which they individually present, of their masters, that were all the domestic slaves of several planters' families transferred to Liberia, or Hayti, they would there constitute a by no means inferior state of African society, whose model would be found in Mississippi. Each family would be a faithful copy of that with which it was once connected: and should their former owners visit them in their new home, they would smile at its resemblance to the original. It is from this class that the friends of wisely regulated emancipation are to seek material for carrying their plans into effect.

The second class is composed of town slaves; which not only includes domestic slaves, in the families of the citizens, but also all negro mechanics, draymen, hostlers, labourers, hucksters, and washwomen, and the heterogeneous multitude of every other occupation, who fill the streets of a busy city—for slaves are trained to every kind of manual labour. The blacksmith, cabinet-maker, carpenter, builder, wheelwright,—all have one or more slaves labouring at their trades. The negro is a third arm to every working man, who can possibly save money enough to purchase one. He is emphatically the "right-hand man" of every man. Even free negroes cannot do without them: some of them own several, to whom they are the severest masters.

"To whom do you belong?" I once inquired of a negro whom I had employed. "There's my master," he replied; pointing to a steady old negro, who had purchased himself, then his wife, and subsequently his three children, by his own manual exertions and persevering industry. He was now the owner of a comfortable house, a piece of land, and two or three slaves, to whom he could add one every three years. It is worthy of remark, and serves to illustrate one of the many singularities characteristic of the race, that the free negro, who "buys his wife's freedom," as they term it, from her master, by paying him her full value, ever afterward considers her in the light of property.

"Thomas, you are a free man," I remarked to one who had purchased himself and wife from his master, by the profits of a poultry yard and vegetable garden, industriously attended to for many years, in his leisure hours and on Sundays. "You are a free man; I suppose you will soon have negroes of your own."

"Hi! Hab one now, master." "Who, Tom?"—"Ol' Sarah, master." "Old Sarah! she is your wife." "She my nigger too; I pay master five hun'red dollars for her."

SAMBO AND CUFFY—A DIALOGUE

(Jackson, 1850) [6]

Sambo. What am de State buildin' dat new house for, Cuffy?

Cuffy. Did you eber hear dat anybody built a old house, nigger? Dat is de armony.

Sambo. What am dey gwine do wid it?

Cuffy. What am dey gwine do wid it? Put de guns ob de State, dat dey calls ahms, into it.

Sambo. Has dey enuf to fill up dat house?

Cuffy. Yawh! yawh! yawh! yoo maholey.*

Sambo. Does dey keep um loaded?

Cuffy. Does dey keep um loaded? Nigger, you mus' be a conteremptious ninny. Dey *was* loaded, but day's all *gone off!*

Sambo and Cuffy. Yawh! yawh! yawh!

[6] *Weekly Southron,* Jackson, Mississippi, July 12, 1850, p. 3.
* This, we understand, is Choctaw for "yes, perhaps so." Many negroes in this State understand Choctaw pretty well.—Editor *Southron.*

BANJO SONG

Recorded by B. L. C. Wailes [7]

[IN THE fall of 1856, B. L. C. Wailes, planter, man of affairs, geologist (author of *Report on the Agriculture and Geology of Mississippi, Embracing a Sketch of the Social and Natural History of the State*), and president of the Board of Trustees of Jefferson College, was voyaging upriver on the Memphis packet. In the evening, he says, the passengers were entertained by one of the negro servants aboard. The black minstrel, with the accompaniment of his banjo, sang variations of "Old Dan Tucker." Two stanzas Wailes kept in his head until he could write them down in his diary.]

> The biggest fool I ever did see
> Was a man what lived in Tennessee
> He put his shirt on over his coat
> And buttoned his trousers round his throat

> Old Parson Adams done his best
> To make himself an Iron chest
> He filled it full of bread & ham
> To carry him on to Promised land.

NOT THE DEVIL, BUT OLD JOHN

By J. F. H. Claiborne [8]

SOME years since a wedding being about to take place in a thinly settled neighborhood, it was necessary to send some twelve miles for an old negro fiddler, who was indispensable at every frolic, quilting, or house-raising for forty miles around. A wild, hilly, unsettled country lay between them.

The company gathered, the *Squire* performed the ceremony, drinks were passed around, and groups of various ages and interests formed in the house. At length some of the girls began to yawn; the pretty bride herself looked drowsy; a scraping of feet was heard in the gallery, and one or two impatient bucks, anxious to show their keeping, commenced shuffling, cracking their heels together and cutting the pigeon

[7] From the MS. diary of B. L. C. Wailes, October 18, 1856, through the kindness of Dr. Charles S. Sydnor, of the University of Mississippi, who has in preparation a biography of Wailes.

[8] "A Trip through the Piney Woods," first published in the *Mississippi Free Trader and Natchez Gazette*, 1841–42; reprinted in *Publications of the Mississippi Historical Society*, vol. IX. I have taken the liberty of abridging the story. For note on Claiborne, see p. 69, *supra*.

wing. *Still no fiddler came.* . . . A wedding without a fiddler was scarcely considered legal.

At length a party of six young men set out to hunt the fiddler.

About four miles distant stood an old waste house, and as they approached an infernal howling as from a hundred chained devils was heard, and occasionally by way of interlude the squeaking of a fiddle. The old house had long been reputed to be "haunted." . . . Davy Crockett himself couldn't have stood it; so they "turned tail and cut dirt" for the place they came from and reported that the devil had caught old John and was then at the haunted house dancing a breakdown with fifty she-wolves for his partners.

Fortified by deep draughts of whiskey, the whole party of menfolk, led by the Squire, mounted and rode to the place. At that moment the moon burst forth and within the building they saw the form of the old fiddler poised in the air playing a Virginia jig while a crowd of demons were leaping, bounding, and howling to the music. The Squire tried to exorcise the demons with the prayer book, left in his pocket after the marriage ceremony; but the howling . . . became terrible; the fiddling grew livelier, until suddenly the yell and din rose to such a tremendous key that the line paused, then broke in every direction, and the Squire, shouting "Devil take the hindmost!" mounted his "singe cat," and was the first to give the alarm to the terrified ladies.

Haggard, gloomy, and disappointed, the company returned to the spot next morning. There still stood the house—there leaped a dozen wolves up and down, panting for breath, their eyes red and fiery, their tails switching to and fro. And there on the joist was perched—not the Devil—but *Old John* himself.

He had been treed there, and in order to keep himself from going to sleep and falling into the mouths of the wolves, he had played till daylight.

A FIDDLER AND A PRAYING FOREMAN

By "A Mississippi Planter" [9]

I MUST not omit to mention that I have a good fiddler, and keep him well supplied with catgut, and I make it his duty to play for the negroes every Saturday night until 12 o'clock. They are exceedingly punctual in their attendance at the ball, while Charley's fiddle is always accompanied with Ihurod on the triangle, and Sam to "pat."

I also employ a good preacher, who regularly preaches to them on the Sabbath day, and it is made the duty of every one to come up

[9] "Management of Negroes upon Southern Estates," *De Bow's Review*, vol. X, New Series, vol. IV (New-Orleans, 1851), p. 625.

clean and decent to the place of worship. As Father Garritt regularly calls on Brother Abram, (the foreman of the prayer meetings,) to close the exercises, he gives out and sings his hymn with much unction, and always cocks his eye at Charley, the fiddler, as much as to say, "Old fellow, you had your time last night; now it is mine."

I would gladly learn every negro on the place to read the bible, but for a fanaticism which, while it professes friendship to the negro, is keeping a cloud over his mental vision, and almost crushing out his hopes of salvation.

A NEGRO SONG

For the *Natchez Courier*

By Thos. J. Shields, of Mobile, Alabama [10]

De ole Virginy nigger,
  He know a ting or two,
And whereber you may meet him
  I'll tell you what he do:—
He brag ob his own country—
  He is de "Upper Crust"—
Ob all de well-born darkies,
  "His family's de fust."
    We meet all kind ob darkie
    As o'er de world we go,
    De highest in de nation,
    And lowest ob de low.

De Norf' Carlina darkie,
  You can't catch him asleep,
He neber talk a great deal,
  But den he tink a heap;—
God bless dat same ole country,
  My brudders all lib dar,
A picking out de cotton,
  Or burning ob de tar:
    We meet all kind ob darkie, &c.

De Souf' Carlina nigger
  To *chivalry* belong—
He lub de "Ole Palmetto,"
  And sing de cornfield song.

[10] Natchez *Daily Courier*, January 19, 1853, p. [3].

Dat am de spunky nigger,
  Dat hab dem windy fights,
Wheneber he's contending
  For his own "Suddern Rights":
    We meet all kind ob darkie, &c.

Den dar's de Georgy darkie,
  Wid little common sense,
For, allers like his massa,
  He's "straddling ob de fence;"
But when he get to trading,
  Den he will hab his fun,
In swapping of "Ole Bullet,"
  He is "A, number one":
    We meet all kind ob darkie, &c.

De gay Alabamy nigger,
  Way down on Mobile Bay,
He lib on fish and oyster,
  And frolics all de day;
Dat am a sprightly darkie,
  Take him in any way—
But, at de game ob "Poker,"
  You cannot wid him play:
    We meet all kind ob darkie, &c.

De Massissippy darkie,
  He will "Repudiate,"
Wheneber he is cheated
  By *sharpers* ob de State;
And if you do insult him,
  Just look out for your life,
He'll chop you into "mince meat,"
  Wid dat ole Bowie knife:
    We meet all kind ob darkie, &c.

Wid Luziana darkie,
  I don't know what to do;
His missus may be Spanish—
  His massa may be Jew—
But den dis much is sartin,
  He spend his money free,

In treating ob de darkie
 Whoeber he may be:
  We meet all kind ob darkie, &c.

Dar's de Tennessee nigger,
 Wid open, honest heart—
Hab he an only hoe-cake,
 He'll gib his friend a part;
And share wid him his blanket
 While da make de whisky fly,
To treat de stranger darkie
 Dat want his lands to buy:
  We meet all kind ob darkie, &c.

De ole Kaintucky darkie,
 "Near Lexington" he stay;
And says he allers lib dar
 Until he come away;—
But dat is quite unsartin
 Wid darkies ob dat State,
Becase da allers come from
 "Scott, Jessamine or *Fayette":*
  We meet all kind ob darkie, &c.

De ole Missoury nigger,
 "A Benton man" he be,
Becase he tink dat darkie
 Will hab all de *soil free;*
Den dar's de *anti* nigger,
 Wid head a little higher,
Who, to kill off dat darkie,
 Did went for "Massa Geyer":
  We meet all kind ob darkie,
  As o'er de world we go,
  De highest in de nation,
  And lowest ob de low.

OSCEOLA, Mo., Jan. 6, 1853.

NATCHEZ RACES [11]

THE *fall* races prematurely opened on the starting ground (corner of
Commerce and Franklin streets,) near Perrin's fruit-stand last Friday
afternoon, without previous announcement.

[11] The *Courier*, Natchez, August 23, 1864, p. [3].

The competitors consisted chiefly of youngish colored volunteers. After considerable *nigging* and false starts from the "dead-line," scratches mostly were made between a chunkey "Double-Smut," and cream-colored "Long-shanks." The "scrouging" was heavy; but by the time Pearl street corner ("coming out place") was reached, Double-smut was "no whar." A variety of impromptu "goes" were then made by inferior "animals." In fact, few, if any "thorough-breds" were visible. Several fist-fights and "bandigos" followed with the usual chaff, and there is no knowing what else had happened, if spectators had not been favored with a *stretch* like (Rollo's)

> —"Ichabod Ide
> Had a good ride,
> And lost his pride."—

Something ahead of Cowper's famous Gilpin—(Jock of Islington?) —by "a citizen

> Of credit and renown."

Howbeit, as the racing "gin out" (several of the foot "cuffs" being "dead-blowed" with heeling it for the "fer corner,") it so chanced that Mynheer Schnickelfritzer's black breeding sow fresh from a fragrant gutter up-street, *greasefully* waddled to rear of that sun-burnt "krowd" all ripe for rascality. In a twinkling, Piggy's caudal app-*end*-age was grabbed by a juvenile Scip (-heigh-ho-) Africanus? And, from grip, optically spanning the space 'twixt head and tail, he leaped on his *Pig*-asus (Irish classic for Pegasus—Jupiter's "winged horse,") and

> —"To horse, my brave boys, and away!"

This was the even-season's "handicap,"—a stern reality, *bristling* with excitement.

What with the thumps and screeching of some fifteen or twenty noisy negro brats, several small white "fellers," a brace of dogs, shouts of armed men and passers by, the result may be imagined.

> Away went nigger, neck or naught,
> Away went boys and pig,
> Who little wot of being "rid"
> In *sich* a style by "nig."

In the words of an old racer, it was the "worstest kind of a scrub," and only a "quarter race," (such as Pharsalia or Metarie never had,) but as a little four year old said: "Oh, my! though wasn't it fun."

Heavy as "Bacon's Works" may be, no bacon (with his "back-up,") worked harder than piggy in question, towards the far corner.

It was a regular "sweep sticks," swiped and lathered as piggy was, nigger on back, over the gravel frantically "pegging away," with the motley troop in hot pursuit. Obstinacy however enters into the porcine nature, and that it was, which abruptly ended the contest—though hog distanced, *fat*-igued, hooted, huffed, tail-pinned and exacerbated beyond all swinish endurance, by the descendants upon Ham—at last "trew to natur," porky stopped short in his "hogs head"-long career, and presto! little nigger was "no whar." Two ebony shin-shanks twinkled in the air, as twilight "twithered" on the dusky "ground and lofty tumbling." While—like a second-hand cracked bomb-conic, on a quarter charge of powder from a short-stock gun—old sousy lumbered on leaving "little nig" with his nose in the mud. Night dropped its Natchez curtain on that sable scene.

> "The dogs did bark, the children screamed,
>   Up flew the windows all;
> And every soul cried out, well done!
>   As loud as he could bawl."

NEGRO RAFFLE

From the *Louisville Journal* [12]

IN MY tour through the Southern States, I have met with many amusing incidents, but do not remember anything that created so great an excitement for the time being as a "negro raffle," in the town of ——, in the State of Mississippi. Mr. ——, the owner of the boy, having a note to pay that day, and not having the wherewith to do it, was compelled to do what he gladly would not have done. The boy to be raffled was a smart, intelligent lad of about 18 years of age. He went by the name of Bill. There was 80 chances, with "three dice," at $10 per chance. I was present when the affair came off; there remained one chance, which I took and gave to Bill on condition that he would throw the dice himself and "shake like oxen." Bill rolled his eyes in an astonished and astonishing manner, and after a hearty wha! wha! wha! in which he displayed two frightful rows of ivory, opening a mouth "like the break of day from east to west," with a low bow, said: "I'll try, massa." As may be supposed, the scene became highly exciting.

The raffling commenced. Bill looked on unconcerned at anything but the idea of leaving his old master. When the chances were all raffled off but the last, Bill took the box; previously to throwing, however, he was offered $100 for his chance; the highest throw yet made being 46, which stood a "tie" between two individuals, but Bill was no "*compromise man;*" he refused the offer, saying "de whole hog or noffin," and made his first throw which was 13. His second was 16. Bill stopped scratching his head, threw again, and up came 18. It was declared off that "Bill was high and free;" and such a shout I never heard in all my life. Bill hardly knew what to do with himself. In a moment, however, he asked the whole party to drink, and no man in ——, 'tis said, ever refused an invitation of the kind except one, and he died soon after; so says *tradition*.

Bill's success induced him to try another speculation of "the same sort," believing that he could do, as a *free man*, as much as he had done; he proposed to set himself up again for a "raffle," and as he had won before, he thought it would be no more than fair that he should put the price at $600 this time. The chances were soon taken, Bill reserving but one chance to himself. He pocketed $590, and the sport again commenced. Bill's original owner and himself were the two highest again, and in throwing off, Bill lost. It proved a very fortunate speculation for Bill and his master both. The master had made $800 clear, and Bill had cleared $590, and remained with his kind master.— They started for home together, the master declaring that no money could induce him to part with him again, unless he was willing to leave, but promised him, if he would be as faithful to him as he always had been, until he was 21, he should have his freedom. They were both well contented, and every one present was satisfied that he had got his money's worth.

"PLEASE WHIP THE BEARER AND OBLIGE"

By T. W. Caskey [13]

A WIDOW who owned a large cotton plantation and lived in a fine, old-fashioned, Southern, country mansion, employed an over-seer to superintend her business. The cluster of cabins, called the negro quarters, was about half a mile from the lady's residence. She kept a few do-

[13] F. D. Srygley, *Seventy Years in Dixie, Recollections and Sayings of T. W. Caskey*, pp. 281-283.

mestic servants at her home, and the over-seer lived near the "quarters" and had charge of all her other negroes. Among the servants she kept about her own residence were two boys—one of them a shrewd mulatto who drove her carriage, and the other a thick-headed black boy who chopped wood, cultivated her garden and kept her front yard and lawn in good order.

When any of her domestic servants needed to be whipped, she merely wrote a note to the over-seer and sent it by the one that had been condemned to the lash, saying: "Please whip the bearer and oblige," etc.

The mulatto carriage driver carried one note and took his whipping, but the second time he was requested to carry a note to the over-seer, he suspected the meaning of it, perhaps because he knew he needed a whipping, and concluded to send a substitute. So he hunted up the thick-headed wood-chopper and said to him:

"See yere, boy! Ole Missus say how you got ter fotch dis yere note to de boss!"

The boy was glad to get off from work for a trip to the "quarters," supposing the note was merely a matter of some general instruction which "ole Missus" wanted to give "de boss" about business matters. But when "de boss" ordered him to prepare for the whipping, the real meaning of it all began to penetrate his thick head. He protested that he had done nothing to be whipped for, and declared it was "dat yaller nigger what ort to be lashed," but the over-seer was accustomed to such protestations of innocence, and hence paid no attention to what he said, but whipped him and sent him back.

"A 'POSSUM SORTER SQUAR' LIKE"

By T. W. Caskey [14]

I bought from a negro boy, in the days of slavery, at Jackson, Mississippi, what he said were two 'possums. Many masters allowed their slaves large liberty, and even encouraged them, in such trafficking, on their own account. One of the so-called 'possums was very large, the other quite small. The smaller one had been cut off at both ends— head and tail. I asked the "nigger" why he had thus shorn it of its fair proportions, and he said:

"Well, boss, I had ter cut off 'is head, 'cause I squashed it up monst'us bad w'en I kill 'im, an' mos' folks don't like 'possum tail much nohow, an' I cut dat off too so de 'possum'd look sorter squar' like."

[14] *Ibid.*, pp. 114-118.

Satisfied with this plausible lie, I paid the price and took the 'possums. I always knew that an experienced and well-trained negro could lie as adroitly as a white man, but I confess I was not expecting to find such originality and ingenuity in a mere child, of either race, as a liar, in an emergency like this.

By chance, Dr. Mitchell, a local scientist of some note, dined with us on the day we ate the abridged animal. When we had completely demolished the thing, except one piece which still remained in the dish, I discovered some peculiarity about the bones on my plate, of which there were not a few. So I said:

"Doctor, these don't look like 'possum bones."

He looked attentively at the bones on his own plate for a moment, and then said:

"All of you please pass your bones to me."

He was evidently getting interested. We all watched him in breathless suspense. He placed the bones together, studied them attentively for several minutes, and reluctantly accepted the only conclusion that was consistent with his knowledge of "boneology" and the facts before his eyes. Finally he said:

"Parson, this thing was a cat."

Perhaps he stated it in even stronger terms than that. He probably used a vigorous adjective just before the word "thing," which it would be an offense to pious ears to repeat. But suppose he did, what of it? I need not give his exact language, if I but state clearly his conclusion, which I have done. Under the excitement of the moment he should have been allowed more latitude, in the selection of adjectives, than I have a right to claim.

I have had many years in which to formulate suitable language to express an idea which burst upon his mind like a clap of thunder from a clear sky. And yet I cannot feel that I have really made any great improvement upon his language.

His conclusion created a panic at the table. Mrs. Caskey beat a hasty retreat, the children laughed, the doctor looked non-plused, and I vowed vengeance upon the negro. After the first shock of surprise and mortification, the practical elements of my nature asserted themselves. It was plain to see that apologies were useless. The cat was all eaten but one piece, and there could be no place found for repentance. Having set my hand to the plow, I was not the man to turn back. It was needless to hesitate or falter at that stage of the case. Procrastination is the thief of time. I wavered no longer, but boldly stuck my fork into the last remaining piece of the misrepresented animal, and quietly finished my dinner.

JOHN TOOK HIS HAT AND JUMPED THE FENCE

By W. C. Smedes and T. A. Marshall [15]

WILLIS (a slave) states, at about one o'clock on the night the murder was committed, John [the accused] came to the shanty where they both slept, and John called Nathan out to take a drink with him, and Nathan soon returned, but John went off, and he did not see him any more until about one hour before daybreak next morning; that, on the day the inquest was held over the body, he saw a number of persons going toward the dead body, and John asked him, witness, where all these people were going to, when he replied that they were going to have a jury and make all the railroad hands go before them and put their hands on the dead body, and that blood would follow the hand of the murderer; that John then took off his cap and asked Nathan to take care of it . . . jumped over the fence about the shanty, and went off, running.

"SHE CAME NOT IN MOURNING WEEDS"

By Henry S. Foote [16]

[A NEGRO slave was condemned to death. He asked that his wife be permitted to see him before he died. Foote interceded with the woman's master. While she was awaiting the master's decision, "She was evidently in the deepest agony of soul. . . . *The blood poured from both nostrils.*" Deeply touched, her master granted the request.] A few weeks elapsed before the convict expiated upon the scaffold the enormous crime which he was accused of having perpetrated. A vast multitude was in attendance on this occasion, of all classes, colors, and conditions. Among others the bereaved wife came to behold the taking away of the life of one who had been to her a source of so much solicitude and so much domestic beatitude. She came not in mourning weeds; she came not shedding tears of nuptial commiseration, and refusing to be comforted. She came not alone, with tremulous step and heart-breaking agony. But she came dressed forth in gay habiliments; with elastic step and hope-gilded visage; and attended by one who so soon as this hanging-scene should be over, was to supply the place of him whom she was about to lose forever.

[15] "John (a Slave) v. the State," *Reports of Cases Argued and Determined in the High Court of Errors and Appeals of the State of Mississippi*, Boston (Charles C. Little and Joseph Brown), 1851, pp. 571-572. [24 *Mississippi*, Annotated Edition, St. Paul (West Publishing Company), 1909.] For this citation I am personally indebted to Professor Charles S. Sydnor, University, Mississippi.

[16] *Bench and Bar*, pp. 101-102. For note on Foote, see p. 159, *supra*.

"IGNO'ANCE OF DE CO'T"

Scene: Biloxi, Mississippi

By Minnie Walter Myers [17]

Judge. What about this case—have you a lawyer to defend you?
Negro. No, sah.
Judge. What are you going to do about one?
Negro. Well, Jedge, Ah went out an' insulted one, an' he tol' me jes' to come in an' th'o' myself on de igno'ance of de co't.

FROM *DIARY OF A MISSISSIPPI PLANTER* (1840–63)

By Dr. M. W. Philips [18]

July 4, 1840. Holiday. Much folks drunk today, reckon so. Patriotism will tell! Our folks all home, and all sober, "case in for one resin, jest case we hasn't got nohow, anything wha fa make drunk come."

October 9, 1846. Amy gave birth to a negro "gall baby" this morning about 2 o'clock.

May 18, 1853. Amy gave birth to 3 girls between 12 and 1 o'clock this morn.

Sunday, July 10, 1853. Peyton is no more. Aged 42. Though he was a bad man in many respects, yet he was a most excellent field hand, always at his post. On this place for 21 years. Except for the measles and its sequence, the injury rec'd by the mule last Nov'r and its sequence, he has not lost 15 days work, I verily believe, in the remaining 19 years. I wish we could hope for his eternal state.

June 1, 1862. Amy gave birth to a girl yesterday, "Rebecca," 19th child.

---

[17] *Romance and Realism of the Southern Gulf Coast*, p. 126.
[18] Ed. by F. L. Riley, *Pub. Miss. Hist. Soc.*, vol. X (1909).

CHAPTER XIX

THE FOURTH ESTATE[1]

THE first newspaper of our region was apparently *Le Moniteur de la Louisiane* (New Orleans, 1794). In Mississippi (Territory then) it was the *Mississippi Gazette* (Natchez, 1799); in Alabama, the *Mobile Centinel,* actually printed at Fort Stoddart (May 23, 1811), because Mobile was then in Spanish territory. The *Mississippi Gazette,* edited by B. M. Stokes, was a foolscap sheet printed on a press bought from Andrew Marschalk, the first printer of Mississippi. Its rival, *Green's Impartial Observer* (of which the Library of Congress has the issue for January 24, 1801), was short-lived. By 1808 there were four newspapers in Mississippi, all at Natchez. Other early Natchez periodicals were *The Natchez,* a newspaper, and *The Ariel* (1825), a literary magazine, edited by James K. Cook. At Woodville, in 1812,[2] was founded the *Republican,* which is still running. The *Mississippi Free Trader* (founded in 1835), edited by J. F. H. Claiborne, Forbes, and L. A. Besançon, and the *Courier* (1837), issued weekly, tri-weekly, or daily until 1860, were the most influential Natchez papers. At Vicksburg, *The Whig,* a daily, was published between 1840 and 1860. *The Mississippian,* first established at Vicksburg, then moved to Jackson, was edited by H. S. Foote and E. Barksdale. In Alabama, early newspapers were the Huntsville *Republican* (1816), the Mobile *Register* (1821, still running), and the Tuscaloosa *Independent Monitor* (1836). In the Alabama-Mississippi-Louisiana region as a whole, the most widely read ante-bellum newspapers were the Natchez *Free Trader* and *Courier,* the Mobile *Register,* and the New Orleans *Picayune* and *Delta.* All these papers clipped liberally from one another and from other papers of national scope, such as the St. Louis *Reveille* and

---

[1] Facts chiefly from Dunbar Rowland's article, "Newspapers," in *Encyclopedia of Mississippi History,* 2 vols., Madison, Wis., 1907, vol. II, p. 860; and Thomas M. Owen's *History of Alabama and Dictionary of Alabama Biography,* vol. II, p. 1075.
[2] Rowland, *op. cit.,* article "Woodville," says "first issue was Sat., Dec. 2, 1823."

Porter's New York *Spirit of the Times*. Apparently their editors were members of one great fraternity, and jibed and robbed and fought and helped one another as their brethren do to-day.

That they sometimes fought and always needed fraternal sympathy and coöperation is only too apparent from reading their news columns and their editorial comments to-day. Theirs was a fighting occupation. One paper, at Grenada, Mississippi, in the thirties, called itself (not inappropriately) *The Bowie Knife*. During the twenty-two-year life of the Vicksburg *Tri-Weekly Sentinel* (1838–1860), five of its editors came to violent ends on account of personal difficulties resulting from editorial utterances. Among gentlemen of the lower South, the only proper redress for libel, the most manly rejoinder to adverse personal criticism, the most effective reply to political differences, was to go out and shoot an editor. In a more genial mood, the gentleman might consider a flogging more humane if considerably more troublesome. These heady days of direct action also made editors as restless as other men, and they gallivanted off to California with the other forty-niners and wrote back tall tales for their papers.

Possibly the only subject on which they could get together among themselves, or with their patrons, was abolition, Yankees, and the War. The war, pulling everybody, from editor to printer and printer's devil, into the ranks of defence, put an abrupt period to most of their papers. In Mississippi, for example, of fifty papers running in 1860, only fourteen were eking out a troublesome existence in 1865. Two of these, the Vicksburg *Citizen* and the Natchez *Courier,* suffered the ignominy of running under supervision by Federal officers. From the latter, the present book, in the chapter "Negroes," extracts a mock-heroic account of "Natchez Races" in 1864.

RESORT TO VIOLENCE UPON THE PERSONS OF EDITORS[3]

ILLEGAL PROCEEDINGS—RESORT TO VIOLENCE—RESPECT FOR THE LAWS—BAD EFFECT OF PUBLISHING THE DETAILS OF STREET ENCOUNTERS, &C. &C.

SOME friends of ours have made request that we should publish a statement of some violent proceedings between Mr. Kendall, a mem-

[3] *Mississippi Free Trader and Natchez Weekly Gazette,* Thursday, March 19, 1840, p. 1.

ber of our legislature, and Dr. Hagan, editor of the Vicksburg Sentinel.
With feelings of ardent friendship to our chivalrous cotemporary and
of friendship to the other party, we have forborne saying any thing
about either.

With regard to a resort to violence upon the persons of editors, we
are very much of the opinion of the editor of the Boston Herald,
who, in speaking of a personal attack made by two brothers in Grand
Gulf upon an editor who had spirit enough to turn the tide of victory
against the stronger and attacking party, thus expresses himself:—

"Editors generally are very peaceable of disposition, and remarkable
for the urbanity of their manners and generosity of heart, and desire
to preserve respected and unsullied the laws; but, as is seen, when
attacked by ruffians, they possess enough of the 'bone and muscle' to
give 'Peter his due.' Heaven preserve us from ever living in Mississippi, if such is the mode of 'conducting business' in that quarter, and
if editors or any other class are obliged to defend themselves otherwise, than with the pen or in a court of law."

As a general rule, we shall refuse to give publicity to details of
street fights and other violent encounters, unless the death of some
one concerned shall make the occurrence a matter of general interest
and publicity.

The resort to personal violence upon the editorial fraternity is about
as wise a proceeding as to attack a hornet's nest with the naked hands.
However heavy may be the war club, the pen is still heavier—and
the blow which it inflicts is seen by thousands of eyes, and has often-
times a poison in its hurt which

"Outvenoms all the worms of Nile."

It is due to the public press to show a deep respect to the laws and
the wholesome morals of society, as well as the decencies of life.
A violation of individual and private character should be followed by
the immediate application of those legal penalties which alone are the
true correctives of any evil of this nature.

FLOGGING AN EDITOR [4]

SOME years ago, a populous town, located towards the interior of
Mississippi, was infested by a gang of blacklegs, who amused themselves at times, when they could find nobody else to pluck, by preying
upon each other. A new importation of these sporting gentry excited
some alarm among the inhabitants, lest they should be completely
over-run; they determined therefore on their expulsion. A poor wretch

[4] Natchez *Daily Courier*, January 25, 1853, p. [1].

of a country editor, who was expected, by virtue of his vocation, to take upon himself all the responsibilities from which others might choose to shrink, was peremptorily called upon by his "patrons"—that is, those who paid him two dollars a year for his paper, and therefore presumed that they owned him, body and soul—to make an effort towards the extermination of the enemy. The unfortunate editor, being gifted with about as much brains as money—skull and purse both empty— said at once that he would indite a "flasher," one that would undoubtedly drive the obnoxious vermin into some more hospitable region. And when his paper appeared, it was a "flasher" sure enough.

In the course of his observations he gave the initials of several of the fraternity, whom he desired to leave town as soon as possible, if they had the slightest desire to save their bacon.

The next morning, while the poor scribe was comfortably seated in his office, listlessly fumbling over a meagre parcel of exchanges, he heard footsteps on the stairs, and presently an individual having accomplished the ascent, made his appearance. His first salutation was slightly abrupt.

"Where is the editor of this dirty lying paper?"

Now, aside from the rudeness of this opening interrogatory, there were other considerations that induced the editor to believe there was trouble on foot. The personage who addressed him bore a cowhide in his hand, and, moreover, seemed to be exceedingly enraged. This was not all; he recognized in him a distinguished leader of the sporting fraternity, with whose cognomen he had taken very irreverent liberties. It was without the slightest hesitation, therefore, that he replied to the introductor's query—

"I don't know."

"Do you belong to the concern?"

"No, indeed, but I presume the editor will be in soon."

"Well," said the visitor, "I will wait for him." And suiting the action to the word, he composedly took a chair, picked up a paper, and commenced reading.

"If I meet him," said the frightened knight of the scissors and quill, "I will tell him there is a gentleman here who wishes to see him."

As he reached the foot of the stairs, in his hasty retreat, he was accosted by another person, who thus made himself known:

"Can you tell me where I can find the sneaking rascal who has charge of this villainous sheet?" producing the last number of "Freedom's Echo, and the Battle-Axe of Liberty."

"Yes," replied the editor, "he is up there in the office now, reading, with his back to the door."

"Thank you," exclaimed the stranger, as he bounced up the stairs.

"I've got you, have I!" ejaculated he, as he made a grasp at his brother in iniquity, and they came crashing to the floor together.

As the combatants, notwithstanding the similarity of their vocation, happened to be unacquainted with each other, a very pretty quarrel ensued. First one was at the top, then the other; blow followed blow, kick followed kick, oath followed oath, until, bruised, exhausted, and bloody, with features resembling Deaf Burke after a two hours' pugilistic encounter, there was by mutual consent a cessation of hostilities. As the warriors sat on the floor contemplating each other, the first comer found breath enough to ask:—

"Who are you? What did you attack me for?"

"You abused me in your paper, you scoundrel!"

"Me! I'm not the editor. I came here to flog him myself!"

Mutual explanations and apologies ensued, and the two mistaken gentlemen retired to 'bind up their wounds.' As the story comes to us, the distinguished individual whose vocation it was to enlighten the world by the aid of that great engine, the public press, escaped scot free.

"O! CARRY ME BACK!" [5]

COL. FALCONER, formerly editor of the Holly Springs Gazette, departed for California about two years since. He announced when on the eve of departure, that he had become poor and ragged during his editorial career—that his white hat had gone to seed, that his elbows were visible through the cloth of his coat, and that his naked toes were exposed to the chilling blast and howling storm. From the valley of the far off Sacramento, *golden* tidings were wafted to our disconsolate craftsman, and instanter he determined to fly to that land, and amass a princely fortune, and return to Mississippi with "a pocket full of rocks."

The Colonel has returned to Mississippi. He announced his arrival at Victoria, Texas, as follows, in a letter to a gentleman in this State:

"Our sojourn in the mines was just 12 months, and though most of the company have been closely engaged in mining during that entire period, I assert without fear of successful contradiction, that not more than twenty have been lucky enough to make a sufficient amount to enable them to return home. No men have labored more diligently, or submitted to greater hardships and privations, than the 'Western Rovers,' and I have no doubt that they have been as successful as most of the companies that have gone to California. Some of the

[5] *The Southern Journal*, Monticello, Mississippi, March 8, 1851, p. [2].

company have died, some have returned, and others are on their
way home, but a large majority are still in California, waiting for
some lucky turn in the wheel of fortune to enable them to raise a
sufficient sum to pay their expenses back home.

"As for my part, Messrs. Editors, if the *'Golden Fever'* should ever
again attack me, if I should have a lucid moment during such attack,
I shall insist that my friends have me put in a straight jacket, and
sent as early as practicable to an insane hospital. If the spirit of adventure should again trespass on my sober judgement, I shall go to
New Orleans, rent me an office, and spend the money I have to spare
in the purchase of lottery tickets, where the chances are equally favorable for realizing a fortune as mining in California, without having to
travel around so much of the 'elephant.' "

And the Helena (Ark.) True Issue announces his passage up the
river to Memphis, as follows:

"T. A. Falconer, formerly editor of the Holly Springs Gazette, who
has been in California nearly two years, passed up the river a few
days since, with the crown of his hat out, flat broke. Well, we suppose Tom has no money; but he has friends, good and true, wherever
he is known. He is worthy of them. Mr. Filmore should appoint him
to some office, if he wants honest men about him."

Alas! poor Tom.

PUFF EXTRAORDINARY [6]

When George W. Kendall, assisted by J. B. Marshall and Denis
Corcoran, was imparting vivacity and spirit to the *New Orleans Picayune,* and winning for it a *prestige* it has never relinquished, he was
called upon by an old friend, whom he seemed very much delighted
to see, and who expressed similar gratification to see him. The conversation ran upon general subjects, but had not progressed far, in a natural, unconstrained, familiar way, before Kendall intimated that he
rather thought his friend had married since he had last seen him, and
inquired for the "old woman." The very unexpected response was
that she was dead. Kendall's friend then went on with a very florid
eulogy of the virtues and excellence of the deceased, and lamented,
with Graves-like gravity, his "sainted Maria." The *contretemps* of
which he had been guilty, rather set George back a little; but it was
all right when his friend said, in the most serious manner possible, and
as a thing not to be denied, "Come, George, can't you give the old
woman a puff?" He doubtless desired to have a feeling obituary notice
written, and took that quaint way of explaining his wish. It need hardly

[6] *The Southern Monthly,* vol. I, No. 2 (Memphis, Tennessee, October, 1861), p. 152.

be said that the *puff* was written, and was exceedingly expressive, but not so *emphatic* as was the loud and prolonged laughter that pealed through the old sanctum, No. 72 Camp street, when the bereaved husband retired. "George, can't you give the old woman a puff?" lasted Kendall a week.

A NEW WAY OF RAISING THE WIND[7]

THERE are various ways of "raising the wind," beside those resorted to by Jeremy Diddler, who by his ready expedients must have been a "son of the sod." I will relate one that is an actual occurrence. About four years ago I lived in the small town of Panola, on the banks of the Tallahatchie, in the State of Mississippi. I superintended the mechanical department of one of those great institutions yclept a "weekly newspaper," and had in my employment an Irishman, who acted not only as compositor but as pressman. Mike (by such name alone I knew him) was full of fun and fond of "the craythur." He took especial delight in expatiating on the importance of having an advertisement at the head of a column to the only two "grocery" keepers in the place, and frequently received a *douceur* for his seeming interest in the prosperity of each. One hot summer's day, while Mike was busily engaged at the press, Mr. L——, one of the grocers, entered the office with a "new advertisement," and requested that it should be placed at the head of the column. Mike heard him, and immediately stopped the press.

"What's that ye says, Mr. L——?" called out the "Exile of Erin."

"Place it at the top of the column, under 'new advertisements,'" replied Mr. L——.

"It can't be did," said Mike drily.

"Why not?" inquired Mr. L——.

"Bekase," said Mike, smiling, "Mr. B——, (the other grocer,) has had the gintlemanly kindness to pay us for our throuble by sinding a bottle of 'the best in the house,' an av koorse his 'advee' goes at the top in preference to yours. I'm sorry for it, you know, but he who pays the printher gets the best place."

"All right," said Mr. L——, laughing; "I'll send over a 'bottle of the best' and a box of cigars."

"Well, thin, if you do," said Mike, "be the powers of Moll Kelly— the Lord have marcy on her soul—but your 'advee' 'll go at the top as shure as my name's Mike."

Mr. L—— went off and sent the bottle and cigars as promised. I asked Mike why he had resorted to an untruth, as Mr. B—— had

[7] *Ibid.*, pp. 153-154.

made no such bargain—in fact, had no advertisement in the paper at the time.

"Och! don't throuble yourself," replied Mike; "it was only an expadient to get the liquor for nothin'."

Perhaps on some future occasion I may "pluck from memory" a few more of the same sort.   Your X-eyed servant,   I. R. ONY.

You will find, says John B. Gough, in London a class of people hardly ever heard of here. They are Jacks-of-all-trades. Ask them what they do. Why, they hold horses, are ready to black boots, write for the paper, run errands, draw up law documents, sweep the crossings, write your letters, &c., &c., reminding you very much of the character of "Belladonna." A man without one ounce of superfluous clothing or flesh upon him, is asked: "Well, my man, what can you do?" "Well, zur, I kin do most anything, zur." "Well, what in particular?" "Well, zur, furst, I'm ov a lit'ary character; does more than that, zur; carries out the newspapers; I 'elps to spread knowledge han hinformation, han no lit'ary character does more than that, zur; an' I goes into the mercantile sometimes; hin dry weather I sells clothes-pins; hin wet weather I goes into the sanitarius, and sweeps the streets, han of nights, partic'larly, I turns wagabond, han I goes to the theater, han I ham a hactor—I ham a pantomime hactor, zur; I ham just hout o' my last hengagement. In fifty-three hengagements I performed the 'ind legs of the helephant;

"You needn't laugh, zur, there is a great deal of genius hin doing that; but I lost my sit'ation."

"You did. How did you lose it?"

"I met with han haccident. The chap what had done the fore legs, me han 'im 'ad a fight while we was hin the helephant, han the consequences was we hupset the whole concern. Oh, my! 'ow the people did laugh, and 'ow the manager did swore! He said he 'ud 'ave no more stupid numeraries hif they was not peaceable han legitimate, han so I got my discharge."

I read the other day, in the *Memphis Argus,* the account of an individual who, like a bee-hunter watching a bee-line, had the curiosity to bend his prying eyes on the repeated flights of a wild goose, till he followed the uncivilized representative of the loquacious *biped,* (which *answer*ing a patriotic impulse, saved the citadel of Rome,) to her nest, that had been with goose-like prudence erected in a hollow stump of twenty feet elevation—the stump, not the nest. Clambering by means of a vine to the summit of the stump, the old goose being gone, the new goose let himself down to secure the eggs, when the frail structure gave way and the spoiler found himself in a tight place. This is an eggstraordinary story, and decidedly rich "on the goose." The misfortune is that the fellow ever got out, because I have heard of several similar stories, in every one of which the chief actor proved himself a goose. A venturous young Nimrod once got into bear-hole, and could never raise a pair of whiskers afterward. The goose-hunter deserved to be converted into a quill-driver!

NEW YEAR'S PRAYER [8]

Postscript. Reader! just remember
You have passed quite through December,
And from cloudy Nova Zembla
    Cometh Winter.
Think of him who coineth news,
Think of all your little dues,
And to buy his baby shoes,
    Pay the Printer.

And forget ye not the Carrier,
He has been no idle carrier,
Let there linger then no barrier
    'Tween your *chink*
And his pocket. For his rhymes,
Give him dollars, bits, and dimes,
So God give you better times,
    Prays Phil. Phlink.

A MISSISSIPPI CORRESPONDENT "DOWN ON HIS LUCK!" [9]

MADISON COUNTY, Miss., July 1st, 1850.

My Dear Sir.—I have now been a subscriber to your invaluable paper for some four or five years, and during that whole time have read it with more pleasure than any other paper I receive. I have never complained of anything in it, and have always looked forward from Saturday to Saturday with more pleasure than to the arrival of any other mail. I

[8] The Woodville *Republican,* January 2, 1847. Given me by Professor Charles S. Sydnor, University of Mississippi, who has in preparation a study of the culture of the old Natchez region.

[9] *Spirit of the Times,* vol. 20 (August 10, 1850), p. 294.

say I have never complained: but now I mean to do it. You have given me cause of complaint. My grievance is hard to bear, and you will say so when I state it. It is this; viz.:—

Item 1st: In the summer of 1847, I sent you, from the Hot Springs, in Virginia, an account of the best thing that took place in the mountains that summer. A capital anecdote; the best of the season. You never noticed either it or me.

Item 2d: Last fall I sent you decidedly the best thing, and one which created more laughter, more real fun, than anything that ever took place in this county. That, also, you neither published or acknowledged.

These are my charges against you. I, with my usual modesty, attributed the whole blame to myself, to my want of talents, to my inability to write intelligibly; until yesterday I received your paper of the 15th June, in which are three *sorter* anecdotes, from Cincinnati, by "Qui Vive," and another immediately below, by "Phi Ro." Now, if you call these pieces better than mine, if *they* are anecdotes, I have nothing more to say; I "pass out." Why, sir, "I say it, who should not say it," that "Qui Vive's" small attempt is no more to be compared to my anecdotes "than I to Hercules." And "Phi Ro" is "nowhere" in the race.

I will leave it to you yourself (provided you take the same view of it I do) whether I have not made out my case against you. If you are unwilling to decide it yourself, I will leave it to arbitration; provided "my brother Tom and my partner are the arbitrators."

With much respect, and many wishes for your continued prosperity, I subscribe myself   Your sincere friend and   SUBSCRIBER.

P.S.—I do not put my name to this, for fear you may think it impertinent; in which spirit, I assure you, upon my honor, it is not intended. By turning to your subscription list, you will be able to find it. If I were to put my name to it, and you were to take it in a wrong spirit (in one in which it is not intended), you might get after me, by name, with a sharp stick with a lightning bug to the end of it; in which category I have no ambition to appear, being, by nature, habit, and education, exceedingly modest and unobtrusive.

———

Note by the Editor.—Of the two communications referred to, we think the first one was an account of a singing master who taught school in winter and kept a stallion in the summer. The success of both man and horse was highly flattering, but the details were quite too spicy for our columns. The other communication we do not remember, but presume it is included in a lot of fifty or more which we have carefully stowed away, while about as many others are now passing from hand to hand among the queer ones of our acquaintance, under solemn promises to be returned to us.

By the way, it must have occurred to any attentive reader or correspondent of this paper that, for nearly two years past, we have refrained almost altogether from alluding to rejected articles. Many of our correspondents themselves solicited the adoption of this course. Of the great number of original communciations received at this office, not two in five are ever published. We should like to hear from our Mississippi friend again. Any article of his which he would venture to read to a company of ladies and gentlemen, we will publish with pleasure, if the subject is neither religious nor political.

LOOK OUT FOR BREAKERS [10]

One of our good citizens has in preparation for the press a work with the following jaw breaking title:

"Scenography of the Celestial Regions, being a treatise on Diosphantasmegorology and Ontology, or a full Diosphantasmeologic Pantography of the Supermundane Domain. The origin of Man, of Language, and of Scripture; the cause of Creation of Life and of Death; the formation of Time and of Eternity; and the reason why it is natural to die, &c. By M. J. Custard."

The author is one of those favored few, like Jo Smith and Parson Miller, to whom it is given to know more of human and superhuman affairs than falls to the lot of most men. He has had a vision, the result of which is that the sealed book has become unsealed, and things heretofore shrouded in darkness are now plainly visible, or will be when the book is printed.

☞ Professors of Theology, we suppose, are rather scarce in the Creek country, as it is a standing law of the nation, "if any person preach or hold religious meetings, he shall for the first offence receive fifty lashes on his bare back, and for the second offence one hundred lashes."

[10] Natchez *Mississippi Free Trader*, September 16, 1846.

CHAPTER XX

MOTLEY'S THE WEAR

To REGIMENT people is always difficult, and often quite futile. Even the docile and disciplined Germans have a way of kicking over the traces and jumping out of gear. Most categories of human character have a tendency to crack up under strain, or to fall short in emergencies. How natural it was that Chaucer's "Wel nyne and twenty in a companye" swelled to one and thirty when the Canon and his Yeoman came puffing up from behind, and thus obligated the Canterbury poet to the task of four more tales (that is, if he were going to be as good as his word).

For the merely genial purpose of this book, it is even more difficult to classify a people as fluent, mercurial, casual, and cantankerous as were the men and women of the lower South a hundred years ago. If not so numerous, they were as ubiquitous as the pigs of a famous story, and in places and times when "Shifty" was the motto they changed calling and character like Proteus. A man grown tired of being an unsuccessful lawyer could knock off for a couple of weeks, rub the paint off his shingle, and devastate the next county as a doctor. Reuben Davis took it the other way round, and about as speedily. The Reverend McGrath was indubitably a big shot gangster of his day; by all contemporary accounts he was an eloquent preacher. David Theodore Hines, M.A., of South Carolina, ran the whole gamut of professions and rifled pockets as well in one as in another. But the most serious impediment to categorizing the people of our region is that many of them were inclined to be just people —not doctors, lawyers, gamblers, steamboat captains, and the like, but just people, very interesting individual human beings.

Thus we have sundry folks and sundry stories by or about them. And, to be safely inclusive in this presentation, it must be admitted that we have some pieces that are not primarily about people; it can be said only that people wrote them.

Of the latter, two are about dogs. Only the maternity of one of these dogs, however, is certain; the secret of paternity is an open question for the reader to solve. The other dogs are nonpareil 'possum dogs, and, presumably, of respectable parentage. One story is about mosquitoes of the Ganniper variety. Another is about sweet potatoes, the most potatoish story ever told. The final one of this subgroup, and the last in our book, is a poetic effusion on bacon and greens.

Of the real folks, bridegrooms, fruit peddlers, Yazoo Swampers, tow-headed ballad-singers, and Warping Bars and Bussing Coons may be shaken in the same sheet or triced in the same pack. Citation of honor is reserved for "The Ugly Man"—a man so ugly that— only he can tell how ugly he was.

Concluding this book and reflecting upon the character types included, the reader may also speculate about those excluded or neglected. On this point, it is to be hoped that two observations will satisfy such a reader.

In the first place, though this book has for its primary purpose a fairly comprehensive representation of the life of the people in the region and the period designated, it has not aspired to be a sociological or economic treatise. Those interested in these aspects will find an excellent book in Ulrich B. Phillips' *Life and Labor in the Old South*, Boston (Little, Brown, and Company), 1929, or in William E. Dodd's *The Cotton Kingdom, A Chronicle of the Old South*, New Haven (Yale University Press), 1921.

In the second place, if the critical reader has specifically in mind the omission, to the extent of a separate chapter, of a character type so important in the life of an agricultural region as the Southern planter, he cannot be any more surprised and disappointed than the editor himself. There were undoubtedly thousands of planters in the region, as there were thousands of plantations, and planters and plantations appear casually in thousands of stories. A few of both appear in the stories and sketches of this book. But they have not appeared in sufficient numbers as distinctive humorous types and *locales* to muster a corporal's guard for a chapter. The larger truths which may explain the cause of this scarcity are not a proper subject for this book. If the reader cares to press the point, perhaps he may find them to his own satisfaction in Francis Pendleton Gaines' *The Southern Plantation, A Study in the Development and the Accuracy of a Tradition,* New York (Columbia University Press), 1925.

A PRODIGY[1]

THE following is an extract from a letter received by a gentleman of this town, from a correspondent in the city of Raleigh, North Carolina:—

"A most curious spectacle was exhibited in this city a few days ago. —A female of the canine species was delivered of the most perfect lusus naturae that has ever been beheld in this part of the world, or, I believe, in any other. I will give you as accurate a description as I can.

"Its shape more resembles that of a child, than anything else I can compare it to; indeed it appears to be a composition of the human and brute parts of the creation. It has three heads, viz., one on each shoulder, and another between them. The one in the middle is the exact representation of the human face; those on the shoulders no way differing from those of a dog. It has six legs, two of which stand upright on its back, and four tails. I forgot to mention that the middle-head instead of being covered with hair similar to that on the body, is furnished with black curly hair, similar to that on the head of a negro; and hands instead of paws, are placed on the ends of those legs or arms, (whichever they may be called) which stand upright on the back.

"The owner of this curious animal expects to make a fortune by it. He sets out in a few days on his travels, and will, no doubt, pass through Petersburgh, when you will see with your own eyes; and I dare say, you will be as little able to account for such a strange appearance as I can be."

To Naturalists,

The following *Quere* is submitted, viz. Whether the foregoing birth originated from an unlawful connection, or from a misconception; or from what other cause.

[1] *Green's Impartial Observer. Free and Unbiass'd,* Natchez:—Printed by J. Green. Vol. I, No. XIX (Saturday, January 24, 1801: American Independence, Twenty-Fifth Year. Federal Government, Twelfth Year).

CUMING'S TOUR

"Of Cuming himself we have no information save such as is gleaned from his book. He appears to have been an Englishman of culture and refinement, who had travelled extensively in other lands —notably the West Indies, France, Switzerland, and Italy. It is certain that he journeyed to good purpose, with an intelligent, open mind, free from local prejudices, and with trained habits of observation." So writes his editor.[2] His journey was taken in 1807–1809. "The journey to Mississippi," we learn from the same source, "appears to have been undertaken with a view to making his home in that territory. The place and date signed to the preface—'Mississippi Territory, 20th October, 1809'—would indicate that he had decided upon remaining where he had found the social life so much to his taste, and some of his former friends and acquaintances had settled." [3] Apparently he left descendants at Bayou Pierre, Mississippi.[4]

"A GANNIPER BY G—"

By Fortescue Cuming [5]

JUNE 4th [1809], in eleven miles we arrived at Crow's nest island, where invited by the beauty of its appearance, some of us landed in a skiff. It is a little narrow island, about a hundred and fifty paces long by forty broad. It is sufficiently raised above inundation, and is very dry and pleasant, with innumerable blackbirds, which have their nests amongst the thirty tall cotton wood trees it contains. It is covered with brush, through which is an old path from one end to the other. A quantity of drift wood lies on its upper end, which projecting, forms a fine boat harbour just below it, quite out of the current. There are but few musquitoes on the dry part, but a low, drowned point, covered with small poplars, and extending a hundred yards at the lower end

[2] Reuben Gold Thwaites, *Early Western Travels, 1748–1846, A Series of Annotated Reprints of some of the best and rarest contemporary volumes of travel, descriptive of the Aborigines and Social and Economic Conditions in the Middle and Far West, during the Period of Early American Settlement*, Volume IV, *Cuming's Tour to the Western Country (1807–1809)*, Cleveland, Ohio (The Arthur H. Clark Company), 1904, Preface, p. 7.
[3] *Ibid.*, p. 9.
[4] *Ibid.*, p. 13.
[5] *Sketches of a Tour to the Western Country, through the States of Ohio and Kentucky; A Voyage down the Ohio and Mississippi Rivers, and a Trip through the Mississippi Territory, and Part of West Florida, Commenced at Philadelphia in the Winter of 1807, and Concluded in 1809* ... Pittsburg ... 1810, ed. cit., pp. 301-303.

swarms with them, and many of the largest size, called gannipers. These venemous and troublesome insects remind me of a humorous story I have heard, which I take the liberty of introducing here.

Some gentlemen in South Carolina had dined together, and while the wine circulated freely after dinner the conversation turned on the quantity of musquitoes generated in the rice swamps of that country. One of the gentlemen said that those insects never troubled him, and that he believed people in general complained more of them than they had occasion to do—that for his part he would not notice them, were he naked in a rice swamp. Another of the company, (according to the custom of the country, where all arguments terminate in a wager) offered him a considerable bet that he would not lie quietly on his face, naked, in the swamp, a quarter of an hour. The other took him up, and all the party immediately adjourned to the place fixed on. The gentleman stripped, lay down, and bore with the most resolute fortitude the attack of the hostile foe. The time had almost expired, and his antagonist, fearing he must lose his wager, seized a fire brand from one of the negro fires that happened to be near, and approaching slyly applied it to a fleshy part of his prostrate adversary, who, not able to bear the increased pain, clapped his hand on the part, jumped up, and cried out, "A ganniper by G—." He then acknowledged he had lost his wager, by that "damned ganniper," and the party returned to the house to renew their libations to Bacchus, and to laugh over the comical termination of the bet.

MISCELLANY [6]

Important Decision.—At a recent village debate, in Vermont, the question, "Ought a young man to foller a gal, after she gives him the mitten," was duly argued pro and con—and then the President decided that he hadn't oughter.

"Bob, I understand you are on a cruise after Dick to cowhide him."
"Yes—I'm off on a *whaling* expedition."

A Lady's interpretation of a Text.—When a man smacks thee on the one cheek, turn, and let him smack thee on the other also.

Elegant   Refinement.—Roosters' tails are now called "fowl's bustles."

[6] Page (unnumbered) of *Louisiana Merchants' and Planters' Almanac* for 1843.

The Bangor Whig is responsible for the following melting stanzas:

TO MISS ——

Methought my heart a roasting lay,
  On Cupid's kitchen spit;
Methought he stole thy heart away,
  And stuck it next to it.

Methought thy heart began to melt,
  And mine to gravy run,
Till both a glow congenial felt,
  And melted into one.

JOHNNY SANDS

A man whose name was Johnny Sands,
  Had married Betty Hague;
Who, though she brought him cash and lands,
  Yet proved a shocking plague.

For she was quite a scolding wife,
  Full of caprice and whim:
He said that he was tired of life—
  And she was tired of him.

Says he, "then I will drown myself,
  The river runs below;"
Says she, "pray do, you silly elf,
  I wish'd it long ago."

Said he, "upon the brink upright
  I'll stand; run down the hill,
And push me in with all your might";
  Said she, "my love, I will."

"For fear that courage I should lack,
  And try to save my life,
Pray tie my hands behind my back—"
  "I will," replied the wife.

She tied them fast, as you may think,
  And when securely done,

"Now go," she cried, upon the brink,
"And I'll prepare to run."

All down the hill his tender bride
Now ran with all her force,
To push him in—he step'd aside,
And she fell in of course.

There, splashing, struggling, like a fish,
"O, help me, Johnny Sands!"
"I can't my dear, though much I wish,
For you have tied my hands."

There is a man in Portland who can never wear a dress coat but once—the skirts always being snapped off by his rapid manner of turning corners.—*Boston Post*.

We know him well. Our Collector has been in full chase of him this six months, but has never been able to come up with him.—*Portland Argus*.

Better than a Yankee Trick.—It is related of a Mississippi Steamboat Captain, that, having lost all patience waiting for passengers in New-Orleans, in July, concluded to hire a dozen hearses, and send them perambulating about the city, whereupon was got up the cry of yellow fever, and in two hours his boat was crowded to suffocation.

Useful Hint.—A graduate who had taken high honors at the university, was elected, on account of his known attainments and learning, as incumbent of a new church in a populous parish. Inexperience, however, in a most important duty, led, much to the surprise of his parishioners, to a failure, which was promptly rectified by an old matter of fact church warden leaving in the vestry room the following note: "Rev. sir, if you would preach 50 per cent. slower and 100 per cent. louder, you would preach with 1,000 per cent. greater effect.

The Scotchman's Prayer.—Keep my purse from the *lawyer*—and my body from the *doctor*—and my soul from the *devil*.

☞ The Picayune says poetry's riz;—as a proof, read the following:

TO KATE

I love you, Kate; I do, by gosh!
As Uncle Ben he loveth squash:

As hens love corn, or pigs potatoes—
I love you as I do tomatoes!

"Oft in the stilly night,
    When slumber's chains have bound me,
I feel the cursed bite
    Of something crawling round me!"

A gentleman, addicted to taking snuff, let fall his handkerchief; stooping to pick it up, he seized hold of a lady's dress, wiped his nose with it, and then commenced stuffing it into his coat pocket. He did not discover his mistake till a somewhat irascible gentleman kicked him out of the house.

T'other day a man in Baltimore, intending to wind up his watch, through a sudden attack of absence of mind, wound up himself. He did not perceive his mistake until his creditors refused to allow him to go upon *tick* any longer!

Major N——, upon being asked whether he was seriously injured when the St. Leonard steamer's boiler exploded, replied, that he was so used to being blown up by his wife that a mere steamer had no effect upon him.

One of the Tallboys Family.—In Slickville, there is a boy, aged ten years, who is so uncommonly tall that he cannot tell when his toes are cold.

Bad Times.—The Wheeling Times says:—"That times are so bad and payments so rare, that the girls down east complain that the young men cannot even *pay* their addresses."

CASH AND THE BEAR

By Nelson F. Smith [7]

Mr. Jesse W. Bryan, the late landlord of the "Exchange," was the next Sheriff, elected in August 1849, over two whig competitors, Mr. B. F. Roper and B. G. McAllister. Mr. Bryan is a native of Kentucky, was born in Christian county, August 17, 1819. His father migrated to Alabama in 1820 and settled in Sumter county, where he was en-

[7] *History of Pickens County, Alabama, from Its Earliest Settlement in Eighteen Hundred and Seventeen, to Eighteen Hundred and Fifty-Six,* Carrollton, Alabama (Printed at the "Pickens Republican" Office), 1856, pp. 101-105.

gaged in business with General Gaines at the Choctaw Agency, and died there when Jesse was only four years old. His mother's maiden name was Hawkins, she being own cousin of the renowned David Crockett.—She settled at this place after the death of her husband and here she died. In 1840, Mr. Bryan married his present estimable lady, who is a sister of Mr. John Alexander of Carrollton. It is stated that the first Carrollton wedding was the marriage of one of Mrs. Bryan's daughters, sister of our present subject. The history of Mr. Bryan is well known, since the last named date, to most of our readers. He engaged in business at Yorkville as a merchant, afterwards went to Mobile, returned to Pickens in 1840, and acted as deputy of W. H. Davis, whom he succeeded in the office, as above stated.

Jesse W. Bryan, Esq., enjoys a more extensive reputation than any of his predecessors, or successors, as we feel bound to set it down, with all deference to other rather celebrated gentlemen. His celebrity is of that enviable character which the Press alone can confer, and without which a great man is nowhere! It would be sheer affectation to *ignore* the clever story of "Cash and the Bear," or "Jess Bryan's Bear Fight" —a tale of three heroes, at least! which has been told, published, nay, stereotyped, from Oregon to Texas, which had its origin on the Gulf of Mexico, was about a "Bar," taken, for aught now known to the contrary, among the Rocky Mountains! The tale originally appeared in the West Alabamian from the pen of Judge A. B. Clitherall, showing how a native came it over a bear man. There is a rich vein of humor in this inimitably told story, which is a much better illustration of Judge Clitherall's ability to write, than anything said in eulogy of his powers. It runs thus:

Every man, woman and child in Pickens county knows Jess Bryan. And to those whose circumstances unfortunately compel them to live elsewhere, we would say that Jesse is the present Sheriff of the county aforesaid. And furthermore, we have the authority of the present Secretary of State, for saying that he was the finest looking Sheriff who carried the returns of the last Presidential election to Montgomery.

On reaching Montgomery, Jess went to the Capitol and was introduced to the Secretary; "I am happy to know you, Mr. Bryan," said the affable Col. Garrett.

"I am happy to find you do," replied the Sheriff, "for since I put on these blacks I hardly know myself."

Jesse is our crack tale-teller, and many side-aches have the boys had from laughing at his nubbin ridge and Sourwood stories. One of his we will now give, premising that the gist of the tale consists in his rich mode of telling it, and that it must lose much by being read.

"Some years ago, before I got to be sheriff of this county, I was in Mobile, and on one day I saw a crowd moving out toward the Orange Grove; I joined it, and learned that a match fight was to come off between Jim Burguss's bull dog and a tame bear, for five hundred dollars a side, one hundred forfeit.

"As soon as the ring was formed, the dog was turned loose at the bear, and after one round he stayed loose—no sort of talk could make him clinch again, and Burguss paid the forfeit and drew off the dog.

"Just as the crowd was about to disperse, a tall, raw boned native from Chickasaha, who was rejoicing in the ownership of a big bony, stump-tailed cur dog, sung out: 'I'll be darned if Cash can't take that bar.'

" 'What will you bet of that?' said the owner of the bear.

" 'I'll go my pile,' said raw-bones, and drawing out the foot of an old stocking, he shelled out twenty dollars. The bear man covered the twenty and the ring was again formed.

" 'Now, gentlemen,' said Chicasaha, 'I wish it to be understood as how nobody goes enter this ring but me an' Cash an' the bar, and nobody ain't got to speak or tetch but me.'

"This was agreed to, and the bear being unmuzzled, the word was given.

" 'Look out, Cash; mind your eyes! Watch him, Cash!' cried rawbones, as Cash, with a prudent regard for his own interests, kept at a respectful distance; his bristles standing up like the teeth of a harrow. As soon as Cash had taken a position a little in the rear of his foe, and out of the range of his paws, his master shouted, 'take him, Cash!'

"With one bound Cash seized the poor brute by the root of the ear, keeping his body side by side with his enemy, so that the latter could not possibly strike him.

" 'Keep outen this ring, gentlemen,' cried the owner of Cash. 'Bring him *here*, Cash!' Cash, by main force, dragged the bear half around the ring, without once exposing himself to the furious blows of the animal.

" 'Shake him, Cash!' Again the brave dog shook his foe until the bear's teeth fairly chattered with pain and rage. Still Cash, by keeping yard-arm and yard-arm with the bear, was as safe as if he had been in his master's cabin.

"The owner of the bear seeing that the bear could not bring his arms to bear, could not bear to see Cash bear the bear in such a bearfaced manner, and gave up the day.

" 'You give it up,' said our man. 'Well, then, gentlemen, clar the ring—Cash leaves when he do leave 'em. Hold him, Cash! You say it's my money, no discounts, no nothing? Watch your time, Cash. Let go, Cash.'

"With a single spring, Cash was ten feet beyond the reach of the bear's paw.

" 'That's a right pert bear,' said raw-bones, 'but he ain't nigh such a good one as me and Cash has tuk. We got one this fall as measured nine feet from snout to tail tip.'

" 'That's a lie,' said the discomfitted owner of the bear, 'you never *saw* a bear that large in your life.'

" 'I haint? Well, I'll go you these two twenty dollars on that branch of the subject.'

" 'It's a bet,' said the bear man.

" 'Well, come down to George Davis', and we'll try the case.'

"The crowd all accompanied the parties, and we soon reached George Davis' Store.

" 'George let me see that biggest bar skin I let you have a spell back,' said our man.

"Davis handed out the skin, and it measured nine feet *one inch and a half!*

" 'Twenty to start on, and twenty are forty, and forty are eighty! Sweet J——s! Whoop! Come *here*, Cash. Good evening gentle*men*,' sang the overjoyed native; and the last I saw of him he and Cash were eating ginger cakes at the market-house."

THAT BIG DOG FIGHT AT MYERS'S

A Story of Mississippi

By a Mississippian [8]

THE writer of the following story is one of the most entertaining companions we ever met. Like the elder Placide, or Gabriel Ravel, he has the keenest perception of the ludicrous imaginable; in him this is combined with an inexhaustible flow of spirits, and a rare fund of wit and humour peculiarly calculated to "set the table in a roar." For several years he has been a most acceptable correspondent of the New York "Spirit of the Times," and while his stories have ranged from "amazin to onkimmon," there is not an indifferent one among them all. His extraordinary merit as a story-teller is only equalled by his modesty; "not for the world" would he permit us to name him. We are free to say, however, that he is a country gentleman of Mississippi, "of about

[8] *The Big Bear of Arkansas, and Other Sketches, Illustrative of Characters and Incidents in the South-West*, Edited by William T. Porter, with Illustrations by Darley, Philadelphia (T. B. Peterson and Brothers), c. 1846, pp. 54-61. For note on *The Big Bear*, see p. 109, *supra.*

our size," and that he resides on a river-plantation nearly equidistant from the regions of "the cotton trade and sugar line."

"Well, them was great times, and *men* lived about here, them days, too!—not sayin' they're all dead, but the settlement is got too thick for 'em to splurge, an' they are old—beside, they're waitin' for thar *boys* to do somethin' when they gits *men!* I tell you what, if they lived till kingdom come *they* wouldn't be men. I'd like to see one single one of 'em that ever rid his horse up two pair of stairs, jumpt him thru—"

"Stop, stop, Uncle Johnny! Do tell us about *that big dog fight at Myers's.*"

"Ha, ha, boy! *You* thar? Had your bitters yet? Well, well—we'll take 'em together; licker *is* better now than it used to was; but people don't drink so much, and that's strange! ain't it? Well, I was talkin' to these men about old Greensville, and about them same men, for they was all at that same dog fite—Featte, the Devil! never be a patchin' to what old Greensville was about the time *'Old Col'* was sheriff! I'll just bet all the licker I ever *expect* to drink, that thar ain't no second story in Featte that's got hoss tracks on the floor and up agin' the ceil—"

"I must stop you again, Uncle Johnny; Fayette is yet in its youth, and promises—"

"Youth, H—l! yes, like the *youth* of some of my old friends' sons —upwards of thirty, an' they're expectin' to make *men* out'n 'em yet! I tell you what, young men in *my* time'd just get in a spree, sorter open thar shirt collars, and shuck tharselves with a growl, and come out reddy-made men; and most on 'em has *staid* reddy for fifty-one year! I ain't failed now, yet, and—"

"Uncle Johnny, for God's sake stick to that dog story: we'll hear all this after—"

"Ah, you boy, you never will let me tell my story *my* way, but here goes:—Let me see—yes, yes. Well, it was a grate dog in Greensville, anyhow—Charly Cox had run old Saltrum agin' a hoss from the Red-licks, and beat him shameful—run rite plum up the street in Greens-ville so as evry body mite see. Well, a power of licker was wasted—nily evry house in town rid thru—women and children skeared out, and evry drink we took was a *ginral* invite, and about night thar was *one* ginral in *town*—Ginral Intoxication. Well, 'bout sundown the old Ginral—God bless him!—called up his troops; some of the same ones who was at Orleans; let's see—thar was the high sheriff, Dick, Bat, Jim, old Iron Tooth, an'—"

"Iron Tooth! who's he?" suggested I.

"Why, *he's* the man what fit the dog! Ain't you never seen a man here in Featte, when he gits *high* up, just pulls out his knife, and goes to chawin' it as if he'd made a bet he could bite it in two?"

"Yes, yes, go on!"

"Well, the Ginral made 'em all mount, formed line, and rid rite into the grocery—formed line agin, had a big stir-up drink handed to 'em all, and when the Ginral raised *his* hat and said 'the Hero of Orleans,' the yell that went up put a bead on that man's licker that staid nily a month, I hearn. We come a rarin' out'n the grocery—charged up and down two or three times, cleared the streets of all *weak* things, then started out home, all in a brest; evry one of us had a Polk stalk—"

"Hel-lo!—Polk stalks that early?"

"Well, well, Hickry sticks—same thing—out of town we went, chargin' evry thing we see—fences, cattle, ox-teams; and at last we got to old Myers's, farly squeelin' to rar over somethin'! Old Myers's dog was awful bad—the worst in anybody's nolledge—why, people sent fifty miles to git pups from him! Well, he come a chargin', too, and met us at the gate, lookin' like a young hyena. Iron Tooth just turned himself round to us, and says he, 'Men, I'll take *this* fite off'n *your* hands;' so down he got, ondressed to shirt, *stock* and boots—got down on his all-fours in the road, walkin' backards and forards, pitchin' up the dust and bellerin' like a bull! When the dog see him at that sort of work, he did sorter stop barkin', but soon as he see *our* animal strut up to the gate and begin to smell, then, like another dog, he got fairly crazy to git thru at him; rarin', cavortin', and tarin' off pickets! Our animal was a takin' all this quite easy—smellin' thru at him whinin' *me-you, me-you, me-you*—struttin' backards and forards, histin' up one leg agin the gate. Well, after a while the dog begin to git sorter tired, and then *our* animal begin to git mad! snap for snap he gin the dog, and the spit and slobber flew, and soon the dog was worse than he *had* been. Thar we was settin' on our hosses, rollin' with laughin' and licker, and thought the thing was rich, as it was; but just then, our animal riz on his hinders, onlatched the gate, and the dog *lunged* for him. Ain't you never noticed when one dog bounces at another, he sorter whirls round sideways, to keep him from hittin' him a fair lick? Well, jist so our animal: he whirled round sideways to let the dog hav a glancin' lick, and true to the caracter, he was goin' to allow the dog a dog's chance, and he stuck to his all-fours. The dog didn't make but one lunge, and he stopt—as still as the picter of the wolf in the spellin' book—for you see our animal was right starn end facin' him, his shirt smartly up over his back, and standin' mity high up on his hind legs at that! We all raised the old Indian yell for you

never did see sich a site, and thar stood the dog with the awfullest
countenance you ever seen a *dog* ware! Our man, sorter thinkin' he'd
bluffed the dog, now give two or three short goat-pitches backards at
him! Ha! ha! ha!"

"What did he do? What did he do?"

"Do? why *run!* wouldn't a d—d hyena run! The dog had a big
block and chain to him, and soon our animal was arter him, givin'
some of the awfullest leaps and yelps—'twarnt but a little squar picket
yard round the house, and the dog couldn't git out, so round and round
he went—at last, turnin' a corner the chain rapt round a stump, and
thar the dog *was fast, and he had to fite!* But he did give powerful
licks to get loose! When he see his inemy right on him agin, and when
Iron Tooth seen the dog *was* fast, round and round he'd strut; and sich
struttin! Ain't you never seen one of these big, long-legged, short-
tailed baboons struttin' round on the top of the lion's cage? Well, so
he'd go—sorter smellin' at the dog (and his tongue hanging out right
smart, for he *was* tired,) *me-you! me-you!* Snap! snap! the dog would
go, and he began to show fite d—d plain agin, for our varmint was a
facin' him, and he seen *'twas a man* arter all! But our animal know'd
how to come the giraffe over *him*—so round he turns and gives him the
starn view agin! *That* fa'rly broke the dog's hart, and he jist *rared*
back, a pullin' and got loose! One or two goat-pitches backards and
the dog was flat on his back, playin' his fore-paws mity fast, and perhaps some of the awfullest barks you ever hearn a dog gin! Old Iron
Tooth he seen he had the dog at about the rite pint, and he give one
mortal lunge backards, and he lit with both hands on the dog's throat,
turned quick as lightnin', div down his head, and fastened his teeth on
the dog's ears! Sich a shakin' and howlin'! The dog was too skeared
to fite, and our animal had it all his own way. We hollered to 'give him
some in the short ribs,' but he only held on and growled at us, playin'
the dog clean out, I tell you. Well, thar they was, rollin' and tumblin'
in the dirt—first one on top, and then tother—our animal holdin' on
like pitch to a waggin wheel, the dog never thinkin' bout fitin' once,
but makin' rale onest licks to git loose. At last our varmint's hold broke
—the dog riz—made one *tiger* lunge—the chain snapt—he tucked his
tail, and—and—but you all know what skeared dogs *will* do!

"Nobody ain't never got no pups from Myers since—the blood run
rite out!"

JOHNSON J. HOOPER

The creator of Captain Simon Suggs of the Tallapoosa Volunteers was an Alabama lawyer and judge. Johnson J. Hooper was one of the brilliant company of local-color humorists—William Tappan Thompson, George W. Harris, W. T. Thorpe, Sol Smith, and Joseph G. Baldwin—who launched out in the wake of A. B. Longstreet. His masterpiece is *The Adventures of Simon Suggs* (1845), whose hero uproariously exemplifies his own motto, "It is good to be shifty in a new country." *The Widow Rugby's Husband, A Night at the Ugly Man's, and Other Tales of Alabama,* contains, besides a few additional episodes of the life of Captain Suggs, about a score of sketches of other backwoods worthies, including old Bill Wallis, the Ugly Man.

"In a previous sketch," says the author of "A Night at the Ugly Man's," "I mentioned that my friend, Dick McCoy, and myself, were brought to a sudden halt, on our 'voyage' to the Horse Shoe, by the capsizing of our boat; and I further mentioned, that we determined, as it was late, to attempt no further progress that day, but to stop until next morning at the house of Old Bill Wallis, the Ugly Man. In accordance with this plan, we bailed the boat and made her fast to a tree on the 'Turpingtine' side of the river, and commenced our walk." The following three pages describe the Ugly Man's cabin on the spring branch, his wife and daughter, and supper with the family. The remainder of the sketch, in the Ugly Man's own words, tells how ugly the Ugly Man is.

A NIGHT AT THE UGLY MAN'S

By Johnson J. Hooper [9]

SUPPER over, old Bill drew out his large soap-stone pipe, and filling and lighting it, placed it in his mouth. After a whiff or two, he began:

"It's no use argyfyin' the matter—I *am* the ugliest man, now on top of dirt. Thar's narry nuther like me! I'm a crowd by myself. *I allers was.* The fust I know'd of it, tho', was when I was 'bout ten years old. I went down to the spring branch one mornin', to wash my face, and I looked in the water, I seen the shadder of my face. Great God! how I run back, hollerin' for mammy, every jump! That's the last time I seen my face—I daresn't but shet my eyes when I go 'bout water."

[9] *The Widow Rugby's Husband, A Night at the Ugly Man's, and Other Tales of Alabama,* Philadelphia: A. Hart, Late Carey & Hart, 1851, pp. 41-51.

"Don't you use a glass, when you shave?" I inquired.

"Glass! Zounds! What glass could stand it?—'twould bust it, if it was an inch thick. Glass!—pish!"

Lucy told her father he was "too bad," and that "he knew it was no sich a thing"; and the old man told her she was a "sassy wench," and to "hold her tongue."

"Yes," he continued; "it's so; I haven't seen my face in forty years, but I know how it looks. Well, when I growed up, I thort it would be the devil to find a woman that'd be willing to take me, ugly as I was—"

"Oh, you was not so *oncommon* hard-favoured when you was a young man," said old Mrs. Wallis.

"ONCOMMON! I tell you when I was ten years old, a *fly wouldn't light on my face*—and it can't be much wuss now! Shet up, and let me tell the 'squire my ixperance."

"It's no use," put in Lucy, "to be runnin' one's self down, that way, daddy! It ain't right."

"Runnin' down! Thunder and lightnin', Luce! you'll have me as good lookin' directly as John Bozeman, your sweetheart."

As he said this, old Bill looked at me, and succeeded in half covering the ball of his left eye, by way of a wink. Lucy said no more.

The old man continued:

"Well, hard as I thort it 'ud be to get a wife, fust thing I knowed, I had Sally here; and she is, or was, as pretty as any of them."

Old Mrs. Wallis knitted convulsively, and coughed slightly.

"However, she never kissed me afore we was married, and it was a long time arter afore she did. The way of it was this: we had an old one-horned cow, mighty onnery (ordinary) lookin', old as the North Star, and poor as a black snake. One day I went out to the lot"—

"Daddy, I *wouldn't* tell *that*," exclaimed Lucy, in the most persuasive tones.

"Drot ef I don't, tho—it's the truth, and ef you don't keep still, I'll send for Bozeman to hold you quiet in the corner."

Lucy pouted a little, and was silent.

"Yes, I went out to the lot, and thar, sure as life, was my old 'oman, swung to the cow, and the old thing flyin' round, and cuttin' up all sorts o' shines! Ses I, 'What the h—ll are you up to, old 'oman?' And with that she let go, and told me she was tryin' to prac*tize* kissin' on old 'Cherry,' and she thort *arter that* she could make up her mind to *kiss me!*"

"Old man, you *made* that! I've hearn you tell it afore—but you *made* it," said the old lady.

"Well, well! I told her, 'squire, ses I, 'Come down to it now!—hang the cow—shet your eyes!—hold your breath!'—and upon that she bussed me so's you might a heard it a quarter, *and since*, nobody's had better kissin' than me! Now, that was my first ixperance about bein' ugly, arter I was grown, and 'twan't so bad neither!

"The next time my ugly feeturs came into play, was in Mobile; was you ever thar! Worst place on the green yearth; steamboats, oysters, free niggers, furriners, brick houses—hell! *that's* the place! I went down on a flat-boat from Wetumpky, with old John Todd. We had a fust-rate time of it, 'twell we got most to Mobile, and then the d—d steamboats would run so close to us, that the *sloshin'* would pretty nigh capsize us. They done it for devilment. My! how old John cussed! but it done no good. At last, ses I, 'I'll try 'em; ef thar's enny strength in cussin', I'll make 'em ashamed!' So the next one come along cavortin' and snortin' like it was gwine right into us, and did pass in twenty foot! I riz right up on a cotton bag, and ses I to the crowd— which there was a most almighty one on the guards of the boat—ses I, 'You great infernal, racket-makin', smokin', snortin', hell totin' sons of thunder—'

"Afore I could git any furder in my cussin', the crowd gin the most tremenjus, yearth-shakin' howl that ever was hearn—and one fellar, as they was broad-side with us, hollered out, 'It's the old HE UGLY HIMSELF! Great G—d, WHAT A MOUTH!' With that, thar was somethin' rained and rattled in our boat like hail, only hevier, and directly me and old John picked up *a level peck of buck-horn-handled knives!* I'll be darn'd this minit if we didn't!"

Old Mrs. Wallis looked to Heaven, as if appealing there for forgiveness of some great sin her ugly consort had committed; but she said nothing.

"So I lost nothin' by bein' ugly *that* time! Arter I got into Mobile, howsever, I was bothered and pestered by the people stoppin' in the street to look at me—all dirty and lightwood-smoked as I was, from bein' on the boat."—

"I think I'd a cleaned up a little," interposed tidy Lucy.

"Old 'oman! *ain't* you got nary cold 'tater to choke that gal with! Well, they'd look at me the hardest you ever seen. But I got ahead o' my story: A few days afore, thar had been a boat busted, and a heap o' people scalded and killed, one way and another. So at last, as I went into a grocery, a squad of people followed me in, and one 'lowed, ses he, 'It's one of the unfortunate sufferers by the bustin' of the Franklin,' and upon that he axed me to drink with him, and as I had my tumbler half way to my mouth, he stopped me of a sudden—

" 'Beg your pardon, stranger—but'—ses he.

" 'But—what?' ses I.

" 'Jist *fix your mouth that way again!*' ses he.

"I done it, just like I was gwine to drink, and I'll be cussed if I didn't think the whole on 'em would go into fits!—they yelled and whooped like a gang of wolves. Finally, one of 'em ses, 'Don't make fun of the unfortunate; he's hardly got over bein' blowed up yet. Less make up a puss for him.' Then they all throwed in, and made up five dollars; as the spokesman handed me the change, he axed me, 'Whar did you find yourself after the 'splosion?'

" 'In a flat-boat,' ses I.

" 'How far from the Franklin?' ses he.

" 'Why,' ses I, 'I never seen *her,* but as nigh as I can guess, it must have been, from what they tell me, nigh on to *three hundred and seventy-five miles!*' You oughter 'a seen that gang scatter. As they left, ses one, 'IT'S HIM. *It's the Ugly Man of all!*'

"Knockin' round the place, I came upon one o' these fellers grinds music out'n a mahogany box. He had a little monkey along—the d—dest peartest, least bit of a critter you ever seed! Well, bein' fond of music and varmints, I gits pretty close to the masheen, and d—d ef 'twarn't hard to tell which got most praise, me or the monkey. Howsever, at last, I got close up, and the darn thing ketcht a sight of me and *squalled!* It jumped off'n the box in a fright, and hang'd itself by its chain. The grinder histed it up ag'in, but it squalled more'n ever, and jerked and twisted and run over the keeper, and jumped off'n his back, and hang'd itself ag'in. *The sight o' me had run it distracted!* At last the grinder hilt it to his bosom, and ses he,

" 'Go ways, oagley man—maungkee fraid much oagley!' Ses I, 'Go to h—ll, you old heathen'—(you see he was some sort of a Dutch chap or another)—'if you compare me to your dirty monkey ag'in, I'll throw it hell'ards, and split your old box over your head!' And ses he right off ag'in,

" 'Maungkee ish petter ash dat oagley mans!'

"Ses I, 'Gentle*men*, you heer this crittur compare me, a free Amerakin, to his d—d heathen dumb brute of Afriky'; and with that, I fetched the monkey sailing that sent him a whirlin' about sixty-five yards, over a brick wall, and the next minit the Dutchman and his box was the worst mixed up pile of *rags and splinters* you ever seen in *one* mud-hole! About that time, too, thar was a pretty *up-country* runnin' on top o' them cussed bricks as you'll commonly see. I lay up two or three days, and at last made my passage up to Wetumpky, *in the cabin!*"

"How was that?" I asked.

"An old lady, that was along, 'lowed that it was dangerous for me to stay on the deack, *as I might scare the masheenery* OUT O' JINT. So they tuck me in the cabin afore we started, and I reckon I was treated nigh on to a hundred times, afore we got to Wetumpky."

"That's not the way you told it the last time," remarked Mrs. Wallis.

"Thunder! 'squire, did you ever hear sich wimmen folks—I've hardly had a chance to edge in a word, tonight. Well, my last ixperance was about a year ago. I got ketcht in a hurricane; it was blowin' like the devil, and the thunder and lightnin' was tremenjus—so I gits under a big red-oak, and thar I sot 'twell the lightnin' struck it! I was leanin' agin the tree when the bolt come down, shiverin' and splinterin' all before it. It hit me right here—and then"—

"Good Heavens! did *lightning* disfigure your face so?"

"Disfigure h—ll! No! The lightnin' struck right here, as I was sayin', and then—IT GLANCED!"

"Good Lord look down!" ejaculated Mrs. Wallis.

"You'd better go to bed now, 'squire," said old Bill; "and in the mornin' I'll go with you and Dick to the Horse Shoe. *That* was the main feetur of old Hickory. He was ugly some, hisself. God bless him, I've seed him—but he didn't have the gift like me. Good night."

A WHOLE LOT THE MATTER

By Francis Bartow Lloyd ("Rufus Sanders") [10]

It was a cold, raw, drizzly, dreary day in the month of January. Way over in one of the western counties of Alabama, not far from the Mississippi line, I was ridin along all alone by myself. The sun didn't shine a single lick all day, but I could tell from the general appearment of things that it was most night. It was wild, rocky country, where you mought ride ten miles on a dead stretch and never see a livin human bein. The big road led over a hill and across a branch, and then over another hill and across another branch all day long. All of a suddent like a bend in the road brought me in sight of a covered wagon and I thought to myself maybe I will now run into a jolly crowd of campers. The wagon stood in a little open clost to the road and the oxen had been unyoked and tied up for the night. But as I rode up the onlyest livin sould I could see was a yearlin boy, which the same he was down on his knees tryin to start a fire and cryin like his heart would break.

---

[10] *Sketches of Country Life: Humor, Wisdom and Pathos: From the "Sage of Rocky Creek." The Homely Life of the Alabama Back Country Has Its Sunny Side: Rough But Wise and Kindly Talk.* Birmingham, Ala., Press of Roberts & Son, 1898. P. 33. For biographical note on Lloyd, see p. 196, *supra.*

He didn't have on many clothes, and them that he had was powerful plain and thin. He never looked at me when I rode up, but went on foolin with the fire and shakin and shiverin and cryin. Naturally of course it was none of my business, but the sight of that boy touched a tender place in me and I had to stop and find out somethin if I could in regards to the circumference of his calamity. I couldn't help it.

"What's the matter with you, sonny?" says I soft and gentle as I could, cause I was might nigh ready to cry myself.

"Nothin much in particlar," says he.

"But there must be somethin terrible the matter to make you cry and take on so," says I, "and you must tell me what it is. Maybe I can help you out of your troubles and tribulations."

"Taint no use, Mister," says the boy between his sobs—"taint a blame bit of use. But if nothin else will do I can tell you how it is. Old Buck has got the holler horn and got it bad, Daddy is layin out there in the wagin dead drunk, Sister Sal she loped off with a strange man last night, Mammy she took and run away wid a sewin machine peddler this mornin, our dog died last week, and the goldarned wood is wet, and dad-blame it I don't want to go to Texas nohow."

I give the boy my pocket knife and two bits in money, told him to brace up and be a man as best he could, and left him alone in his troubles. That was all I could do.

HANDY STRIBBLIN'S DOG

By Francis B. Lloyd [11]

Now Handy Stribblin, that married one of the Cross girls, had a fine lookin possum dog and his name was Bulger. The Stribblin boys bought him of Slim Jim Blevins when he was nothin but a three-months-old pup. They all chipped in and paid six bits for him, spot cash. But they soon found out that a possum dog want a very good piece of family property.

When they got married and settled off to themselves, they all wanted to keep Bulger. They had went snooks to buy the dog, and each man owned an undivided one-third interest in him. Bulger couldn't stay with all three of the boys at one and the same time, and they couldn't divide him out and keep him in good shape for runnin possums. And there they had it, till it begins to look like they might stir up a family feud.

William and John at last agreed if they could trade Handy out of his share of the dog they would settle it. They could buy or sell, or divide the dog's time half and half between themselves. They were

[11] *Ibid.*, pp. 275-276.

both smart in books and could make poetry right along. Handy was rather dull, but powerful bull-headed. So they fixed up a scheme to beat Handy out.

"Boys, we have all got to say a piece of poetry in order to settle this dog question," says William to John and Handy, "and every piece of poetry has got to have something about possum in it. Me and John will say our piece. If you can't come to time, Handy, the dog is ourn. But if you can come to time right prompt on a piece of poetry, with somethin about possum in it, the dog is yourn."

"I am willin," says John.

"I am sorter skittish about it," says Handy, "cause I ain't much on poetry, but if that's the game you are goin to play I reckon I will have to try my hand."

"Well and good," says William, "so here:

> "Possum is a cunnin thing,
>   He ramble in the dark,
> But never knows what runnin is
>   Till he hear old Bulger bark."

"My time comes next," says John, and he blazed away:

> "Possum is a sly old chap,
>   He drags a long, slick tail,
> He eats up all our new ground corn
>   And husks it on the rail."

By this time Handy was tremblin like a man with the buck ager. He was afraid he couldn't make up a piece and say it, and accordin to the trade he would lose Bulger if he didn't. He stuttered and stammered some at the start, and then braced up and went on as follows:

> "Possum up a simmon tree,
> Rabbit on the ground,
> Rabbit say you dad-blame
>   slou-footed, box-ankled,
>   bench-legged, long-tail,
>   gray-headed, blaze-faced,
>   grass-bellied son-of-a-gun,
> Shake some simmons down!"

Handy didn't know very much about cuttin across lots, you notice, but he kept his eye on the wire and finally pulled in ahead of the distance flag, and the dog was his.

TALL TALES OF THE FORTY-NINERS

By H. S. Fulkerson [12]

THE California stories of the wonderful fecundity of soil and climate in that distant land, current since its earliest settlement, have largely taxed the credulity of our people, accustomed though they be to wonders in the natural world. Some of our returned gold-hunters have laid us under many obligations for these veracious stories; and they apply not alone to vegetable growths, but to other remarkable things which have been witnessed there.

For instance, my friend G. H. T., of Vicksburg, who, in the halcyon days of his youth, sought fortune and the "bubble reputation" in the golden fields of California, has, thanks to his tenacious memory, treasured up some recollections which, as a historian, I desire for the benefit of posterity, to put on record.

When in the mountains of California in search of gold, in the region of the growth of those monarchs of the forest, the Redwood, my friend said, on one occasion sixteen couples danced a cotillion on the stump of one of these felled trees. Not far from this tree was another immense one still standing, but decayed away until there was but an outer rim left. Into this hollow tree one of the party drove his horse and buggy. An incredulous listener, a sturdy old bachelor, when this was being told, enquired how the horse and buggy were turned around to be driven out. The answer was they were not turned round at all, but were driven out at a *knot-hole* on the other side of the tree.

Returning to San Francisco after some months spent in the mountains, he encountered a large party who had just dined off the half of a large watermelon, so large that a rip-saw would not go through it, making it necessary that it should be sawed, on opening it, *on both* sides. He and his friends were invited to help themselves, to the other half. They did so, and after finishing it, the rind was used in ferrying the party across an unfordable stream near by.

This party, as they journeyed, encountered a happy family in the shape of a prairie dog, an owl, and a rattlesnake, all living *in the same hole*. They also passed in their journey a garden from which the housewife was gathering into the market basket on her arm, beets and turnips, which weighed from fifty to eighty pounds each.

After reaching San Francisco, my friend took a situation in a wholesale crockery house. His first duty was to receive a large consignment of wares just arrived by ship, the freight bill against which amounted

[12] *Random Recollections of Early Days in Mississippi*, Vicksburg, 1885, pp. 156-158. For biographical note on Fulkerson, see p. 307, *supra*.

to near ten thousand dollars. The merchant's account at bank was over-drawn and he was greatly perplexed about the payment of the bill. My friend's suggestiveness relieved the embarrassment. He sought and got permission from the Captain of the vessel to open some boxes of French tumblers belonging to the consignment, to retail on the wharf. In a short time he retailed enough of them to pay the freight bill, and the merchant was happy.

The old bachelor, before referred to (he was a Hibernian by descent), on hearing my friend tell this story one day, said, excitedly, "I would not tell such a lie as that *even if it was true!*" There was no disposition on his part to question the correctness of my friend's state-ment. It was only a peculiar way in which he sought to express his astonishment.

What a privilege it is to live in so great a country, to be part and parcel of such marvels in nature, and to be contemporary with so much genius and inventive talent in all the arts and sciences which con-tribute so largely to man's comfort and enjoyment. *Vive la Americano!*

LATE FROM CALIFORNIA [13]

WE HAVE been permitted to peruse a letter written by a friend in Nevada City, California, dated March the 24th. The rainy season, which usually commences in November, had just set in, and the miners were in fine spirits. Nevada City, which had been almost destroyed by fire a few weeks previous, was being rebuilt, and rich deposits of gold were still found occasionally in the vicinity of the town. The Rev. Samuel Davidson had not completed his tunnel, which he has been en-gaged in cutting for several months, and did not expect to complete it before the 1st of June. H. & B. Ferrell, and several other of our Mis-sissippi friends, were also at or near Nevada, in fine health and spirits, and doing better than they had previously done for several months. The rain had fallen in sufficient quantities to supply the miners with water in abundance to wash the dirt they had thrown from the gulches, and many of them were doing a fine business. Several lumps of gold, averag-ing from ten to sixty dollars, had been found near the mouth of Mr. Davidson's tunnel. One or two quartz veins had been discovered in the neighborhood of Nevada, which our friends out there were sanguine would prove very rich.

The two Messrs. Grider are on the Middle-fork of the Yuba river, on the "Mississippi Bar," where they have spent most of the winter. Dr. Williams of Tippah, when last heard from, was on his way up there.

[13] *Mississippi Palladium*, Holly Springs, May 23, 1851, p. [3].

Our old friend Grider has had a terrible rumpus with a Grizzly Bear. He writes that he was out "prospecting" when a noise in the thicket near him, attracted his attention, and he stopped a moment, when he perceived a very large Bear rushing out of the thicket to attack him. He dashed off at his greatest speed, but had not ran over a hundred yards before he was overtaken, knocked down, and his pants torn off of him by the bear. The blow that he received was so severe that he was unable to move or speak for several moments. When he recovered from the shock he beheld the bear seated in a few feet of him, gazing intently upon him, and deliberating what he should next do in the premises. G. (who is a splendid looking man when well dressed, and is ugly enough, however, in his California rigging to scare wolves or bears,) caught the bear's eye and commenced making mouths at him, which produced such a fright that he ran off immediately. G. writes that he did not mind the blow the bear had given him, although it made his ears ring for a week, half so much as he did the loss of his only pair of pantaloons.

AFFAIRE PATHÉTIQUE; OR,
LAUNDERING THE BABY [14]

MR. JOSEPH LEAVITTE, one of our citizens, returned from California. In speaking of sights and scenes in California, he mentions the following incident, which speaks eloquently of the true humanity of hearts even in California, where selfishness and passion are supposed to reign with unwonted force.

During the raging of the cholera in California, a young man from the State of Mississippi (Jesse Cook,) about twenty-three years of age, who was engaged in the laborious work of mining, chanced to meet with a family from Missouri, consisting of husband, wife and two children, one of them an infant. Disease had attacked one of the children, a little boy, and he was soon stricken down by the cholera, and laid by the sorrowing parents in a little grave dug in the bank of the river. Soon after, the father of the child died, leaving only the mother and her infant daughter. Her grief was great—she was in a strange land— The husband of her youth and the first born son of her hope had departed to the land of spirits, and their remains were lying in their graves in the quiet valve of the river. Her earthly support had failed, and yet she clung to life for the sake of her infant. Strangers proved kind, and the hand of benevolence provided for her wants, and the voice of kindness greeted her ears. But disease preyed upon her, and

[14] *The Southern Journal*, vol. XII, No. 37 (Monticello, Mississippi, March 20, 1852).

death tore her away from her tender infant, and by strange hands she was buried.

The sweet loving eyes of an infant looked up confiding into the face of young Cook, and a smile wreathed its beautiful face, and its delicate little hand stretched forth confidingly. No female was there to caress and care for it, and the young miner, with a swelling heart, and with a trust in God and his own resources, took the nameless infant then only seven months old, in charge, and provided for it with a father's care and a mother's love.

He daily fed and washed and pressed it, and gave it the fond name of his mother, Mary; by day he cradled it near him in his toils, and at night huddled it as an angle-child to his bosom.

After a while he made application to various families at Sacramento City, to have the child taken care of, and offered to pay five dollars a week, but none were disposed to undertake the care of it, and he abandoned mining and resolved to proceed to Oregon and there take up land for a farm and make a home for the little orphan.

The simple, unadorned facts in this case are sufficiently touching and suggestive without any comment from our pen.—*Memphis Christian Advocate.*

POTATOES, POTATOES, POTATOES!

By J. F. H. Claiborne [15]

THE repast was abundant, excellent, and scrupulously neat, but almost every dish was composed of *potatoes* dressed in various ways. There were baked potatoes, fried potatoes, bacon and potatoes boiled together—a fine loin of beef was flanked around with potatoes. . . . A hash of wild turkey was garnished with potatoes mixed up in it. A roast fowl was stuffed with potatoes; beside us stood a plate of potato biscuit, as light as sponge; the *coffee*, which was strong and well flavored, was made of potatoes, and one of the girls drew from the cupboard a rich potato pie. In about an hour a charming blue-eyed girl brought us a tumbler of potato beer that sparkled like champaign and rather archly intimated to us that there were hot potatoes in the ashes if we felt like eating one. The beer was admirable, and we were told that good whiskey, molasses, and vinegar were sometimes made of potatoes.

At length we turned in. . . . The bed itself, though soft and pleasant, was made of *potato vines.* . . . After falling into a troubled sleep, we dreamed that we had *turned into big potatoes*, and that some one was *digging us up.*

[15] "A Trip through the Piney Woods," first published in the Natchez *Free Trader and Gazette* in 1841–42; reprinted in *Publications of the Mississippi Historical Society*, vol. IX. For note on Claiborne, see p. 69, *supra.*

SHAKING THE BRIDAL SHEET
By R. C. Beckett [16]

MR. MESEROLE, of Miffleton and Meserole, the carriage and harness firm, was the smallest man in Aberdeen and Miss Simpson, the milliner, was the largest lady in the community. They were married. A day or two afterwards, when my eldest brother, Newton, was passing their residence he saw the bride shaking a sheet out of a back window. He called to her, "What you doing—hunting for Meserole?"

ASK AUNT MARIAH
By R. C. Beckett [17]

MR. WILKES lived about a mile and a half from the business part of the city [of Aberdeen] and supplied it with fruits and early vegetables. He had a little spring wagon for the purpose, driven by an old mulatto woman named Aunt Mariah. He made money and finally bought a carriage in which the family drove to Sunday-school and church. One night some bad boys secured a paint bucket, and while the team was hitched and the family in church, they painted on the vehicle in bold letters:

> "Who'd a thought it?
> Apples bought it.
> If you think I'm a liar,
> Just ask Aunt Mariah."

THEY BOTH SWORE OFF
By R. C. Beckett [18]

NEGROES were also brought through for sale from Virginia and colder climates. Negro traders were called "speculators" by the white people and "speckled ladies" by the negroes. The most prominent negro trader was old Ned Herndon, who was hard to get money out of. After selling a number of negroes one day, he felt so good that he got on a little private spree with some of his friends. He slept that night at the hotel, and next morning raised a terrible "rumpus," claiming that he had been robbed. One of these friends stepped in and, hearing the row, told him that he had not been robbed, but had simply paid an honest debt, and had a receipt somewhere for it. The old man examined his pocket-

[16] "Antebellum Times in Monroe County," *Publications of the Mississippi Historical Society,* vol. XI, p. 94.
[17] *Ibid.,* p. 96.
[18] *Ibid.,* pp. 92-93 and 95.

book more closely and, sure enough, he found this gentleman's receipt for the money. Of course, this man had taken out the exact amount of the drunken man's debt and placed the receipt in the pocketbook. The old man looked astounded. He exclaimed, "If I'm that big a fool I'll never drink again"; and he never did. This was his own explanation of his later habit of total abstinence.

Old man Charley McClellan was postmaster. He was short, fat and "stumpy," had straggling snow-white hair and beard and a sour disposition. He kept a keg of liquor, the contents of which would sometimes cause him to lose his equilibrium, and when he was feeling bad from his attempts to "sober up," he would get a stick and lambast his keg, exclaiming vehemently, "Make Charley drunk, eh! Goin' to give you a good beatin'. Don't think you'll do it any more when I git through with yer." He always wore the same blue suit, the blue coat buttoned up in front with brass buttons, and was a most striking reminder of "Old Grimes is dead."

SCENES AND CHARACTERS IN ARKANSAS

From the *Spirit of The Times* [19]

PETER WHETSTONE's real estate operations—The "Benton's mint drops" currency—The "chaps" of the Devil's Fork and the Racoon Branch of the War Eagle—Peter Whetstone's rifle, dog, and sister—Red-headed Jim Cole—Race between "Warping Bars" and "Bussing Coon"—The Banter, the Acceptance, the Treat, and the Consequences.

————

DEVIL'S FORK, OF LITTLE RED RIVER,
(Arkansas,) Feb. 14, 1837.

Dear Mr. Editor,—Excuse my familiarity, for you must know us chaps on the Devil's Fork don't stand on ceremony; well, week before last, daddy sent me down to the Land Office, at Batesville, with a cool hundred shiners, to enter a piece of land—I tell you, it took all sorts of raking and scraping to raise the hundred.—Squire Smith let him have forty, but he would not have done it, but for a monstrous hankering he has, after sister Sal. Dad has got right smart paper money, but the great folks at Washington have got so proud they turn up their noses at the best sort of paper now-a-days. While I was at Batesville, I saw your *paper*, and the way I did love to read it, was nobody's business.—

[19] *Arkansas Times and Advocate,* Little Rock, May 1, 1837, p. [1].

Captain —— lent them to me every day, and I just made up my mind, that no matter what Daddy said, I would take it myself.

I just wish you could come to the Devil's Fork. The way I would show you fun, for I have got the best pack of bear dogs; the closest shooting rifle, the fastest swimming horse, and perhaps, the prettiest sister you ever did see. Why, those fellows on the Racoon Fork of the War Eagle, ain't a priming to us boys of the Devil's Fork. They aint monstrous friendly to us, ever since I laid out *Warping Bars,* with the *Bussing Coon.* I tell you, we used them up that hunt—red headed Jim Cole drove home twenty-four of the likeliest sort of cows and calves, and Bill Spence walked into a fellow for three good chunks of horses.

I'll tell you how that race was made. Monday evening of the election, I was standing talking to Squire Woods—we were just outside of the Doggery, when I heard somebody cavorting—I stepped right in—there stood big Dan Looney, the Racoon Fork Bully. I said nothing, but stopt right still—Says Dan, "I say it publicly and above board, that the Warping Bars can beat any nag from the Gulf of Mexico to the Rocky Mountains, that is now living and above ground, that drinks the waters of the Devil's Fork, one quarter of a mile with any weight, from a gutted snow bird to a stack of fodder."

Before I had time to say a word after Dan got through, in jumped Jim Cole—Says he, "Dan, the Bussing Coon can slam the Warping Bars this day three weeks, one quarter of a mile, with little Bill Allen's weight on each; for fifty dollars in cash, and two hundred in the best sort of truck."

"It is wedding," said Dan, "and give us your hand."

They shook hands and agreed to put up two good horses as forfeits. No sooner was the race made, than the boys commenced drinking and shouting. Dan said Jim Cole owed a treat—Jim Cole said Dan owed a treat. They agreed to leave it to Squire Woods; now Squire Woods is up to snuff and makes no more of belting a quart, than a methodist preacher would of eating a whole chicken, so says he, "boys, taking all things into consideration, I think it but fair that both should treat to a gallon, and sugar enough to sweeten it." "Hurrah for Squire Woods," roared every chap except Dan and Jim.

It didn't take more than twenty minutes to make some of them feel their keeping. I knew what was coming, and you may depend I kept my eye skinned. Dan soon became uproarious, and made out he was a heap drunker than he was. After a little while he couldn't hold in—Says he, "I can pick the ticks off of any you hell-fire boys," (meaning the Devil's Fork chaps)—the words were hardly out of his mouth before Jim Cole cried out, "you are a liar, Dan," and *cherow* he took him just above the butt of the ear—Dan realed, and ere he recovered, several persons rushed between them.—"Come boys," says one, "there is Squire Woods, and have some respect for him." "Damn Squire Woods," says Dan, "a Squire is no more than any other man in a fight!"

The physic was working—there was no chance to control it—coats were shed—hats flung off—shirt collars unbuttoned—but one thing was needed to bring about a general fight—that soon happened, for Bill Spence jumped right upon the table and shouted "hurrah for the Devil's Fork!" Dan answered him by yelling "go it my Coons"—the Doggery was on about half way ground, and the two settlements were about equally represented. The fight commenced; I tell you there was no time to swap knives—I pitched into Dan—'twas just like two studs kicking—we had it so good and so good for a long time—at last Dan was using me up, when Squire Woods (who had got through whipping his man) slipped up and legged for me, and I rather think gave Dan a slight kick—Dan sung out and the Devil's Fork triumphed.

I reckon there were all sorts of 4th July's cut over the fellows' eyes —and bit noses and fingers were plenty. We started home just about dark, singing Ingen all the way. I didn't want Daddy to see me that night, so I slipped to the stable loft—next morning I started out bear hunting, the particulars of which I will write you some of these times.

Ever yours,
PETER WHETSTONE.

CURIOSITIES OF LITERATURE [20]

WOLF RIVER, Eastern Mississippi, June 1st., 1849.

Mr. Editor.—The way that the *literati* in these diggins hump themselves occasionally is hard to beat. Allow me, dear 'Spirit,' to inflict upon you and your readers a few specimens of their productions which I have met with in my travels. Here is a copy of an advertisement 'posted' on a pine tree by the road side, which may perhaps be rendered more *intelligible* by the explanation which was furnished me in the neighborhood, and which throw much light upon what might otherwise appear somewhat a mystery. The chap whose name is subscribed to the advertisement is a groggery keeper, who claims that there is about $500 due to him in the neighborhood, but, wishing to go to Mobile for supplies, he thinks that if he can raise $250, that sum will do to start on. But let us read this curious document:—

[20] *Spirit of the Times,* New-York, June 30, 1849, p. 217.

NOTIS

Gentlemen if you Will Vote For Me to Goe to Mobeal I will Goe on the 20 Day of January 1849 I am intitle to five Hundred votes But two hundred and fifty votes Will Elect Me to Mobeal   My Kind Benevilent Frends oner Brite Sae the Same the electhin commence this Day wich the 10 Day 1848 Holds untill 20 Day of Jenuary 1849

Respectfully Yours   WILLIS JONES.

The Ballet Box redy At Eny time to take votes

W. JONES.

Hard hearted indeed must be the customers of Jones's groggery if that 'notis' didn't make 'some come' from their pockets; they were bound to shell out the rhino to so eloquent an appeal as that.

Not long since I had the pleasure of meeting a goodly assemblage of our piney woods sovereigns, male and female, at a grand 'Innfare' held in this vicinity. The frolic lasted all night, and as the concourse of people was large, and the house of our hospitable host quite too small for his company, while the dance and 'revel' were going on within doors, little groups assembled in various places outside, amusing themselves as they best could. Among the rest, my attention was drawn to a small circle of lads and lasses, surrounding a bright 'lighted' fire in the yard. The boys were plaguing the girls, and the latter were holding their handkerchief before their faces, partly as if to screen them from the blazing fire, and partly to ward off the kisses which the boys seemed disposed to inflict. At length a proposition was made to a youth, whose most remarkable features were a head of very long flaxen hair, and a pair of slender legs, encased in tight linsey woolsey unmentionables. After a great deal of coaxing to sing 'that song,' the vocalist complied with the request, and with a shrill piping voice, elevated to the highest pitch of which it was capable, with nasal twang, and accent 'more easily felt than described,' he perpetrated a 'song ballat,' a copy of which, at my urgent request, he furnished me, in his own 'hand write,' on the following morning. Here it is, as furnished to me *verbatim et literatim*:—

A SONG BALLAT

1 Come all you youths of evry State
  Listen a while and I'll relate
  A mournfull tale to you ile tell
  And which of late has me befell

2 I am by birth a georgion
  Parents to me there duty done
  Hansomly they instructed me
  And raised me up in piety

3 But from their counsil I have fled
And a most wreched life ive led
Which soon will end disgrased you see
It will a worning to you bee

4 Come nearer youths whilst I relate
To you the cause of my sad state
Which will to you a worning bee
When I am gone to eternity

5 Now marke you all my dismel end
Caused by a faulse pretended friend
Persuaded me from home to flee
In search of a new country

6 My greedy heart disceaved me
In pride of wealth and vanity
Led me a captive like you see
In iron bands as cold as clay

7 None of my friends would come as near
Who onct to me was vary dear
They said in Jail let him be hangd
A rebel of the christian land

8 Then oh my heart it greaved me sore
To think of seeing them no more
For now the time is drawing neer
When they will see me no more heare

9 Its on the 6th November next
My Bodyse laid with in the dust
When to a world of Sperits I
Will flap my wings and sore on hi

10 Then fare you well my Father dear
This world no longer holds me hear
And you my brothers sisters to
I bid you all a long ado
Farewell my loving friends

There, Mr. 'Spirit,' if you can beat that, you may shoot
Your humble servant,   RANSUMHEEL.

BACON AND GREENS

By Bakus W. Huntington [21]

BAKUS W. HUNTINGTON, the author of "Bacon and Greens," the culinary epic which I reproduce below, came to Tuskaloosa when he was quite a youth, and commenced the practice of law. He was an educated gentleman, of modest and prepossessing appearance, with prompt and ready business habits, having the best aptitudes of an office lawyer. . . . It was a great practical merit in him to suppress his literary inclinations and make them subordinate to his business. . . . The poem below first appeared anonymously in the *Southron*. Only a few persons knew who was the author. The newspapers of the day gave it the rounds at the time. . . .

I have lived long enough to be rarely mistaken,
    And borne my full share of life's changeable scenes,
But my woes have been solaced by good greens and bacon,
    And my joys have been doubled by bacon and greens.

What a thrill of remembrance e'en now they awaken,
    Of childhood's gay morning and youth's merry scenes,
When, one day, we had greens and a plate full of bacon,
    And, the next, we had bacon and a plate full of greens.

Ah! well I remember when sad and forsaken,
    Heart-wrung by the scorn of a miss in her teens,
How I rushed from her sight to my loved greens and bacon,
    And forgot my despair over bacon and greens.

When the banks refused specie and credit was shaken,
    I shared in the wreck and was ruined in means;
My friends all declared I had not saved my bacon,
    But they lied—I still had my bacon and greens.

Oh! there is a charm in this dish, rightly taken,
    That, from custards and jellies, an epicure weans:
Stick your fork in the fat—wrap your greens round the bacon,
    And you will vow there is nothing like bacon and greens.

[21] Note and text from William R. Smith's *Reminiscences of a Long Life; Historical, Political, Personal, and Literary*, Vol. I, Washington, D. C., c. 1889, pp. 270-274.

If some fairy a grant of three wishes would make one
  So worthless as I, and so laden with sins,
I'd wish all the greens in the world—then the bacon—
  And then wish a little more bacon and greens.

POSTSCRIPT

I return to confess that for once I'm mistaken,
  As much as I've known of this world and its scenes,
There's one thing that's equal to both greens and bacon,
  And that is a dish of—good bacon and greens.